AF792103

EDITORS

Charles Sheridan
University of Missouri
Kansas City, Missouri, USA

Joseph Sargent
The Menninger Foundation
Topeka, Kansas, USA

ASSOCIATE EDITORS

Kenneth Anchor
Vanderbilt University
Nashville, Tennessee, USA

Jeffrey Barth
University of Virginia
Charlottesville, Virginia, USA

EDITORIAL BOARD

David B. Adams
W. Stewart Agras
Frank Andrasik
Bruce Bongar
Steven N. Broder
Wilbert E. Fordyce
Michael Freeman
Antonio Celso de Noronha Goyos
Ted A. Grossbart
David L. Johnson
Bruno Kappes
Arnold A. Lazarus
Steven E. Locke
James Lynch
Leila Regina de Paula Nunes
Eugene G. Peniston
Thomas Pruzinsky
Sally Radmacher
Donald B. Rinsley
Bertram Rothschild
Wencke Jensen Seltzer
Margaret E. Texidor
Richard S. Weiner

ABMP PROFESSIONAL ADVISORY COUNCIL

Richard E. Easton, Executive Officer
Kenneth Anchor, Administrative Officer
Jeffrey Barth, Scholarship & Publications Coordinator

W. Stewart Agras
Patricia Andrise
J.D. Ball
Aaron T. Beck
Merrill I. Berman
Larry Beutler
V.D. Bhatt
Murray Bowen
Elizabeth W. Bradley
Laurence A. Bradley
Steven N. Broder
Renald C. Eichler
Albert Ellis
Wilbert E. Fordyce
Michael Freeman
Richard L. Grant
Dorothy Gronwall
Ted A. Grossbart
Diana Guthrie
W. Rodney Hammond
Cagle Harrendorf
Paul E. Jarvis
Bruno Kappes
Robert A. Kovan
Arnold A. Lazarus
Robert Leftwich
Lester M. Libo
Karl L. Manders
Ronald B. Margolis
Michael McElroy
Donald Meichenbaum
Leo Richard Miller
Roger Patterson
Thomas G. Paulter
Thomas H. Peake
Cecil P. Peck
Eugene G. Peniston
Myron Prescott
Karl H. Pribram
Donald B. Rinsley
William Peter Schofield
C. Norman Shealy
Leonard Silverstein
Charles L. Sheridan
B.F. Skinner
W.W. Spradlin
Richard B. Stuart
William T. Tsushima
Dennis C. Turk
Paul L. Wachtel
D.H. Webb
Michael L. Zarr

Student Editor: Deborah A. Abraham
Administrative Manager: Felicia Figlarz Anchor
Administrative Assistants: Janet Dearman and Susan Prosch
Managing Editor: Anne Stilman

Library of Congress Cataloguing-in-Publication Data
Medical psychotherapy.

Includes bibliographies.
1. Psychotherapy. 2. Medicine, Psychosomatic. 3. Somatoform disorders. I. Sheridan, Charles L., 1937- . II. Sargent, Joseph. [DNLM: 1. Psychotherapy. WM 420 M489]
RC480.5.M355 1988 616.89'14 88-842
ISBN 0-920887-21-X (soft)

Canadian Cataloguing in Publication Data
Main entry under title:

Medical psychotherapy

Bibliography: p.
ISBN 0-920887-21-X

1. Psychotherapy. I. Sheridan, Charles L., 1937- . II. Sargent, Joseph.

RC480.M43 1988 616.89'14 C88-093478-6

This publication serves as the official organ of the American Board of Medical Psychotherapists.

Copyright ©1988 by Hans Huber Publishers, Inc.

No part of this publication may be reproduced, stored in a retrieval system, or transmitted, in any form or by any means, electronic, mechanical, photocopying, microfilming, recording, or otherwise, without written permission from the publisher.

Printed in Canada

ISBN 0-920887-21-X Hans Huber Toronto • Lewiston, NY
ISBN 3-456-81652-9 Hans Huber Bern • Stuttgart

ISSN 0835-3069 Hans Huber Toronto • Lewiston, NY

Medical Psychotherapy: An International Journal

Volume 1 1988

1. Collaboration of plastic surgeon and medical psychotherapist: Elective cosmetic surgery
Thomas Pruzinsky 1

2. Psychotherapy with head-injured patients
J.D. Ball 15

3. The chronic pain patient: Multimodal assessment and psychotherapy
Bruce N. Eimer 23

4. Millon Clinical Multiaxial Inventory (MCMI) clusters for alcohol abusers: Further evidence of validity and implications for medical psychotherapy
Dennis C. Donat 41

5. The relationship between absorption capacity and electromyographic biofeedback relaxation training with a male clinical sample
Harold Kelso, Kenneth Anchor, and Michael McElroy 51

6. A clinician's guide to differential diagnosis between physical and psychiatric disorders
Chris E. Stout 65

7. Body symptoms and the medical psychotherapist
Thomas G. Pautler 73

8. Stress and headache in the workplace: The role of caffeine
Joseph Sargent and Patricia Solbach 83

9. Medical psychotherapy with elderly psychiatric inpatients: Uses of paraprofessionals in treatment
Peter A. Lichtenberg 87

10. Somatic Communications: Interpersonal theory and therapy of psychosomatic disorders
Robert Sanders 95

11. Understanding learning disabilities: A primer for the psychotherapist
Marijanet Doonan and Roy E. Ehrlich 113

12. Brief versus extended relaxation: Relationship to improvement at follow-up in mixed headache patients
Alvin E. Lake III and Jeffrey D. Pingel 119

13. Group assertion and contingent time-out procedures in the control of assaultive behaviors in schizophrenics
Eugene G. Peniston and Paul J. Kulkosky 131

14. Crisis in midlife among osteopathic physicians
W. Randall Ratliff, James R. Hall, Jerry C. McGill, Joel Wyatt, and Kate Wyatt 143

15. Evoking vocal imitation in at-risk infants: An experimental analysis
Leila Regina de Paula Nunes and Claire L. Poulson 151

16. The emotional distress of the artificial insemination patient
Aline P. Zoldbrod 161

17. **Position Paper:**

Professional regulation: Issues and problems in current credentialing practices
Kenneth N. Anchor and Deborah A. Abraham 173

Discussants:

Counseling and credentialing in the field of diabetes mellitus
Diana Guthrie 181

Professional regulation: A critique
Larry E. Beutler 183

Comment on "Professional regulation: Issues and problems in current credentialing practices"
Alan H. Roberts 187

Credentialing practices: Resistance to innovation
Richard S. Weiner 191

Response to ABMP Task Force position paper on "Professional Credentialing"
Louis A. Pagliaro 203

Competency: Self-imposed professional discipline
Raymond F. Hanbury 207

Medical Psychotherapy
1988, Volume 1, pp. 1-13
© 1988 by
Hans Huber Publishers, Toronto

Collaboration of Plastic Surgeon and Medical Psychotherapist: Elective Cosmetic Surgery

THOMAS PRUZINSKY
University of Virginia School of Medicine

This article describes the role of a medical psychotherapist in a department of plastic surgery. Characteristics of a medical psychotherapy model of practice are described with reference to patients seeking elective cosmetic surgery. Clinical observations and empirical reviews are utilized to describe patient motivations for cosmetic surgery, the process of patient selection, patient problems in the pre-, intra-, and post-operative periods, and potential negative psychological reactions to the surgery. Medical psychotherapist interventions for these situations are described. Emphasis is placed on the range of consistent positive psychological outcomes resulting from undergoing elective cosmetic surgery.

Introduction

This is the first article in a two-part series describing the collaboration of the medical psychotherapist and the plastic surgeon.[1] These articles have three major goals: (a) defining the characteristics of a medical psychotherapy model of practice; (b) describing the medical psychotherapist's work in a department of plastic surgery; and (c) reviewing and summarizing the psychological literature on cosmetic and reconstructive surgery.

Elective cosmetic surgery refers to surgical changes resulting in aesthetic improvement; i.e. the presurgical appearance of these patients is unlikely to have been viewed as deviating significantly from normal (Goin & Goin, 1986). The surgical procedures requested include rhinoplasty, breast augmentation and reduction, and facelift. This

---

Inquiries or reprint requests should be directed to Thomas Pruzinsky, Ph.D., Box 203, University of Virginia, School of Medicine, Charlottesville, VA., 22908.

1. Part II will appear in a future edition of this journal.

first article reviews the process of patient screening, critical intra-operative concerns, and the potential positive and negative effects of elective cosmetic surgery.

The second article will describe the psychological aspects of *reconstructive* surgery, which involves a change from an objectively evident abnormal appearance to a more normal one (Goin & Goin, 1986). The medical psychotherapist's role in evaluating and treating children with major craniofacial anomalies (e.g. cleft lip and palate) and with children and adults needing reconstructive surgery after injury (e.g. burns) or disease (e.g. cancer) is described.

Medical Psychotherapy Practice

Medical psychotherapy is a hybrid discipline composed of many sub-disciplines including: consultation-liaison psychiatry, clinical psychology, nursing, pediatric psychology, medical psychology, health psychology, and behavioral health. It is defined in terms of the basic areas of knowledge within these sub-disciplines (e.g. personality development, psychopathology, and psychotherapy techniques).

Characteristics of Medical Psychotherapist Practice

Three characteristics of medical psychotherapy in the University of Virginia Department of Plastic Surgery are collaboration, specialization, and integration. These characteristics may have general applicability to defining medical psychotherapy as a whole with regard to three general roles: prevention, direct patient service, and rehabilitation (Medical Psychotherapist Newsletter, 1986).

Collaboration

Collaboration involves extensive interaction between medical psychotherapists and physicians in the areas of prevention, provision of direct services, rehabilitation, research, and training. A medical psychotherapist working full-time in plastic surgery has a wide range of contact with surgeons and patients (Deaton & Langman, 1986) by attending surgical planning conferences and surgery clinics, conducting research, and training plastic surgery and clinical psychology residents.

Furthermore, a collaborative model of interaction emphasizes a proactive approach to patient care by focusing on problem anticipation and prevention. By contrast, a *consultation* model is a reactive approach to patient care involving "calling in" the medical psychotherapist from the outside when a difficult situation develops.

A collaborative model of medical psychotherapy enhances the quality of patient care by facilitating medical psychotherapist-primary physician communication, a greater degree of trust between the disciplines, and an attitude of cooperation. However, to develop a collaborative model of interaction, medical psychotherapist specialization is essential.

Specialization

As a medical specialty, plastic surgery is a world unto itself. Consequently, to be optimally effective, a medical psychotherapist working in this setting needs a clear understanding of the practice of plastic surgery (e.g. the types of surgical procedures conducted and the psychological aspects involved). This information is available through interviewing a range of plastic surgery patients (Edgerton & Langman, 1982) and interacting extensively with surgeons.

Specialization entails developing a very specific set of base rates (e.g., What is the normal level of anxiety in the initial consultation with the plastic surgeon? What is the normal range of anxiety following an elective surgical procedure?). Without these base rates the medical psychotherapist cannot make fully informed treatment decisions.

Specialized knowledge of plastic surgery facilitates medical psychotherapist and surgeon collaboration by providing a common language for both to speak, and creating a common ground of information. Furthermore, specialization and collaboration facilitate integration of knowledge common to these two disciplines.

Integration

Two somewhat contradictory sounding questions best exemplify the characteristic of integration: What does the plastic surgeon teach the medical psychotherapist about personality development and change, psychopathology, body image, human coping, and defense mechanisms? Conversely, what does the medical psychotherapist teach the plastic surgeon about patient selection, the process of rehabilitation, and general care of plastic surgery patients?

In the "laboratory" of the plastic surgery clinic, many opportunities exist to observe mechanisms of defense in action, the impact of body image changes on personality, the role of physical attractiveness in determining the quality of life, and the constant interplay between developmental issues and human change processes. Conversely, knowledge of psychotherapy, psychopathology, and personality development are applied daily in the surgery clinic. Thus, knowledge within these two apparently distinct areas is integrated.

Summary

Medical psychotherapists typically apply knowledge of personality functioning and change to highly specialized areas of medicine, thus facilitating prevention, rehabilitation, and provision of direct services. Close collaboration with medical colleagues leads to clear and consistent communication, an attitude of working together, and a proactive as opposed to a reactive approach to problem prevention and problem-solving. Medical psychotherapist specialization within a particular medical discipline enhances collaboration and facilitates the integration of the knowledge between the disciplines. The remaining portions of this paper exemplify these characteristics of medical psychotherapist practice.

General Considerations in Elective Surgery

Stage One: Decision to Seek Consultation

Increasingly large numbers of individuals request elective cosmetic surgery (Rees, 1987). This is not surprising given the general population's expressed dissatisfaction regarding their body image (Cash, Winstead, & Janda, 1986), and increase in knowledge about and availability of plastic surgery (Rees, 1987).

Individuals requesting plastic surgery report strong feelings of self-consciousness (Buss, 1985; Harris, 1982b). Their perception of personal appearance negatively influences their self-concept and self-esteem, and is associated with avoidance of social situations as well as behavioral inhibition (Harris, 1982b).

Questioning patients reveals that feelings of self-consciousness are the major motivation to seek consultation with a plastic surgeon. These individuals often have thought about seeking surgical help for a number of years. They typically express fears of being "vain" or in other ways express guilt about requesting surgery (Courtiss, 1980). In general, males have greater difficulty seeking help than do females (Edgerton & Langman, 1982).

Stage Two: The Initial Consultation

In this section, the process of patient selection is described. Careful selection is critical to insure patient appropriateness for surgery (Goin & Goin, 1986; Lavell & Lewis, 1984). While the majority of patients have reasonable motivations and requests, there are instances when requests must be examined. It is in the area of patient selection that the medical psychotherapist is primarily involved, in *prevention* and *provision of direct services*.

Many older reports on the personality characteristics of individuals seeking elective surgery portray them as psychologically disturbed (e.g. Linn & Goldman, 1949; Meerloo, 1956). As Goin & Goin (1986) stated in a reference to psychological reports of rhinoplasty patients: "As a rough rule, the older the date of the publication, the more disturbed the patient appears to be" (p. 91). Generally, in earlier eras the motivation for surgery was characterized as neurotic (Wengle, 1986a).

Later, more empirically based examinations of elective plastic surgery patients considered a range of variables influencing the decision to seek surgery, including: personality variables, level of psychopathology, coping styles, previous history of cosmetic surgery or psychiatric problems, current life stresses, and others (Wengle, 1986b). A basic conclusion of these studies was that patients seeking elective surgery are individuals; all have their unique motivations for surgery and styles of coping with stress (Wengle, 1986b). It is the responsibility of the medical psychotherapist and surgeon to discover these motivations and coping styles in the initial consultation.

Patient perspective on the initial consultation. It is common for patients to have high anxiety levels in the initial consultation (Rees, 1987). The meeting has long been anticipated and the outcome is very important to them. Patients are concerned with whether the changes they desire can be achieved, and about the cost and timing of surgery.

Surgeon perspective on the initial consultation. The surgeon first evaluates the degree to which the deformity the patient perceives is evident. The deformity is often small, though the psychological reaction to it is large. It is a general principle of plastic surgery that the level of psychological concern regarding a deformity is *not* necessarily correlated with the size or conspicuousness of the deformity. Small, less noticeable deformities can cause great distress. This is *not* necessarily an indication of psychopathology. When evaluating a patient for elective surgery, understanding the *patient's perception* of his or her deformity is essential (Edgerton & Langman, 1982).

Once the patient and surgeon agree on the nature and degree of the deformity and that surgical improvement is possible, the operation of choice is presented to the patient along with its anticipated outcomes and potential limitations and complications. The surgeon assesses the patient's understanding of these possible problems, as well as ability to withstand the stress of surgery (Edgerton & Langman, 1982).

It is also necessary to assess the patient's motivation for surgery. The surgeon is most comfortable with and reassured by internal motivations (i.e. the desire to feel better about oneself). Motivations involving the desire to please someone else (i.e. motivations external to the self) are of concern (Edgerton & Langman, 1982).

The surgeon also assesses the amount of stress the patient is experiencing. For example, if he or she is in a period of mourning the death of a loved one, it is often prudent to postpone surgery until these stressors have abated (Edgerton & Langman, 1982).

Of critical importance in the selective process is the surgeon's *intuition* about the interaction occurring with the patient. The surgeons assess the degree to which they are comfortable working with individual patients and their particular requests (Edgerton & Langman, 1982).

Medical psychotherapist perspective on the initial consultation. In our department, the medical psychotherapist often accompanies the surgeon at the initial patient consultation to observe the interview, and intervenes primarily if there is evidence of patient psychological distress.

Severe psychological problems in patients requesting elective surgery are uncommon (Goin & Goin, 1986). The surgeon and the medical psychotherapist become more concerned about patient appropriateness for surgery if, for example, there is evidence of psychiatric disorder, a history of unsatisfactory cosmetic surgery, unreasonable expectations for the outcome, or lack of clarity about the change desired.

Formal psychological testing (e.g. MMPI, Rorschach) is sometimes employed to provide a clearer picture of the patient's current level of functioning and information regarding diagnosis. Individuals requesting elective surgery often experience mild to moderate levels of depression (e.g. Edgerton, Jacobson, Meyer, 1960). Diagnoses of depressive disorders, therefore, need consideration. In the context of the plastic surgery clinic, an important concern is the degree to which depression is related to feelings of self-consciousness regarding appearance or to other life concerns, and the degree to which the patient is hoping that his or her depression will be relieved by surgery.

Consideration of a diagnosis of Body Dysmorphic Disorder is also important.

> "The essential feature of this disorder is preoccupation with some imagined defect in appearance in a normal-appearing person. The most common complaints involve facial flaws, such as wrinkles, spots on the

> skin, excessive facial hair, shape of the nose, mouth, jaw, or eyebrows, and swelling of the face.... In some cases a slight physical anomaly is present, but the person's concern is grossly excessive." (American Psychiatric Association, 1987, p. 255).

A preoccupation with some body part that is delusional in nature is not to be diagnosed under this category. In this situation, the diagnosis of "Delusional Disorder, Somatic type" (American Psychiatric Association, 1987) is more accurate.

The category of Body Dysmorphic Disorder previously fell under the rubric of dysmorphophobia (Thomas, 1984). Approximately 2% of patients requesting elective cosmetic surgery could receive the diagnosis of dysmorphophobia (Andreasan & Bardach, 1977). This figure is consistent with our clinical experience (i.e. the situation where overconcern about a body part is nondelusional, but "excessive" given objective evaluation of the "deformity"). It is worth repeating, however, that the degree of the deformity is *not* necessarily correlated with the degree of psychological distress regarding it.

Thus, while most individuals requesting surgery are psychologically stable, there are a significant number who come to the plastic surgeon with emotional problems. With these patients, the critical question is not one of diagnosis but: What is the fate of such a person seeking plastic surgery (Edgerton, 1975; Edgerton & Langman, 1982)?

Patients evidencing psychological problems are often rejected for treatment by plastic surgeons (Edgerton, 1975; Wray, 1986). This is partly due to surgeon fears of litigation or concern that the patient is seeking a physical solution to psychological problems. These individuals are usually referred to psychiatrists for consultation. However, most resist such referrals. They often react defensively and perceive the surgeon as "blocking" what they desire, and usually do not follow up on the psychiatric referral. Consequently, they feel they cannot return to the surgeon, and are left frustrated in their desire for surgical change. These troubled patients often travel from plastic surgeon to plastic surgeon seeking help (Edgerton & Langman, 1982).

However, patients with psychological disorders should *not* be eliminated from consideration for surgery. It is the plastic surgeon's obligation to assure that these patients receive the highest standard of care possible (Edgerton, 1975).

In our clinic, this goal is achieved by presenting patient consultation with the medical psychotherapist as part of clinic routine. The medical psychotherapist usually has witnessed the interaction between the surgeon and patient, and intervenes with a clear perspective of the concerns of both parties.

The most frequent type of direct service provided in this situation is a brief course of psychotherapy. This entails postponement of surgery-related decisions until a thorough evaluation of the patient's current life situation is conducted. During this evaluation the patient maintains contact with *both* the surgeon and the medical psychotherapist, often over a period of months.

Contact with the surgeon is essential so that patients feel they are still being considered for surgery. Multiple surgical evaluations also clarify the physical change desired, and a stronger surgeon-patient alliance develops.

In this approach, the medical psychotherapist assesses the psychological status of the patient and can often assist in clarifying his or her surgical goals. A brief course of psychotherapy is often helpful in ascertaining the patient's motivations and expectations. Furthermore, this contact allows a therapeutic relationship to develop, which is utilized as a support if surgery is eventually performed.

In the vast majority of cases, this intermittent contact with the type of patient we are particularly concerned about (e.g. those who are depressed) tempers both surgeon and medical psychotherapist concerns about patient appropriateness for surgery, and allows the patient to obtain the desired surgery. The case study at the end of this article demonstrates this therapeutic approach.

Summary. Careful patient selection is essential in preventing possible negative reactions to cosmetic surgery. Very clear guidelines exist for assessing people's perceptions of their deformities and motivation for surgery. Standard assessments of psychological status are also critical in order to screen for depression, Body Dysmorphic Disorder, or somatic delusions that may be indicative of more severe psychological disorders. If psychological screening results in concern regarding patient appropriateness for surgery, the medical psychotherapist and surgeon should collaborate on an in-depth assessment of the patient, and attempt to develop a stronger doctor-patient alliance.

Stage Three: The Pre- and Intra-Operative Periods

There are major concerns for the medical psychotherapist in these two time periods: pre-operative patient anxiety, and the occurrence of traumatic intra-operative psychological reactions.

Patient anxiety. Patients undergoing surgery experience high levels of anxiety. Treatment programs involving stress inoculation, relaxation training, or hypnosis (Stayman, Norman, Tucker, & Virnelli, 1987) exist to reduce anxiety and/or to manage pain. Though the effectiveness of such programs is unclear, patients who are more anxious in the pre-operative period do tend to have longer periods of recovery (Johnston, 1986). It is an ideal role of the medical psychotherapist to attempt interventions to reduce this pre-operative anxiety.

Traumatic intra-operative reactions. A small minority of patients experience psychological trauma during the intra-operative period. Significant emotional reactions during elective cosmetic procedures have been documented (Burgoyne, Goin, & Goin, 1977). This may be due to misperceptions of conversation overheard while in the anaesthetized state (Hawtof & Smith, 1987) or the result of other factors (e.g. sensory restriction). These reactions are usually short-lived, but can be disturbing and potentially harmful.

Importantly, surgeons are often *unaware* of these negative intra-operative reactions (Burgoyne et al., 1977). In the case of face-lift patients, their existence was discovered via post-operative psychiatric interviews. The following point emphasizes the importance of close collaboration between the medical psychotherapist and the surgeon.

> "This high rate [10 percent] of significant emotional reactions is unreported elsewhere, most likely because the patients hide them so well. Were it not for the fact that these psychiatric interviews were conducted . . . by a psychiatrist *with whom previous rapport had been established*, we would not have discovered them either" (Burgoyne, Goin, & Goin, 1977, p. 582, emphasis added).

Medical psychotherapists are in the best position to evaluate whether such reactions occurred. At the first meeting with the patient after surgery, when alone with the patient, they inquire about unusual experiences during the operation, and explain that some people experience these.

Stage Four: The Post-Operative Period

Transient experiences of depression and anxiety are fairly common in the post-operative period, often following initial periods of euphoria (Edgerton & Langman, 1982; Goin & Goin, 1986). These result from uncertainty regarding the outcome of surgery, strange physical sensations, and the general stress of surgery. Furthermore, the patient often does not remember the surgeon's warnings about the normal occurrence of post-operative events (e.g. bleeding, swelling, discoloration, unusual skin sensations, etc.), which can be frightening (Goin & Goin, 1986).

These emotional reactions are best handled through reassurance and empathy as opposed to medication. Contact with the surgeon in this period is a powerful palliative. However, in a teaching hospital, resident physicians often handle routine post-operative care, which can be disconcerting to the patient and his or her family. In this situation, the medical psychotherapist often serves as the bridge between the attending physician and the patient, providing continuity of care. The likelihood of being effective in this situation is enhanced by the degree to which rapport and credibility were established in the pre-operative period.

Stage Five: Long-term Effects of Elective Plastic Surgery

Negative Effects of Elective Surgery. Negative psychological experiences in the follow-up period can occur in the context of either a positive or a negative surgical outcome. In cases of an objective shortcoming, surgeons must handle the situation with great care. They must take responsibility for mistakes if they have occurred, listen and empathize with the range of emotions expressed by the patient, remain available, and generally treat the patient in the most humane manner possible (Goldwyn, 1984).

Prevention of severe psychological reactions is accomplished via clear *pre*-operative communication. Patients must be assessed in terms of their ability to withstand the stress of positive outcome surgery, as well as surgery that is less than ideal. A positive surgeon-patient relationship established in the pre-operative period facilitates coping with this difficult situation.

In situations where there is a less-than-ideal surgical outcome, the medical psychotherapist plays a supportive role. There are often opportunities for individual meetings where patients ventilate the emotions, especially anger, that they feel toward the surgeon. Reassurance and simply listening are in the best interests of both the patient and the surgeon.

Negative psychological reactions to a technically successful surgery include patient dissatisfaction, loss of identity, and onset of psychosis. Patient dissatisfaction can result from: the existence of significant psychological problems, lack of understanding regarding the realistic outcome of the surgery, or the need for external approval of the surgical changes that do not occur (Macgregor, 1981).

Patient dissatisfaction can often be prevented via thorough pre-operative consultation (Macgregor, 1981). However, "secret motivations" for change, revealed only in the post-operative period, make clear the impossibility of preventing all problems (Goin, Burgoyne, & Goin, 1976).

Persistent dissatisfaction with the outcome of surgery may indicate an "insatiable" cosmetic surgery patient (Knorr, Edgerton, & Hoopes, 1967). "Insatiable" patients are those who, despite technical surgical success, *repeatedly* ask for re-operations on a particular body part so as to "get it right." These patients differ from the ones undergoing multiple surgical procedures who are satisfied with each successive operation. Insatiable patients are especially challenging and difficult to work with, and often have a borderline personality organization (Groenman & Sauer, 1983).

Negative reactions to successful surgery also include loss of identity. The patient reports "not looking like myself" for an extended period of time post-surgically. Loss of identity occurs with greater frequency with some operations than with others.

Surgical procedures can be classified as "type changing" or restorative (Goin & Goin, 1986). Restorative operations (e.g. standard face-lifts) return the person's physical features to the way they once were, whereas "type changing" procedures bring about basic alterations (e.g. rhinoplasty).

Subjective loss of identity is more often associated with type changing operations. It appears to result most frequently from rhinoplasty (Knorr, 1972), though similar experiences have been reported with other procedures (e.g. blepharoplasty) (Goin & Goin, 1986). Overall, it is a rare occurrence and appears more common in older patients (Goin & Goin, 1986).

Another negative reaction to surgery is the development of psychosis (e.g. Goin & Goin, 1986; Schweitzer & Hirschfeld, 1984). It is difficult to predict but thankfully rare (Goin & Goin, 1986). Medical psychotherapist intervention is critical in this situation. Intervention focuses on crisis intervention and patient stabilization in the post-operative period, and insuring adequate post-operative psychological care.

The positive effects of elective plastic surgery. The effects of elective cosmetic surgery are for the most part very beneficial, and patients are usually satisfied with the surgical and psychological gains (Goin & Goin, 1986; Marcus, 1984; Wengle, 1986a). These positive changes occur with face-lifts (Goin, Burgoyne, Goin, & Staples, 1980), breast reductions (Hollyman, Lacey, Whitfield, & Wilson, 1986), breast augmentations (Ohlsen, Ponten, & Hamberg, 1979), rhinoplasties (Marcus, 1984), and other procedures (Goin & Goin, 1986).

These positive effects maintain over significant follow-up periods (Wengle, 1986a) and have been documented via psychological testing (e.g. Hay & Heather, 1973; Marcus, 1984). Surgery can also result in the objective perception of patients as more attractive (Cash & Horton, 1983; Kalick, 1979), though findings in this area are inconsistent (Marcus, 1984).

The purpose of elective surgery is to reverse the cycle of self-consciousness and inhibition via change in self-perception of body image (Edgerton, 1973). As Edgerton and Langman (1982) state: "*...the only legitimate indication for purely aesthetic surgery is to improve the emotional health of the patient*" (p. 23). Or, in the words of Harris (1982a): "Plastic surgery is psychotherapeutic" (p. 281).

Follow-up data support this contention. Reduced feelings of depression and self-consciousness and increased self-esteem are frequently reported post-surgically (cf. Goin & Goin, 1986; Marcus, 1984; Wengle, 1986b). Reduction in discrepancies within the self-concept are also achieved (Burk, Zelen, & Terino, 1985); a finding consistent with psychotherapeutic perspectives on growth and change (cf. Higgens, Klein, & Strauman, 1987).

Documentation also exists regarding positive changes in behavior. For example, Marcus (1984) reported reductions in behavioral manifestations of anxiety in social situations for individuals undergoing cosmetic rhinoplasty. Clinical experience also strongly supports the idea that behavior change occurs.

Rehabilitation and Elective Surgery. A large majority of patients undergo a period of psychological rehabilitation in the post-operative period (i.e. reductions in self-consciousness, release of behavioral inhibitions, and the subsequent changes in social interaction). These changes occur with little or no medical psychotherapist or surgeon contact, as there is usually little talk about psychological symptom relief during the post-operative period. Psychological rehabilitation is done by the patients themselves: i.e. it is self-facilitated.

However, not all patients report a decrease in negative psychological symptoms (e.g. Meyer & Jacobsson, 1986). This is understandable. Even with the successful completion of surgery, there cannot be an automatic release from long-standing and habitual patterns of emotional experience, thoughts, and behaviors.

Are there methods to facilitate the process of rehabilitation in the post-operative period? Perhaps similarities in the ways that personality changes occur after plastic surgery, psychotherapy, or life experience (Viederman, 1986) can be documented to facilitate our understanding of this process.

Presently, we only infrequently engage in brief psychotherapy with patients with the explicit intent of maximizing and integrating the positive psychological effects of surgery. It is our impression, however, that this type of psychotherapeutic interaction is beneficial.

Case Presentation

The following case presentation exemplifies surgeon-medical psychotherapist collaboration in the treatment of elective surgery patients.

> A 30-year-old unmarried woman, DF, requested that her face be "made thinner." DF had undergone previous cosmetic surgeries involving her nose, cheeks, eyes, and chin. She was pleased with the outcome of these operations, though she stated that the one aspect of her face that was always the most troublesome *to her* was *her* perception of its wideness. Physical examination by the surgeon revealed a widening of the features, though this was not likely to be noticed by most observers.

In the initial interview, DF was unusually anxious and defensive and appeared depressed. She denied any history of psychiatric hospitalization, though she did report that she had been in psychotherapy for a brief period of time for depression. She described her childhood in very negative terms, with special emphasis on her feelings of being "ugly." She described these feelings as continuing into adulthood, at which time she began to seek out plastic surgeons. Though she benefited from the surgeries, she was still very self-conscious, socially isolated, and kept her face camouflaged with a somewhat unusual hair style.

The nature of DF's request, the existence of previous surgeries, and concern regarding her mental status led the surgeon and psychologist to conduct multiple evaluations and a brief course of psychotherapy before making decisions regarding her requests for surgery. The focus of the therapy was on DF's hopes for change in her life via surgery, and how old images of herself as "ugly" could be effectively confronted both before and after surgery.

The surgeon's meetings with DF focused on specification of her surgical request. These meetings also kept the patient motivated to work with the psychologist, by assuring her that her surgical requests were being taken seriously, despite concerns about her mental status and expectations for changes in her life after surgery.

With this combined approach to treatment, we assured ourselves of the patient's ability to withstand the stress of surgery, and clarified her motivations for expectations of the procedure. Future integration of the surgical changes into her existing body image was also addressed. With these precautions, the surgeon then proceeded to narrow the areas of DF's face that she perceived as deformed.

At eight-month follow-up, DF was very pleased with and grateful for the surgery. She reported a marked reduction in self-consciousness, and reported going out in public more frequently and making plans to develop her employment skills. Some minor modifications were made in her hair style so that her face was not as camouflaged as it previously had been. She did not request any other surgical change. Of course, a much longer term follow-up is needed to see if these gains maintain or if there is any change in her level of functioning.

Summary

Medical psychotherapist collaboration with plastic surgeons can be very fruitful. Most importantly, medical psychotherapist specialization in this fascinating area facilitates a higher standard of patient care. This collaboration also fosters an integration of knowledge available from the two worlds, and this integration of knowledge, in turn, can shed light on the complex area of the process of human change.

ACKNOWLEDGEMENTS. I would like to thank Dr. M.T. Edgerton and Dr. M.W. Langman for their support and major contributions to the manuscript. I thank Dr. Langman and Rhonda Pruzinsky for reviewing the manuscript.

References

AMERICAN PSYCHIATRIC ASSOCIATION (1987). *Diagnostic and Statistical Manual of Mental Disorders III-Revised*. Washington D.C.: American Psychiatric Association.

ANDREASAN, N.C. & Bardach, J. (1977). Dysmorphophobia: Symptom or disease? *American Journal of Psychiatry, 134*, 673-676.

BURGOYNE, R.W., Goin, J.M. & Goin, M.K. (1977). Intraoperative psychological reactions in face-lift patients under local anesthesia. *Plastic and Reconstructive Surgery, 60*, 582-588.

BURK, J., Zelen, S.L., Terino, E.O. (1985). More than skin deep: A self-consistency approach to the psychology of cosmetic surgery. *Plastic and Reconstructive Surgery, 76*, 270-280.

BUSS, A.H. (1985). Self-consciousness and appearance. In Graham, J.A. & Kligman, A.M.(Eds.) *The psychology of cosmetic treatments* (pp.125-132). New York: Praeger Scientific.
CASH, T.F. & Horton, C.E. (1983). Aesthetic surgery: Effects of rhinoplasty on the social perception of patients by others. *Plastic and Reconstructive Surgery, 72*, 543-548.
CASH, T.F., Winstead, B.A. & Janda, L.H. (1986). The great American shape-up. *Psychology Today, 20*, 30-37.
COURTISS, E.H. (1980). Doctor, am I being vain? [Editorial]. *Plastic and Reconstructive Surgery, 65*, 819.
DEATON, A.V. & Langman, M.W. (1986). The contribution of psychologists to the treatment of plastic surgery patients. *Professional Psychology: Research and Practice, 17*, 179-184.
EDGERTON, M.T. (1973). Deformity is a disease. *Transactions and Studies of the College of Physicians of Philadelphia, 41*, 124-130.
EDGERTON, M.T. (1975). The plastic surgeon's obligation to the emotionally disturbed patient. *Plastic and Reconstructive Surgery, 55*, 81-83.
EDGERTON, M.T., Jacobson, W.E. & Meyer, E. (1960). Surgical-psychiatric study of patients seeking plastic (cosmetic) surgery: Ninety-eight patients with minimal deformity. *British Journal of Plastic Surgery, 13*, 136-145.
EDGERTON, M.T. & Langman, M.W. (1982). Psychiatric considerations. In E.H. Courtiss (Ed.) *Male Aesthetic Surgery* (17-37). St. Louis: C.V. Mosby Company.
GOIN, M.K., Burgoyne, R.W. & Goin, J.M. (1976). Face-lift operation: The patient's secret motivations and reactions to 'informed consent'. *Plastic and Reconstructive Surgery, 58*, 273-279.
GOIN, M.K., Burgoyne, R.W., Goin, J.M. & Staples, F.R. (1980). A prospective psychological study of 50 female face-lift patients. *Plastic and Reconstructive Surgery, 65*, 436-442.
GOIN, M.K. & Goin, J.M. (1986). Psychological effects of aesthetic facial surgery. *Advances in Psychosomatic Medicine, 15*, 84-108.
GOLDWYN, R.M. (1984). The dissatisfied patient. In R.M. Goldwyn (Ed.) *The unfavorable result in plastic surgery: Avoidance and treatment (Second Edition)* (pp.11-14). Boston: Little, Brown & Company.
GROENMAN, N.H., & Sauer, H.C. (1983). Personality characteristics of the cosmetic surgical insatiable patient. *Psychotherapy and Psychosomatics, 40*, 241-245.
HARRIS, D.L. (1982a). Cosmetic surgery-where does it begin? *British Journal of Plastic Surgery, 35*, 281-286.
HARRIS, D.L. (1982b). The symptomatology of abnormal appearance: An anecdotal survey. *British Journal of Plastic Surgery, 35*, 312-323.
HAWTOF, D.B. & Smith, D. (1987). Language in the operating room. *Annals of Plastic Surgery, 18*, 186-187.
HAY, G.G. & Heather, B.B. (1973). Changes in psychometric test results following cosmetic nasal operations. *British Journal of Psychiatry, 122*, 89-90.
HIGGENS, E.T., Klein, R.L. & Strauman, T.J. (1987). Self-discrepancies: Distinguishing among self-states, self-state conflicts and emotional vulnerabilities. In K. Yardley & T. Honess (Eds.). *Self and Identity: Psychosocial Perspectives (pp. 173-186).* New York: John Wiley & Sons.
HOLLYMAN, J.A., Lacey, J.H., Whitfield, P.J. & Wilson, J.S. (1986). Surgery for the psyche: A longitudinal study of women undergoing reduction mammoplasty. *British Journal of Plastic Surgery, 39*, 222-224.
JOHNSTON, M. (1986). Pre-operative emotional states and post-operative recovery. *Advances in Psychosomatic Medicine, 15*, 1-22.

KALICK, S.M. (1979). Aesthetic surgery: How it affects the way patients are perceived by others. *Annals of Plastic Surgery, 2*, 128-

KNORR, N.J. (1972). Feminine loss of identity in rhinoplasty. *Archives of Otolaryngology, 96*, 11-15.

KNORR, N.J., Edgerton, M.T. & Hoopes, J.E. (1967). The "insatiable" cosmetic surgery patient. *Plastic and Reconstructive Surgery, 40*, 285-289.

LAVELL, S. & Lewis, C.M. (1984). SAFE: A practical guide to psychological factors in selecting patients for facial cosmetic surgery. *Annals of Plastic Surgery, 12*, 256-259.

LINN, L. & Goldman, I.B. (1949). Psychiatric observations concerning rhinoplasty. *Psychosomatic Medicine, 11*, 307-314.

MACGREGOR, F.C. (1981). Patient dissatisfaction with results of technically satisfactory surgery. *Aesthetic Plastic Surgery, 5*, 27-32.

MARCUS, P. (1984). Psychological aspects of cosmetic rhinoplasty. *British Journal of Plastic Surgery, 37*, 313-318.

MEDICAL PSYCHOTHERAPIST NEWSLETTER (1986). Emergence of medical psychotherapy: The new role of the mental health practitioner in the health care system (Part II). *Medical Psychotherapy Newsletter, 2*, 1-3.

MEERLOO, J. (1956). The fate of one's face. *Psychiatric Quarterly, 30*, 31-43.

MEYER, S. & Jacobsson, S. (1986). The predictive validity of psychosocial factors for patients' acceptance of rhinoplasty. *Annals of Plastic Surgery, 17*, 513-520.

OHLSEN, L., Ponten, B. & Hamberg, G. (1979). Augmentation mammoplasty: A surgical and psychiatric evaluation of the results. *Annals of Plastic Surgery, 2*, 42-52.

REES, T. (with Simmons, S.) (1987). *More than just a pretty face: How cosmetic surgery can improve your looks and your life.* Boston: Little, Brown & Company.

SCHWEITZER, I. & Hirschfeld, J.J. (1984). Post-rhytidectomy psychosis: A rare complication. *Plastic and Reconstructive Surgery, 74*, 419-422.

STAYMAN, J.W., Norman, H.G., Tucker, K.R. & Virnelli, F.R. (1987, May). *Clinical hypnosis: An adjunct to aesthetic surgery*. Paper presented to the American Society of Plastic and Reconstructive Surgery, Atlanta, GA.

THOMAS, C.S. (1984). Dysmorphophobia: A question of definition. *British Journal of Psychiatry, 144*, 513-516.

VIEDERMAN, M. (1986). Personality change though life experience (I): A model. *Psychiatry, 49*, 204-217.

WENGLE, H.P. (1986a). The psychology of cosmetic surgery: A critical overview of the literature 1960-1982-Part I. *Annals of Plastic Surgery, 16*, 435-443.

WENGLE, H.P. (1986b). The psychology of cosmetic surgery: Old problems in patient selection seen in a new way-Part II. *Annals of Plastic Surgery, 16*, 487-493.

WRAY, R.C. (1986). "The buck stops here" [Editorial]. *Plastic and Reconstructive Surgery, 77*, 85-86.

Medical Psychotherapy
1988, Volume 1, pp. 15-22

© 1988 by
Hans Huber Publishers, Toronto

Psychotherapy with Head-Injured Patients

J.D. BALL, Ph.D.
Eastern Virginia Medical School

Despite a long-standing reluctance on the part of many psychotherapists to treat brain-damaged patients, these patients need and stand to benefit from a variety of psychotherapeutic services and modalities. This paper presents the rationale for therapy with head-injured patients, discusses characteristics of this population, and offers a case example of brief psychotherapy with a head injured adolescent to illustrate the content and process of treatment for these individuals.

Introduction

Many psychotherapists and some popular texts (e.g., Yalom, 1986) regard brain-damaged patients as poor candidates for their treatments. This bias has contributed to severe psychosocial stress for head-injury victims and their families. Fortunately, two forces are coming together to highlight the benefits of psychotherapy for this population. First, advances in both neuropsychology and psychotherapy show brain-injured patients to be a varied group who can profit from a variety of tailor-made therapies. Second, the incidence of head injury and the severity of subsequent adjustment problems are creating a large and growing demand for a wide range of rehabilitative services. This paper presents an overview of these influential forces, discusses a specific psychotherapy model to employ with this population, and offers a case example to tie these ideas together.

Advances in Neuropsychology and Psychotherapy

Modern advances in understanding brain-behavior relationships have exposed the wide variability among brain-damaged patients. As a result, clinicians now ask more

Inquiries or reprint requests should be directed to J.D. Ball, Ph.D., Eastern Virginia Medical School, Department of Psychology and Behavioral Sciences, 205 Business Park Drive, Virginia Beach, Virginia 23462.

informed questions than simply whether or not brain damage is present. Neuropsychological test batteries describing specific ability patterns now have established validity as diagnostic aids and treatment planning tools (Boll, 1978; Reitan & Davidson, 1974). With respect to head injuries, neuropsychology has evolved through the development of psychometric tools, to investigations of the cognitive sequelae of head injury, and finally to more recent research into psychosocial adjustment problems of head-injured patients. Studies of related psychosocial disabilities, though long in coming, show these problems to be more long lasting and perhaps more devastating than cognitive impairments (Brooks, 1984; Brooks & McKinlay, 1983; Lezak, 1978; 1987). Consequently, literature reports of forms of psychotherapy with brain-injured patients are on the increase (Lezak, 1978; Morris & Bleiberg, 1986; Prigatano, 1986; Sbodorne, 1984).

Psychotherapy research has shown no one school of intervention to be superior (see Borduin, 1984; and Stiles, Shapiro, & Elliot, 1986 for reviews), but patient selection has been based too often on such psychodynamic prerequisites as psychological-mindedness, capacity for insight, verbal fluency, and a language of feelings. While many head-injured patients are candidates even for psychodynamic therapy, a still greater number can make substantive gains through other approaches. Directive behavioral and systemic strategies, for example, often work through other family members and do not depend for their success on the patient's early memories, verbal associations, or ability to follow complex social interactions. Frank (1974, 1985) has defined psychotherapy as an effort to combat demoralization through: (1) an emotionally charged confiding relationship with a helper, (2) a healing setting, (3) a rationale that allows the therapist to derive a procedure for symptom resolution, and (4) active participation and faith from both patient and therapist. Under this definition, many brain- impaired persons have been receiving psychotherapy for years, even if it has not until recently been delivered by medical psychotherapists.

Psychotherapy Needs of Brain-Injured Patients

Head-injured patients are a special subgroup of neuropsychologically impaired individuals. While highly variable, they share characteristics that should interest psychotherapists: (1) they are a large and needy group whose life adjustment may hinge on the success (or availability) of psychotherapy; and (2) they suffer from predictable emotional and behavioral problems.

Incidence

The National Head Injury Foundation (1983) has estimated that 50,000-90,000 people a year suffer functional impairments from head injuries in the United States alone. There is a steep rise in the incidence rate for young adults between the ages of 15 and 24, and males may outnumber females by 4:1 (Field, 1976; Kerr, Kay, & Lassman, 1971; Kraus, 1980). Motor vehicle accidents account for 70% of closed head injuries that result in coma (Kalsbeek, McLaurin, Harris, & Miller, 1980), and the most firmly established risk factor has been the use of alcohol shortly before injury (Field, 1976; Kerr et al., 1971). Modern medical science has dramatically improved survival rates (Levin,

Benton, & Grossman, 1982), leaving large numbers of survivors and their families with massive medical and emotional needs.

Psychosocial Adjustment Problems

Cognitive and sensory/motor abilities show predictable recovery patterns after head injury (Barth & Boll, 1981; Miller, 1984), but longer-lasting psychological changes may severely impact family interactions and may be associated with psychiatric morbidity in particular family members (Brooks, 1984; Levin et al., 1982). Families of head-injured patients have reported an easier adaptation to the survivor's cognitive changes than to alterations in behavior and personality (Brooks & McKinlay, 1983). Listed below are samples of typical adjustment hurdles that these families may encounter.

Loss. Brain-injured patients and their families must accommodate to a unique and profound loss. While most of us have experienced incapacitating illnesses or injuries, we have learned to expect that medical treatment and/or time will lead to near total recovery. There are few precedents for the substantive and lasting changes to one's core identity that brain injury precipitates. As the brain is the organ of adaptive behavior, lost functions after brain injury may dramatically alter both personality and ability patterns. Functional losses may include the loss of those very skills normally used to contend with loss itself.

Uncertainty. Superimposed on this massive loss is continued uncertainty over just what has happened (Peake, Ball, & Lucci, 1986; Prigatano, 1986). As brain functioning can be observed only indirectly (through its effects on behavior), there is enormous confusion over what an individual can and cannot do, how long any disability will endure, and what can be done to help. The complexity and multiplicity of brain functions helps explain the rush of additionally confusing rehabilitation specialists after brain injury, which led one of my own patients to comment recently, "I've been doctored to death!"

Family role shifts. Behavioral changes of this magnitude also precipitate dramatic family role shifts. For example, some families are stymied completely when their most responsible member no longer shows good judgement. Shifting another family member into a leadership role even while the brain-impaired person fights to keep his or her status is fertile ground for tense conflict. Patients who have regressed in their behavioral capabilities often throw loved ones into chaos. There may be mutual resentment between caretakers and the dependent victim, especially if there is no outlet for expressing these feelings or if compensatory guilt leads to years of persistent caretaker self-sacrifice.

Pervasive lifestyle changes. Chronic, severe disabilities usually precipitate reduced financial status and social isolation. Family members often focus their lives around the victim, staying home more and losing contact with other people. The patients' awkward social skills serve to further distance themselves and their families from needed sources of social support. Of course, this devotion to the victim's needs often produces increased resentment and family tension, and guilt may win over reason, especially in the absence of professional help.

Developmental crises. Prior to their accidents many young adult patients were amidst age-appropriate issues of gaining independence, exploring personal identities, and establishing intimate heterosexual relationships. These developmental struggles are disrupted severely by the injury, which thrusts them back into an unnatural dependency on the family they were preparing to leave. Family conflicts around individuation reemerge with renewed intensity, regardless of how well they had been resolved before the accident. Similarly, problems with physical attractiveness, social acceptance, and sexual security propel renewed crises in relationships with peers. Many head injury victims experience behavioral and personality changes that include increased impulsivity, deficits in judgement, and awkward social skills, all of which complicate these issues. Preliminary vocational plans may require dramatic revision, triggering additional identity crises.

A Model for Psychotherapy

In light of the massive and chronic needs of brain-injured patients, psychotherapy for them runs a grave risk of becoming chronic itself and thereby becoming a drain rather than a support to family resources. From another angle, therapist fears of being engulfed by these families may account more than anything else for their tendency to exclude such patients from treatment. Psychotherapists might avoid both engulfment and fostering unhealthy dependencies by adopting a clinical care model in which they function much like family practitioners. Proponents of brief therapy have argued for a similar model, highlighting the advantages of a series of brief, developmentally geared interventions during age-specific life crises (Budman, 1985; Kovacs, 1982; Peake, Borduin, & Archer, in press). The model proposed here draws from those ideas, and adds the additional twist that the therapist has clinical responsibilities to both the individual patient *and* to the rest of the family. Like the family physician, the therapist functions as care provider, educator, and treatment coordinator, continually monitoring the patient's (and family's) needs for a variety of other services (occupational therapy, physical therapy, speech and language therapy, cognitive retraining, participation in self-help groups, group psychotherapy, family psychotherapy, etc.). Also like the family practitioner, the therapist may undergo long periods when he or she remains quietly but reassuringly in the corner during the "off season."

Neuropsychological testing at scheduled intervals serves important therapeutic functions in this model. These assessments are critical to the educational process as the patient (and family) struggles to answer the first and most central question, "What has happened to me?" (Prigatano, 1986). Comprehensive testing also provides a blueprint for treatment planning, lending the therapist needed credibility for the active advice-giving role he or she will assume. Data from test results aid the coordination of an interdisciplinary treatment plan and facilitate communications between specialists. Repeat evaluations provide built-in check points that cue patient and therapist alike that it is time to monitor the recovery process. Finally, testing helps the patient change his or her point of reference so that level of functioning is compared to the time of first testing after the accident rather than to the patient's ability levels prior to the accident.

To demonstrate many of the foregoing issues, a case example is presented below. While this case illustrates work with a mild case of head injury, more severely injured patients too can benefit from forms of psychotherapy. This case presentation is intended to debunk the final vestiges of the myth that all brain-damaged patients are alike (and are never psychotherapy candidates).

Case Example

The patient, Jane, was 17 years old and a high school senior when she fell down a flight of steps in her home. She was amnestic for the fall, but experienced post-traumatic amnesia of no more than thirty minutes. Subsequently, she experienced headaches, vertigo problems, serious memory deficits, and right-sided ataxia. She was seen in a hospital emergency room and released, but complaints over the next several days led to CT scans, a skull x-ray, EEG, and a glucose tolerance test, all of which were normal. She was referred for neuropsychological assessment two months after her injury when these symptoms had not abated.

There had been no difficulties with Jane's birth or early development, and she had achieved average grades through twelve years of school. However, she showed significant impairment on neuropsychological testing. Her chief deficits were marked attentional and memory problems, and right-sided motor weakness. She obtained a WAIS-R Performance IQ score of 69 and a Verbal IQ score of 85. Her Impairment Index on the Halstead Reitan Neuropsychological Test Battery was 0.6, implying moderate brain dysfunction with impairment on 4 of 7 major subtests. Personality testing suggested no psychiatric diagnosis, but indicated characteristics of repression, social approval seeking and a high incidence of somatic complaints.

Test results were interpreted to Jane, her family, and her physicians as indicative of mild head injury, and she was recommended for retesting in six months to chart her recovery and assist a more definitive diagnosis. Lateralized motoric weakness of this degree without evidence of brain hemorrhage or prolonged unconsciousness were considered unusual after a mild head injury, and Jane's personality testing raised questions about the role of emotional factors in her symptoms. Jane was encouraged to undergo individual psychotherapy and intermittent adjunct family therapy to support her through this depressing event, to address how newfound deficits might interfere with her efforts to gain independence, and to assist her with headache control through relaxation training and biofeedback. Jane and her family agreed to all of these recommendations.

While Jane was guarded in therapy, her memory problems and weak right side triggered uncharacteristic emotional lability. She frequently teared in frustration, grief, and rage over her mysterious disabilities and their injustice. She blamed herself for falling and behaved bitterly toward her parents. (Her older sister had left for college the preceding year, but her parents were having difficulty letting her go, particularly after the accident.) On the other hand, Jane rarely expressed her feelings directly and often provoked her parents into increased restrictiveness by denying real limitations. For example, her injury left her at least temporarily unable to drive a standard shift car that lacked power steering. She demanded these driving privileges anyway, until she frightened herself by being unable to extract the car from a tight parking space that she formerly would have handled easily.

Therapy was brief by design (six months). Contracted goals were to help Jane with accident-related depression, family conflict, headache discomfort, and self-acceptance. Much of this work was supportive, expressly focused on helping her ventilate a host of feelings associated with so mysterious and disruptive an injury. At the same time, she was helped to recognize and use previously successful coping mechanisms to contend with her loss. For example, as she formerly had relied upon high levels of activity to fend off underlying resentments or depression, these coping skills were tapped again in therapy by referring her to a physical therapist and a local health club. Increasing physical activity had dual objectives of helping Jane gain strength on her right side and helping her physically discharge her rage and frustration rather than displace them onto her parents. However, conflict with her parents also seemed based on accumulated resentments that preceded her injury, and therapy focused on helping Jane express her feelings more directly. Behavioral methods of assertiveness training and related cognitive restructuring prepared her for intermittent family meetings where she was afforded "safe" opportunities to try out new skills in direct communications with her parents.

A major focus of psychotherapy was to help Jane and her family understand and accept her head injury. Repeated references to her first neuropsychological evaluation clarified what she could and could not be expected to do for herself. For example, when her parents were so fearful of another fall that they insisted on constant adult supervision, they were informed that Jane was fully able (and needed) to engage in age-appropriate peer activities. On the other hand, when Jane insisted that she was ready to begin her freshman year at a rigorous engineering school only a few months after her injury, test results provided important evidence of her inability to manage the cognitive or attentional requirements of long and arduous class days. Within this context, Jane and her family were provided with realistic hope by informing them that the typical process for significant recovery of cognitive functions after head injury is over at least a two-year period, quickest at first and gradually slowing.

As Jane became more comfortable with therapy, she reported resentments toward other physicians for failing to take her symptoms seriously. The therapist gently suggested that anger at caretakers for discounting her beliefs and abilities seemed to be a pattern that related to her relationship with her parents. Jane found this interpretation to be both interesting and accurate. She was asked how it might apply to her relationship with the therapist, and was able to discuss annoyance with the therapist for holding her back and for not curing her memory and motor weaknesses. With the therapy transference explicit, Jane's communications grew increasingly more direct and meaningful. In addition to "here and now" discussions of the therapy relationship, Jane was encouraged to attend a support meeting of a regional head-injury group. She then realized first-hand the difference between her disabilities and those of patients whose impairments were more severe. She became a support figure to a severely brain-injured student from her own school, and spontaneously noted how difficult it must be for those who had been trying to help *her*. Jane also underwent relaxation training and biofeedback (EMG and thermal training) to assist her with headaches, which seemed to have a tension component. She was quite taken with the biofeedback technology, and responded well to this intervention with a diminution of the frequency and intensity of her headaches.

Six months after initial testing, Jane was readministered a comprehensive neuropsychological evaluation. She showed dramatic improvements in cognitive and sensorimotor areas, which reflected both spontaneous recovery and her work in physical therapy and cognitive retraining. Her WAIS-R Performance IQ score had moved from 69 to 118, and her Verbal IQ score moved from 85 to 100. Her Impairment Index improved from 0.6 to 0.3. Some right-hand motor weakness persisted, and there were still mild difficulties on tasks of concentration and verbal memory. However, Jane witnessed through comparisons of the two testings the significant progress she had made. Cognitive and sensorimotor changes were attributed to predicted spontaneous recovery and physical therapy, and kept distinct from progress with emotional adjustment issues, attributable to work in psychotherapy. Seeing the recovery predictions come to pass gave her renewed confidence in herself, the therapist, and the therapy process.

With regard to subjectively determined psychotherapy gains, Jane made significant progress in her self-acceptance and in the direct expression of her feelings. She received emotional support through a very difficult time in her life, the effects of which are difficult to measure. She avoided the discouraging experience of academic failure in her first year of college and any resultant misconceptions about her own abilities. She responded well to stress management techniques, with significant improvements in the frequency and intensity of her headaches. She was able to individuate better from her family, and seemed to have altered a maladaptive behavior pattern of expecting too much from others while rarely expressing resentments. At termination, her parents reported vast improvements from her earlier levels of irritability. Jane was making plans to attend a limited number of classes at a local four-year college and had decided to take an apartment nearby. She understood that she could renew therapy at any time without fear that this would be seen as a failure of the earlier treatment to have taken. Rather, therapy was framed as something she might utilize intermittently throughout her life as her personal needs and life circumstances dictated.

Summary

The foregoing case illustrates the value of psychotherapy for head-injured patients and the need for special considerations in this work. This is a fairly dramatic example of both the severity of dysfunction that may be present after a seemingly benign injury, and the degree of natural recovery that patients may experience. Victims of more serious injuries are also candidates for help of this kind, and psychotherapists increasingly are involved in this care. Head-injured patients must contend with a major life stress, and are at particular risk during recovery for developing counterproductive coping mechanisms that contribute to serious depression and additional behavior problems. Head-injury victims represent a large and needy group of individuals who stand to profit substantially from the services of enlightened psychotherapists.

References

BARTH, J.T., & Boll, T.J. (1981). Rehabilitation and treatment of central nervous system dysfunction: A behavioral medicine perspective. In C. Prokovand and L.A. Bradley (Eds.), *Medical psychology: Contributions to behavioral medicine*. New York: Academic Press, Inc.

BOLL, T.J. (1978). Diagnosing brain impairments. In B. Wolman (Ed.), *Diagnosis of mental disorders: A handbook*. New York: Plenum.

BORDUIN, C.M. (1984). Problems, progress, and prospects in psychotherapy outcome research. In T.H. Peake & R.P. Archer (Eds.), *Clinical training in psychotherapy*. New York: Haworth.

BROOKS, D.N., & McKinlay, W.M. (1983). Personality and behavioral changes after severe blunt injury: A relative's view. *Journal of Neurology, Neurosurgery, and Psychiatry, 46*, 336-344.

BROOKS, N. (1984). *Closed head injury: Psychological, social and family consequences*. New York: Oxford University Press.

BUDMAN, S.H. (1985). Psychotherapeutic services in the HMO: Zen and the Art of Mental Health Maintenance. *Professional Psychology: Research and Practice, 16,* 798-809.

FIELD, J.H. (1976). *Epidemiology of head injury in England and Wales: With particular application to rehabilitation.* Leicester: Printed for H.M. Stationery Office by Willsons.

FRANK, J. (1974). *Persuasion and healing.* New York: Schocken Books.

FRANK, J. (1985). Therapeutic components shared by all psychotherapies. In Mahoney, J.J. & Freeman, A. (Eds.), *Handbook of psychotherapy and behavior change: An empirical analysis.* New York: John Wiley & Sons.

KALSBEEK, W.D., McLaurin, R.L., Harris, B.S.H., III, & Miller, J.D. (1980). The national head and spinal cord injury survey: Major findings. *Journal of Neurosurgery (Suppl.), 53,* 19-31.

KERR, T.A., Kay, D.W.K., & Lassman, L.P. (1971). Characteristics of patients, type of accident, and mortality in a consecutive series of head injuries admitted to a neurosurgical unit. *British Journal of Preventative Social Medicine, 25,* 179-185.

KOVACS, A.I. (1982). Survival in the 1980's: On the theory and practice of brief psychotherapy. *Psychotherapy: Theory, Research and Practice, 19,* 142-159.

KRAUS, J.F. (1980). Injury to the head and spinal cord: The epidemiological relevance of the medical literature published from 1960 to 1978. *Journal of Neurosurgery (Suppl.), 53,* 3-10.

LEVIN, H.S., Benton, A.L., & Grossman, R.G. (1982). *Neurobehavioral consequences of head injury.* New York: Oxford University Press.

LEZAK, M.D. (1978). Living with the characterologically altered brain injured patient. *Journal of Clinical Psychiatry, 39,* 592-598.

LEZAK, M.D. (1987). Relationships between personality disorders, social disturbances, and physical disability following traumatic brain injury. *Journal of Head Trauma Rehabilitation, 29,* 57-70.

MILLER, E. (1984). *Recovery and management of neuropsychological impairments.* New York: John Wiley & Sons.

MORRIS, J. & Bleiberg, J. (1986). Neuropsychological rehabilitation and traditional psychotherapy. *International Journal of Clinical Neuropsychology, 8,* 133-135.

PEAKE, T.H., Ball, J.D., & Lucci, K.A. (October, 1986). *Broad and narrow band neuropsychology services: A useful distinction.* Paper presented at the annual Neurology by the Sea Conference, Norfolk, Virginia.

PEAKE, T.H., Borduin, C.M., & Archer, R.P. (in press). *Changing frames of mind.* Sage Publishers.

PRIGATANO, G.P. (1986). Psychotherapy after brain injury. *Neuropsychological rehabilitation after brain injury.* Baltimore: John Hopkins University Press.

REITAN, R.M., & Davidson, L.A. (1974). *Clinical neuropsychology: Current status and applications.* Washington, D.C.: V.H. Winston & Sons.

SBORDONE, R.J. (1984). Rehabilitative neuropsychological approach for severe traumatic brain injured patients. *Professional Psychology: Research and Practice, 15,* 165-175.

STILES, W.B., Shapiro, D.A., & Elliot, R. (1986). Are all psychotherapies equivalent? *American Psychologist, 41,* 165-180.

YALOM, I. (1986). *The theory and practice of group psychotherapy, 3rd edition.* New York: Basic Books, Inc.

Medical Psychotherapy
1988, Volume 1, pp. 23-40

© 1988 by
Hans Huber Publishers, Toronto

The Chronic Pain Patient: Multimodal Assessment and Psychotherapy

BRUCE N. EIMER
Abington Memorial Hospital

This paper elaborates a comprehensive, multimodal framework for assessing the chronic pain patient, constructing a modality profile, and implementing psychotherapy. Behavioral, affective, sensory, imaginal, cognitive, interpersonal, and medical dimensions of chronic pain are discussed, and therapeutic interventions for targeting problems in each modality are described. Interpersonal ramifications of living with pain are examined. Taking into account factors underlying patients' resistances to forming a working alliance, a schematization of the psychotherapeutic process is introduced that emphasizes developmental tasks and milestones. Clinical guidelines are presented for addressing such resistances and for motivating patients to learn self-help techniques for coping more effectively and rebuilding their debilitated lives.

Introduction

Chronic pain is a major public health problem. Millions of individuals suffer from one or another type of long duration, intensive pain that remains intractable in the face of efforts to treat the inferred physical cause. As a result, many people are unable to lead productive lives, as pain leaves them physically and emotionally dysfunctional. Recently, there has been an emergence of interest in the development of multimodal psychological treatment approaches designed to address the varied dimensions of chronic pain (Barber & Adrian, 1982; Catalano, 1987; Holzman & Turk, 1986).

Following Melzack and Wall's (1970) "gate-control model," chronic pain can be seen as involving the interaction between three major systems in a psychophysiological interface. These are the cognitive-evaluative system, the emotional-motivational system, and the sensory-physiological system. This conceptualization suggests that effective interventions for pain control must deliberately take into account each of these three

Inquiries or reprint requests should be directed to Bruce N. Eimer, Department of Rehabilitation & Physical Medicine, Abington Memorial Hospital, Abington, Pennsylvania 19001.

systems. Mental health clinicians who evaluate and treat chronic pain patients therefore require a flexible framework for organizing their interventions within each of these systems. Lazarus's (1981, 1985a) comprehensive modality profile, represented by the acronym "BASIC I.D.," provides such a framework, allowing the clinician to conceptualize the chronic pain experience in terms of seven specific modalities. These modalities are: behavior, affect, sensation, imagery, cognition, interpersonal relationships, and drug-related and biological factors. The first letters of each of these modalities spell out the acronym.

The construction of a modality profile is a way of listing and systematically organizing the problems and complaints to be targeted for intervention, and facilitates the adaptation and fitting of psychotherapy to the patient's unique needs (Lazarus, 1985b). In this paper, I shall describe how the multimodal BASIC I.D. framework can be utilized in the psychological assessment and treatment of the chronic pain patient, taking into consideration both the commonalities inherent in this population across all seven modalities, and each patient's unique modality profile.

Given the difficulties that living with chronic pain creates interpersonally, commonalities tend to coalesce within the interpersonal modality. Many chronic pain sufferers are angry and resentful, and a great deal of this resentment finds direction in its expression towards a health care system that is perceived as having failed them. Therefore, the clinician must pay special attention to building rapport during initial contacts, and must assume an action-oriented role to encourage patients to cease blaming themselves and others, and help them to redefine their complaints in terms amenable to problem-solving and coping (Bellissimo & Tunks, 1984; Turk, Meichenbaum & Genest, 1983).

The chronic pain patient, despite pessimism and hopelessness that can spell "resistance" to straight behavior change efforts, must develop affection for the therapist. If this affection is not present, the patient will resist the clinician no matter how skillfully the latter is able to administer his or her armamentarium of techniques. This relationship forms the soil in which the seeds of change take root. The therapist must work to help patients feel good when they leave the office. If patients feel better, they are more likely to be motivated to get better through practicing the coping techniques that the therapist eventually teaches.

Conceptualizing Pain

Following Merskey's (1982) citation of the definition put forth by the International Association for the Study of Pain (1979), pain is herein defined as "an unpleasant sensory and emotional experience which is associated with tissue damage or described in terms of tissue damage." Pain is a complex subjective experience influenced by the setting, the individual's attentional set, and a host of motivational, attitudinal, cognitive, interpersonal, affective, behavioral, and sensory variables. Whereas acute pain is of short duration, usually following tissue injury, and serves as a signal that something is wrong, chronic pain is continuing discomfort of long duration that no longer serves as a signal of immediate threat.

When acute pain does not subside, the ramifications can be psychologically debilitating. Individuals whose lives are seriously disrupted and who center their attention on their pain come to occupy a chronic "sick role" (Bellissimo & Tunks, 1984; Engel, 1959; Gallagher & Wrobel, 1982; Sternbach, 1974; Violin, 1982).

Table 1
Modality Profile of the Chronic Pain Patient

MODALITY	PROBLEMS
Behavior	Preoccupation with pain, complaining, whining, sympathy-seeking, argumentativeness, irritability, explosive outbursts, loss of patience, restlessness, impulsivity, overreactivity, underreactivity, indifference, aggression, uncooperativeness, social withdrawal, avoidance of activities, overactivity, poor pacing, dependency behaviors, inactivity, medication abuse, oversolicitation of medical attention, inability to relax, lethargy, decreased work performance, difficulty coping, crying easily and frequently.
Affect	Sadness, depression, social anxiety, guilt, feelings of vulnerability, anger, resentment, inability to express emotions, unmet nurturance and dependency needs, discouragement, disappointment, anticipatory anxiety, traumatic anxiety, helplessness, fears of disapproval and rejection, deprivation feelings, emotional lability, edginess, loss of motivation, frustration, fear of failure, loss of self-confidence, loss of interest, general malaise, boredom, emotionally drained, exacerbation of pre-existing emotional problems and difficulties.
Sensation	Pain sensations in different parts of the body: head, face, neck, shoulders, extremities, back, buttocks, chest, stomach, groin, genital region; fatigue, insomnia; motor tension: shakiness, muscle aches, muscle weakness, strain, twitches, tics, easy startle; autonomic overactivity: increased and erratic heart and respiration rates, increased skin conductance response manifested by excessive sweating, cold extremities, flushing, pallor, paresthesias, dizziness, light-headedness, upset stomach, urinary and bowel irregularities, throat and chest discomfort, tinnitus, aphonia, oversensitivity to stimuli, visual disturbances.
Imagery	Nightmares, morbid daydreams, intrusive recollections, images of future suffering, images of being disapproved of and rejected, negative self-images, images of self as invalid, distorted interpersonal images.
Cognitions	Negative self-talk, negative attitudes, guilty thoughts, pessimism about the future, ruminations about the unfairness of having chronic pain, punitive thoughts, cognitive distortions: catastrophizing, overgeneralization, selective focus on pain, misattribution, all-or-nothing thinking, negative prediction, disqualifying the positive, magnification and minimization; fears of not getting better; fears of getting worse, fears of certain activities exacerbating pain, negative self-appraisals, constant worrying, confusion, memory disturbances, concentration difficulties, intrusive recollections, self-conscious thoughts, suicidal thoughts.
Interpersonal	Mistrust, conflictual and strained relationships, ambivalence, social withdrawal, social isolation, increased dependency, hostility and resentment, argumentativeness, overreactivity, marital discord, fears of rejection and abandonment, fears of social censure and disapproval, oversensitivity, decreased cooperativeness, abruptness, exacerbation of pre-existing interpersonal problems, trouble meeting others' expectations, "out of synch" with others, unmet expectations, inability to communicate needs and feelings assertively, polarized and labile interactions, feeling misunderstood, feeling unappreciated, feeling stuck in the "sick role," loss of customary social role, others placed in adversarial role, secondary gains for pain, decreased libido.
Drugs and Biology	Medication abuse, drug and alcohol abuse; lack of exercise, poor physical conditioning, improper nutrition, lack of rest and relaxation, overexertion; underlying medical problems: musculoskeletal disorders; low back pain, tension headaches, rheumatoid arthritis, osteoarthritis, myofascial pain; dental pain, nasal pain, sinusoidal pain, ophthalmological pain, otological pain; ischemic disorders: angina pectoris, peripheral vascular disease; neurological disorders: neuralgia, causalgia, neuritis, postoperative neuromas, phantom limb pain, scar tissue pain, nerve entrapments; neoplastic disorders causing nerve compression or invasion.

Hendler (1984) has delineated four stages of response to unremitting pain. During the first two months, or *acute* stage, the sufferer generally expects the pain to subside as the injury heals. Therefore there are no significant psychological changes. During the next four months, or *subacute* stage, when the pain does not remit, the sufferer becomes concerned and frightened. When pain persists beyond six months, the individual's anxiety becomes pervasive and a major reactive depression is likely to develop. Hendler terms the period between six months and three years the *chronic* stage. Pain lasting for longer than three years is termed *subchronic*. People whose pain lasts for more than three years frequently are observed to have recurrent depressions and somatic preoccupations. Those who become chronic pain patients often develop a lengthy history of unsuccessful medical and non-medical treatments to remove their pain. Their psychological profiles reveal a host of behavioral deficits and excesses, self-defeating habits, negative affective states, painful sensations, dysfunctional images, negative cognitions, interpersonal deficits, and bio-physical vulnerabilities.

A prototypical modality profile listing the gamut of problems within each modality presented by chronic pain patients is given in Table 1. It is important to note that individual modalities are not mutually exclusive, although the categories are distinct conceptually, and problems are often categorizable under more than one modality. Complex concepts such as "emotion" or "pain" are really best conceptualized as the interaction among the different modalities, and it is important to look at the whole picture. Nevertheless, for the sake of simplicity and providing a logical structure, therapeutic interventions are organized to target specific problems listed under individual modalities.

Assessment of the Chronic Pain Patient

Effective psychotherapy with chronic pain patients necessitates that each of the seven aforementioned modalities be assessed for deficiencies or "negative symptoms," excesses or positive symptoms, and disruptions. Within the first few sessions, a BASIC I.D. modality profile should be compiled, which then can serve as a "road map" for setting treatment goals. The choice of techniques to be employed should follow logically and systematically from the assessment data (Lazarus, 1985b). Lazarus (1981, 1985a) offers detailed guidelines for constructing a modality profile. Some useful structured paper-and-pencil self-report instruments to supplement a structured interview are the Multimodal Life History Questionnaire (Lazarus, 1981), the Patient Pain Questionnaire (Turk, Meichenbaum & Genest, 1983), the McGill Pain Questionnaire (Melzack, 1975) and the Beck Depression Inventory (Beck, 1967).

Two psychometrically validated self-report inventories for assessing the effects of chronic pain on personality functioning are the MMPI and the much shorter Symptom Checklist-90 (SCL-90). On the MMPI, patients with persistent pain of recent onset tend to show elevations on scales 1 and 3 (hypochondriasis and hysteria) reflecting their concern and anxiety about their bodies (Hendler, 1984). When pain continues beyond six months and becomes chronic, individuals begin to show elevations on the depression scale so that scale 2 (depression) becomes more elevated than scales 1 and 3. Hendler (1984) makes the point that many patients whose pain has lasted for more than three years eventually show a lowering of their elevations on the depression scale while their somatic concerns persist, reflected in continued scale 1 and 3 elevations. On the SCL-90, patients with persistent pain of relatively recent onset show positive symptom clusters for anxiety and somatization. With increasing pain chronicity, they also show positive symptom clusters for depression and interpersonal sensitivity on the SCL-90.

The specific categories of information that need to be collected in an initial multimodal assessment include: the patient's medical and psychiatric treatment history; current living situation; family demographics and history; precipitating events; circumstances surrounding pain onset; characteristics of the pain; information about pain location, intensity, and frequency; duration of pain episodes; the course of the pain episodes over time; the effects of situations and activities on the pain; and related physical and psychological symptomatic complaints. It is important to gather information concerning the patient's personal theories of why he or she has pain, and to inquire about the personal meanings that are assigned to its occurrence. In addition, the clinician ought to gather information about the ways in which the patient has coped thus far with the recurrences of pain, and the ways in which the pain has restricted activities and affected interpersonal relationships. Last but not least, it is always important to ask patients to consider what they are willing to do to learn how to manage their pain, how hard they are willing to work, and how they expect that life will be different after some skills in pain management have been learned. Several excellent sources are available for detailed presentations of structured interview assessments (Cinciripini & Floreen, 1983; Getto & Heaton, 1985; Holzman & Turk, 1986; Melzack, 1975; Tollison, 1986; Turk et al., 1983).

Once an adequate assessment is conducted, the patient needs to be socialized to the therapist's therapeutic model. Actually, the socialization process starts from the initial clinical contact.

Socializing the Patient to the Therapeutic Model

The therapeutic model advocated here is a relationship-oriented psychoeducational one. From the first contact, the patient is socialized to the conceptual framework of self-management through the effective utilization of coping skills. The rationale underlying the construction of a BASIC I.D. is taught, and pain is discussed as a complex multimodal phenomenon. The notion that pain is experienced in many interactive modalities is highlighted as an advantage, by making the point that there are many portals of entry for coping with it and ameliorating it. Pain management is conceptualized as a set of skills, and the idea is presented that the patient may have more of a knack for refining some skills than others. Given the multimodal nature of pain this is considered advantageous, as strengths in one modality can compensate for weaknesses in others.

As many patients are unaware of underlying psychological or environmental stressors that may exacerbate their pain, from the outset of therapy they are encouraged to record their pain-related symptoms in a diary (Turk et al., 1983). In this diary, they are asked to make pain intensity ratings for each hour of the day; to keep track of the circumstances under which their pain is most severe and least severe; and to record associated thoughts, feelings, and coping behaviors, including medication use. By providing clear rationales for such homework assignments, as well as for specific therapeutic interventions, the therapist facilitates rapport and promotes a more positive relationship.

Developmental Tasks in Psychotherapy: Recreating a New Identity

In standard applications of cognitive-behavior therapy with neurotically depressed and anxious individuals (Beck & Emery, 1985; Beck, Rush, Shaw & Emery, 1979; Lazarus, 1981, 1985a), therapy is generally time-limited. The therapist employs time-management strategies during each session, and in setting therapy goals by focusing with the patient on manageable problems, setting task-relevant agendas, and assigning self-help homework to do between sessions. Effective psychotherapy with chronic pain patients often necessitates a more open-ended time perspective. While the psychotherapist is well advised to maintain a systematic and structured focus on problems targeted for solution, it is essential that his or her expectations be adjusted to the reality that the patient is likely to have a great deal invested in maintaining the chronic sick role. In a sense, helping people relinquish a sick role is a developmental task that involves helping them recreate a more functional identity. What follows is an adaptation of Erik Erikson's (1950) stage model of psychosocial development for schematizing developmental milestones in the therapeutic process of identity reformation.

Developmental schematization rests on two assumptions. The first assumption is embodied in the principle of the "psychological double" (Beck & Emery, 1985; Horney, 1950; Kelly, 1955), which holds that people think in terms of contrasting polarities. The second assumption holds that a therapist can give patients the freedom to shift their thinking to the positive poles of their conceptual dimensions, by sharing with them hypotheses concerning the variables maintaining their negative expectations and feelings. The patient is seen as holding a triad of cognitions about self, world, and future (Beck, 1967) that have been repeatedly validated but are dysfunctional.

Often in the initial phases of therapy the essential task is to resolve negative transference. Many hopeless and angry pain patients begin therapy with beliefs such as, "I can't trust anyone to believe that my pain is real and I am not faking," or "They sent me to a shrink because they think the pain is all in my head." The hurdle at this point is to get the patient to develop "hope" that maybe once and for all, help can be given. In order to negotiate this task successfully, the therapist must be able to convey an understanding for the basis for the patient's hopelessness. The goal is to lead the patient to cognize on the positive (i.e., trust) pole of the dimension of *trust vs. mistrust*.

If the therapist cannot help the patient acquire hope, then treatment is likely to end before it begins, because the patient is likely to drop out. If the therapist is successful at this, then the therapy can proceed to the next phase. The second phase may be conceptualized using Erikson's model as a battle of "will." The patient is likely to want the therapist to validate his or her negative cognitions of self in the "sick role." Although the goal is eventually to lead patients to view themselves as autonomous, at this point they have to be offered some validation of their feelings of shame stemming from the activation of long-held cognitions of self-doubt. Paradoxically, by doing so, the therapist is granting the patient autonomy. Again, therapy can reach a premature end if the patient drops out because of a belief that the therapist lacks understanding and acceptance of the exigencies of his or her customary role.

The next phase may be conceptualized as the beginning of a purposive working alliance and collaboration. If the therapeutic relationship has progressed to the point of mutual acceptance, the patient might be ready to share his or her guilt about years of failure at implementing socially constructive, purposive behaviors, having in a sense dropped out of the functional role as a member of society. The therapist needs to acknowledge this guilt and collaborate in an examination of the patient's cognitions about it. This might also be an opportune time to explore the idiosyncratic meanings that the sick role has held for the patient. The goal of this phase of the program is to explore options and alternatives, to develop motivation to change, to accept some responsibility for changing, and to move towards the positive pole (i.e., initiative) of the *initiative-guilt* dimension.

If this phase is negotiated successfully, then therapy might proceed to a more advanced phase of true collaboration and a productive working alliance. At this point, the patient might be open to recognizing his or her sense of inferiority regarding skills and lack of competence in the context of a purposeful, collaborative, and safe relationship. This may now be an opportune time for building coping skills and concomitantly nurturing developing cognitions of "competence," through implementing active cognitive and behavioral interventions. The therapist wants to encourage the patient's industriousness in becoming more active and productive, at the same time relinquishing the sick role. Interventions might include, among others: distraction techniques (Tollison, 1986; Turk et al., 1983), thought stopping (Cautela, 1977), cognitive disputation (Ellis & Grieger, 1977), rational-emotive imagery (Maultsby, 1984), self-instructional training (Turk et al., 1983), relaxation training and self-hypnosis (McKay, Davis, & Eshelman, 1982; Zilbergeld & Lazarus, 1987), biofeedback training (Schwartz, 1987), guided imagery (Lazarus, 1977), contingency management (Fordyce, 1976), assertiveness training (Lange & Jakubowski, 1976), systematic desensitization (Goldfried & Davison, 1976), and muscle-strengthening exercises (Catalano, 1987).

Even if treatment is progressing successfully at this stage, both patient and therapist need to expect periodic lapses marked by reactivation of powerful negative beliefs about self and future, and concomitant recurrences of the negative transference (e.g., thoughts such as, "you don't really understand me after all," "I haven't changed one bit," "I can't really change, nothing helps after all, and we have wasted our time"). In reality, this is likely to be a very difficult transitional phase. The patient is faced with the task of reconciling budding cognitions of an industrious, competent self with powerful old beliefs of a self-doubting, sick self. The therapist has to be sensitive to this, and is well-advised to frame such therapeutic lapses as occasions for "turning adversity into advantage" (Freeman, 1987). Depending on the patient's idiosyncratic meanings and the nature of the lapses, it may be necessary to review the changes made up to this point. Adversity may be reframed as an opportunity for the patient to employ new skills in identifying and disputing cognitive distortions, and to identify, challenge, and restructure dysfunctional core assumptions concerning major issues such as acceptance of pain, personal competence, and control (Beck & Emery, 1985). In terms of Erikson's model, this phase can be conceptualized as a time of identity reformation.

In the following section, various therapeutic techniques for addressing the major problems likely to be identified within each of the seven modalities are briefly discussed. It is important to keep in mind that techniques are not used best in a rote or mechanical fashion. Their successful clinical administration demands flexibility, sensitivity, proper timing, clinical intuition, and knowledge. As Turk, Meichenbaum, & Genest (1983) point out, "a spontaneous, flexible approach will help to establish an atmosphere of rapport, confidence, and alliance" (p. 194).

Therapeutic Techniques

The therapist needs to model a systematic approach to problem-solving, and to combat globalizing, catastrophizing, and all-or-nothing thinking about problems. Therapeutic techniques are logically selected based on an analysis of the problems identified and targeted for intervention in the patient's modality profile (Lazarus, 1985b). Problems are addressed in terms of their urgency, priority, and amenability to solution. It often helps to address "easy" problems early in the therapy in order to promote the patient's sense of self-efficacy and competence (Beck, Rush, Shaw & Emery, 1979). Vague problems are defined in concrete cognitive and behavioral terms; global complaints are made more specific by breaking them down into their component parts so that they become less overwhelming.

Different components of each problem are addressed in their idiosyncratic context and at opportune times. For example, a depression would be addressed in terms of its behavioral components (e.g., inactivity and inertia), affective components (e.g., feeling sad, disappointed, and hopeless), cognitive components (e.g., self-condemning and blaming thoughts, negative expectations, lack of hope), interpersonal components (e.g., social withdrawal, putting people off), and biological components (e.g., vegetative symptoms, response to medication). Each of these components is assessed in terms of the "five W's," these being: What does the problem involve? What maintains the problem? Where does the problem occur? When does it occur? and With whom does it happen? Interventions are then chosen to address the factors involved in maintaining the problem at given times in given situations with particular people.

What follows is an outline of the major techniques that are employed for targeting particular categories of problems within each modality.

Techniques for Shaping Functional Behaviors

Behavioral deficits such as withdrawal, inactivity and avoidance are approached through the implementation of contingency management and behavioral shaping procedures such as graded task assignments (Beck et al., 1979; Fordyce, 1976). Behavioral excesses such as complaining, whining, sympathy-seeking, and argumentativeness are also best addressed in this manner. As behavioral problems frequently occur in an interpersonal context, it is important to involve family members in the treatment. With the patient's approval, family members can be taught behavioral extinction, selective reinforcement, and response-cost procedures for decreasing behavioral excesses (Bellack & Hersen, 1985; Cameron, 1982; Fordyce, 1976).

The patient also needs to learn these procedures to employ as self-management strategies. Many pain patients are unable to modulate their activity levels; they either engage in spurts of excessive activity or are completely inactive, which results either in physical deconditioning from a lack of activity or additional injuries from overexertion. Therefore, it is important to teach such people to pace themselves. This task often demands that the underlying cognitions of all-or-nothing thinking and perfectionism be pinpointed and restructured. Patients need to practice setting limits on the intensity and duration of their efforts in performing chores, duties, and obligations. They need to learn when to stop and rest when they begin to feel pain. Also useful are self-instructional strategies (Turk et al., 1983), and contingency management involving the self-administration of rewards for effort rather than solely for performance or outcome.

Techniques for Altering Negative Emotions

In the affective sphere, chronic pain patients often have difficulty expressing emotions and are frequently emotionally needy. It is therefore helpful to encourage them to ventilate feelings during therapy sessions. Such ventilation can be included in a session's agenda. In addition, assertiveness training (Lange & Jakubowski, 1976) through role-modeling and behavioral rehearsal are frequently indicated for shaping assertiveness and expressive skills.

Rational-emotive imagery (Maultsby, 1984) can be a useful technique for helping the patient learn to change painful emotions to more neutral or positive emotions. In addition, the therapist ought to teach the "rational-emotive A-B-C's" of emotional disturbance (Ellis & Grieger, 1977) and various cognitive techniques such as thought stopping (Cautela & Kearney, 1986), cognitive disputation (Ellis & Grieger, 1977) and self-instructional training (Turk et al., 1983). These techniques are aimed at helping the patient identify and alter dysfunctional cognitions that create and maintain negative affects. They will be addressed in more detail in a later section.

Another very powerful affective technique involves accessing positive affective states by recalling positive memories of past successes and pleasant experiences. Kall (1987) suggests building a "library" of positive experience memories. The basic idea is that positive affects are incompatible with negative ones, and that by learning to replace the latter with the former, one in effect "displaces" negative emotional states. Zilberfeld & Lazarus (1987) offer detailed instructions for hypnotically recalling past successes, which is a useful coping strategy for combatting depression and anxiety. Positive affects from past successful experiences can mobilize hope and conviction and dispel hopelessness and helplessness in the present.

The hypnotic technique known as the "affect bridge" is a powerful method for uncovering the origins of current negative affective states (Edelstien, 1981). The patient is put into a trance and instructed to experience the troublesome feeling in moderate intensity, and then to indicate through ideomotor signaling when the feeling has been attained. Then, the therapist gives the patient permission to hold onto the feeling so that it can be used as a bridge to the past, and to utilize the feeling state as a cue for reconstructing the circumstances under which that particular feeling and associated cognitions originally emerged. Once the original circumstances are reconstructed, they can be restructured so that more positive feeling states can replace the negative ones.

Techniques for Re-regulating Sensory-Physiological Dysregulation

Most chronic pain patients suffer from chronic psycho-physiological dysregulation. Their autonomic overreactivity to stressful situations actually makes for more tension and stress, which perpetuates and exacerbates the pain. Therefore, the sufferer who is caught in a vicious pain-tension-pain cycle needs to learn strategies for re-regulating his or her physiological response system and for breaking out of the negative cycle.

Also, most chronic pain patients complain primarily in somato-sensory terms. Therefore, somatically-oriented interventions are useful for "tracking" patients' "firing orders" for construing their problems (Lazarus, 1985b).

Chronic pain patients often benefit from learning relaxation skills for reducing muscle tension levels that exacerbate musculoskeletal pain and for quieting autonomic nervous system activity. These strategies include progressive muscle tensing and letting-go exercises in the tradition of Jacobson (1977) and passive deep muscle relaxation solely emphasizing letting go of muscle tension (Zilbergeld & Lazarus, 1987). In addition to muscle relaxation, other forms of relaxation for achieving the "quieting response" (Stroebel, 1982) are various forms of meditation and deep, diaphragmatic breathing.

The inclusion of a biofeedback component (Stroebel, 1982), often makes it easier to learn relaxation skills. In this form of therapy, behavioral shaping procedures are employed for feeding back to the patient precise data on his or her progress in lowering sensory and physiological arousal levels (Basmajian, 1983; Schwartz, 1987). Biofeedback-assisted relaxation training teaches one to notice when one is unnecessarily tensing different parts of one's body, and to relax those parts that do not need to be tensed. Such "differential relaxation" helps to break the pain-tension cycle as patients learn to mobilize only those muscle groups that are necessary for a given activity and to relax all others, thus conserving energy. In addition, they are taught to regulate peripheral blood flow so that they can warm their extremities at will. By learning hand- and foot-warming techniques, they indirectly learn how to lower central and autonomic nervous system arousal (Schwartz, 1987).

In the somatic sphere, the therapist should also discuss the necessity of starting a graduated physical exercise program for increasing muscle strength, joint flexibility and range of motion. As this is the domain of the physical therapist and the physician, permission should be obtained from the patient to consult with these specialists.

Techniques for Working with Imagery

Self-hypnosis and guided imagery are useful techniques that can be taught in a skills-based program for learning to alter pain perceptions and images (Hilgard & Hilgard, 1983). Patients can be taught how to "re-program" their negative images, sensations and self-suggestions in a receptive state of relaxation (Zilbergeld & Lazarus, 1987).

Basically, self-hypnosis depends on the acquisition and reinforcement of three skill components (Golden & Friedberg, 1986; Zilbergeld & Lazarus, 1987). These are: inducing a state of relaxed wakefulness, learning to focus one's attention, and refining the ability to generate vivid images and covert verbalizations. Hypnotic techniques capitalize on the phenomenon of distraction; learning to become re-absorbed in something other than pain-related perceptions.

Turk, Meichenbaum and Genest (1983) categorize attention-diverting strategies into those that simply involve shifting attentional focus and those that involve the evocation of imagery. Purely attentional strategies would include the refocusing of attention externally on selected physical characteristics of the environment (e.g., counting ceiling tiles or noticing how many cars of each make you pass on the highway), or internally on thoughts that are unrelated to pain or paradoxically, on the subtle nuances of the pain sensations themselves. The rationale of the latter strategy is to be able to view the pain sensations objectively so as to reduce catastrophizing about them and to lower emotional arousal.

Attention-diverting strategies that involve the deliberate utilization of imagery would include techniques such as imagining oneself in a comfortable pleasant place, re-interpreting the pain sensations as something other than pain (e.g., mentally transforming a stabbing sensation into a tickle), and producing hypnotic analgesia (e.g., imagining that the affected body parts have been injected with Novacain, or visualizing them as made of some artificial substance such as rubber or metal, rendering them incapable of transmitting pain sensations). Another form of imagery involves the imaginative transformation of the context in which the pain is experienced. For example, the sufferer might imagine himself or herself as an athlete or hero who can endure or ignore pain in the midst of an action episode.

Bresler (1979) discusses a guided imagery technique that involves finding an "inner advisor" or guide. In a state of relaxation, the individual takes a "mental trip" to a pleasant and private place where he or she is guided to find a special friend. This special friend is then utilized as an advisor to help the sufferer find new meaning in his or her suffering. A key assumption of this approach is that chronic pain is a signal from the body that needs to be addressed and understood, and the individual is guided to become more attuned to these signals. The kind of guided imagery employed in the inner advisor technique has many similarities to Simonton's (Simonton, Simonton, & Creighton, 1978) visualization approach to mobilizing the body's immunity against the malignancies of cancer. A key similarity is that in both contexts one is guided to tap previously untapped psychological resources for mobilizing hope and self-efficacy.

Another useful imagery technique is termed process or action imagery. In behavior therapy parlance it is also known as mental rehearsal (Zilbergeld & Lazarus, 1987). It involves imagining oneself performing a desired set of behaviors or action sequence. Mental rehearsal is usually employed for the purposes of training in order to shape one's performance to a desired level of proficiency. However, it can also be utilized as a substitute for the activity itself, and this is where it is relevant for the chronic pain patient who for medical reasons may be unable to engage in a certain desired physical activity.

For example, the author saw a depressed and very anxious young man who was recovering from an acute lumbar sprain and strain. He was medically advised to cease running for an indefinite time period. This young man had been running on the average of five times per week for over nine years and he thrived on it! As a result, the physician's proscription contributed significantly to his anxiety and depression. The author commiserated with his plight, and took the soonest opportunity to suggest a constructive alternative for coping, which involved the use of action imagery. The patient was taught how to induce a state of physical and mental relaxation through deep diaphragmatic breathing and progressive muscle relaxation. He was then coached to generate a vivid imagery of himself running from start to finish. This therapeutic team also discovered certain advantages to the use of imagery, the main one being that reality constraints could be slightly violated, and the patient could actually enhance the experience of joy and mastery associated with running, by visualizing himself running better than he ever had run in reality. Another advantage was that the imagery could be used along with biofeedback in order to train him to calm his overreactive nervous system. Electromyographic, heart rate, respiration rate, and blood volume pulse were the biofeedback modalities employed to assist the training. Utilizing these modalities, he was trained to maintain a state of low arousal while generating his arousing images.

Initially, his electromyographic activity, heart rate, and respiration rate rose and blood flow to his extremities constricted when he imagined his scenes. However, with practice, he was able to maintain a low arousal state while imagining himself performing smoothly or performing poorly. His successes in building these skills enhanced his sense of self-efficacy and at the same time provided him with concrete skills for managing his anxiety and depression.

The next section describes cognitive self-instructional strategies that were utilized for coping with negative thoughts and images and for re-programming positive ones.

Cognitive Strategies

Chronic pain sufferers evidence specific patterns of mistaken cognitive appraisals in a "downward spiral" of depressogenic thinking (Catalano, 1987; Lefebvre, 1981). These patterns of cognitive distortion were originally described by Beck and his colleagues (Beck, 1976; Beck et al., 1979; Burns, 1980; Freeman, 1987). They include: catastrophizing about one's limitations, magnifying the negative aspects of pain-related situations, expecting the worst to happen, making negative predictions that reinforce hopelessness and helplessness, overgeneralizing about the negative ramifications of pain-related limitations and their implications, selectively focusing on pain to the exclusion of other things, misattributing blame for pain to one's own insufficiencies, evaluating the implications of one's pain-related condition in all-or-nothing or "black and white" terms, disqualifying positive features of one's situation, and minimizing one's functional resources.

Cognitive techniques for pain control serve several important functions for the sufferer. These include providing motivation for coping, guiding coping efforts, setting limits on self-defeating thoughts and images, and identifying and restructuring cognitive distortions and dysfunctional beliefs. Motivation for coping is enhanced to the extent to which the individual is successful at countering negative self-talk and generating positive self-talk. Given that success increases the probability of more success, effective copers are those who make positive interpretations of their coping efforts and avoid catastrophizing (Turk et al., 1983).

Turk, Meichenbaum, and Genest (1983) have adopted the work of Meichenbaum (1977) to develop a self-instructional training program for chronic pain patients. This program is geared towards enhancing patients' motivation for coping by teaching them how to talk positively to themselves during the different circumstances in which pain is present. For example, to prepare for the eventual onset of pain, they are coached to remind themselves that their predicament is a workable one, and taught to plan out how they are going to cope and to review techniques that might be employed. Anxiety is re-interpreted as a cue for staying on task. For confronting pain and coping with exacerbations of discomfort, patients are taught to focus on coping, to stay on task, to refuse to catastrophize, and to manage physical tension through muscle relaxation and deep breathing. They are helped to compile a "library" of self-statements to facilitate coping in the above situations, and are taught to self-monitor and self-reinforce performance.

Limits are set on self-defeating thoughts and images by learning to abort them before they become overwhelming. The basic technique employed for this purpose is "thought-stopping" (Cautela, 1977), which simply involves interrupting a sequence of negative ideas by vocalizing or subvocalizing the words "stop" a number of times and then substituting an alternative flow of thoughts or images. Golden and Friedberg (1986) describe two other variants of thought-stopping. The first technique simply involves noticing when one is having negative thoughts or images and then reminding oneself to "let go" of them and refocus on positive ideas. A second is derived from the Zen meditation tradition, and emphasizes passively allowing any negative thoughts to flow through one's "stream of consciousness" and then gently going back to thinking positive thoughts. In practice, these cognitive limit-setting techniques are best utilized along with self-instructional strategies. The latter provide the "backbone" and guide the individual's efforts at coping with pain.

Freeman (1987) describes a number of cognitive strategies for testing the reality of negative cognitions and for restructuring cognitive distortions, which can be grouped into five conceptually distinct but overlapping categories. These are: uncovering strategies, problem-solving strategies, hypothesis-testing strategies, re-interpretive strategies, and cognitive rehearsal strategies.

Uncovering strategies include searching for the idiosyncratic meaning of patients' statements, utilizing the "downward arrow" technique to help them follow their reasoning to the underlying schematic issues, guiding them to fantasize their worst concerns, and labeling cognitive distortions.

Problem-solving strategies include examining options and alternatives for coping, and listing the advantages and disadvantages of retaining particular beliefs or engaging in particular behaviors.

Hypothesis-testing strategies include questioning and examining the evidence supporting particular ideas and beliefs, and having patients estimate the probabilities of the worst possible circumstances occurring and then questioning the evidence supporting their fears related to these circumstances.

Re-interpretive strategies include helping patients to scale their evaluations of events so as to see things as existing on a continuum rather than solely in terms of good or bad, identifying their misattributions of blame for their difficulties and reassigning responsibility more realistically, and helping them to replace depressogenic and anxiety-provoking images with more functional ones.

Finally, cognitive rehearsal strategies include guiding patients to practice particular behaviors or ways of thinking mentally in order to consolidate newly formed skills and identify trouble spots, and giving them practice in disputing aloud dysfunctional thoughts verbalized by the therapist. Actually, this latter strategy first involves the therapist modeling the disputation procedure for the patient, whose role is to verbalize dysfunctional thoughts. This is followed by a role-reversal wherein the therapist verbalizes the dysfunctional thoughts and the patient disputes them.

Following the pioneering work of Ellis (Ellis & Grieger, 1977) and Beck (Beck, 1976; Beck & Emery, 1985; Beck et al., 1979), the procedure of cognitive disputation is based on the cognitive model of emotional disturbance. This model holds that situations and events do not make people disturbed, but it is rather their beliefs about them that give rise to emotional disturbance. Therefore, cognitive disputation with pain patients would involve first helping them to identify their underlying beliefs about pain-related situations. Then, they would be coached to utilize cognitive strategies to test the reality of these beliefs and argue against them. The goal of the disputation procedure is to help the patient restructure irrational and dysfunctional beliefs in order to produce a healthier set of emotional consequences.

Interventions in the Interpersonal Modality

In addition to disregulating sensory-physiological, cognitive-evaluative, and motivational-emotional systems, living with chronic pain often dysregulates interpersonal relationships (Roy, 1986). Behavioral, emotional, cognitive, and self-image disturbances strain the fabric of interpersonal interactions. Chronic pain sufferers often have difficulty meeting others' expectations. Their relationships are frequently characterized by ambivalence, mixed messages, strain, and tension. The length of time that the sufferer has lived an emotionally and physically debilitated existence is pathognomic of the degree of disturbance in the interpersonal modality. Avoidances and dependencies become conditioned, ambivalencies become fixated, hostilities and resentments are suppressed, fears are reinforced, and the sufferer becomes more entrenched in living out the "sick role."

Once a good therapeutic relationship has developed, the therapist ought to examine with the patient the interpersonal ramifications of living a debilitated lifestyle. Secondary gains and primary losses of living with pain need to be evaluated. Patients often benefit from coaching in interpersonal cognitive problem-solving skills (Spivack, Platt, & Shure, 1976), to develop the ability to look at their relationships, generate alternative solutions to interpersonal problems, choose and implement solutions, and evaluate the consequences of their choices. Assertiveness and communications training (Lange & Jakubowski, 1976), also are often indicated when patients are unable to communicate with significant others effectively or to express their feelings.

It is often necessary to implement interventions in the marital or family system to resolve tensions arising from the exacerbation of dysfunctional relationship patterns (Roy, 1986). Family members often need to be educated about chronic pain and the patient's underlying medical condition in order to bring their expectations in line with reality. When such efforts are made, the pain patient is more likely to feel understood and accepted. Understanding and acceptance are frequently necessary prerequisites for motivating behavioral change efforts.

Marital interactions between the chronic pain patient and his or her spouse are invariably disturbed (Block, 1981; Maruta, Osborne, Swenson & Holling, 1981; Roy, 1982; Shanfield, Heinman, Cope & Jones, 1978). The pain patient frequently feels that his or her spouse does not understand or does not do enough. The spouse frequently feels drained in that he or she is not getting enough in return for what is given. Expectations are often unspoken and unclear; demands are perceived as unfair. In sum, an adequate quid pro quo is likely to be non-existent. Given these factors, a number of important therapeutic principles emerge for reharmonizing disturbed marital relationships.

The moderation principle refers to the importance of communicating feelings, needs, and gripes, but all in moderation. Excessive complaining, demanding, or griping just builds resentments and reinforces pain-related, dysfunctional roles. Therefore, the therapist should work with the couple to help them learn and rehearse how to communicate their mutual feeling, needs, and complaints in moderation.

The principle of reciprocity refers to the importance of compromise. The therapist needs to help the couple establish a contractual quid pro quo so that neither party continues to feel exploited in the relationship: both need to accept the importance of giving something in return for what is received. At the outset, it often helps to construe the marriage as a sort of business relationship wherein nobody gives or gets anything in return for nothing.

The principle of explicit expectations relates to both of the first two principles. It refers to the importance of avoiding "mind reading" by learning how to communicate expectations clearly. Members of dysfunctional marital and family systems often hold unspoken expectations of other members, or express their expectations indirectly. Thus, expectations are often unmet, grievances accumulate, and resentments linger. It is important for the therapist to help family members make their expectations explicit and then negotiate agreements. Contracts detailing duties and obligations of each involved person relative to contested issues need to be formulated. In addition, licenses and limits for sick and well behaviors need to be agreed upon.

In conducting these interventions, it is always important to avoid joining family members in reinforcing the pain patient's status as a "scapegoat" for other problems. There is a delicate balance to be negotiated between focusing on presenting problems related to pain, and becoming over-involved in pursuing other tangentially related issues. Sticking to the "game plan" provided by the modality profile of the patient's problems is the key to staying on task and remaining focused on relevant and workable treatment goals.

As was mentioned earlier in this paper, the chronic pain sufferer's interpersonal difficulties cut across the modality profile. The modality profile provides a holistic picture, but the key to therapeutic success is modeling for the patient how to break global problems down into manageable chunks. The modality profile provides a coherent organization for accomplishing this. By tracing the patient's progress with the modality profile, each small success in resolving specific problems within given modalities can be noted. Small changes add up to big changes and gradually alter the total picture.

Summing It All Up in the Biological Modality

As mentioned previously, chronic pain patients generally construe their problems in medical terms; they take analgesic medications and visit physicians to obtain pain relief. The multimodal therapist should deliberately respond to the patient in his or her preferred modality (i.e., the biological or medical one) before branching off into other modalities that show therapeutic promise (Lazarus, 1985a). The therapist needs to be able to talk in medical terms to help the patient achieve a basic understanding of the medical issues, and medical treatment alternatives need to be sorted out and evaluated. Only if the therapist validates the medical and physical realities of the patient's suffering will the patient be open to examining the emotional issues. The pain patient is hypersensitive to having the authenticity of his or her pain complaints questioned, and this sets up an initial roadblock that must be negotiated successfully for therapy to proceed.

"First things first" requires that the psychotherapist be available as a sort of medical case manager. Discussing previous diagnoses and treatment and reviewing medical treatment options is the first step. Examining patients' usage of pain medications and educating them about drug indications and contradictions is another important component in medical management. For the non-physician psychotherapist, it is useful to consult with the patient's physician.

Providing some guidance to help patients improve their level of physical conditioning is important, as is conducting interventions that address the mind-body connection and the pain-tension cycle. These interventions (e.g., relaxation training and biofeedback), have already been discussed in the section on re-regulating sensory-physiological dysregulation.

This paper has elaborated a comprehensive multimodal approach to psychotherapy with the chronic pain patient, and points to a unique tension or polarity in the psychotherapeutic context. On the one hand, effective therapy necessitates a high level of therapist activity, direction, and medical relevance. Yet on the other hand, adequate timing requires that the therapist be patient in allowing the patient to progress at his or her own pace, especially early in the treatment. Chronic pain patients present a unique therapeutic challenge. The work is often very trying and necessitates a great deal of empathy on the therapist's part. Yet the potential rewards are great. The therapist is in a position to appreciate the predicament of formerly functional individuals who feel let down by the medical system and by their significant others, and to teach self-help techniques for coping more effectively and rebuilding a debilitated life. This is a very heart-warming role to play as a psychotherapist.

References

BARBER, J. & Adrian, C. (1982) (Eds.), *Psychological approaches to the management of pain*. New York: Brunner/Mazel Publishers.

BASMAJIAN, J.V. (1983). *Biofeedback: Principles and practice for clinicians*. Baltimore: Williams & Wilkins.

BECK, A.T. (1967). *Depression: Clinical, experimental and theoretical aspects*. New York: Hoeber.

BECK, A.T. (1976). *Cognitive therapy and the emotional disorders*. New York: International Universities Press.

BECK, A.T., & Emery, G. (1985). *Anxiety disorders and phobias: A cognitive perspective*. New York: Basic Books.

BECK, A.T., Rush, A.J., Shaw, B.F., & Emery, G. (1979). *Cognitive therapy of depression*. New York: Guilford.

BELLACK, A.S. & Hersen, M. (1985) (Eds.), *Dictionary of behavior therapy techniques*. New York: Pergamon Press.

BELLISSIMO, A., & Tunks, E. (1984). *Chronic Pain: The psychotherapeutic spectrum*. New York: Praeger.

BLOCK, A.R. (1981). Investigation of the response of the spouse to chronic pain behavior. *Psychosomatic Medicine, 43*, 415-422.

BRESLER, D.E. (1979). *Free yourself from pain*. New York: Simon and Schuster.

BURNS, D.D. (1980). *Feeling good: The new mood therapy*. New York: Morrow.

CAMERON, R. (1982). Behavior and cognitive therapies. In R. Roy & E. Tunks (Eds.), *Chronic Pain: Psychosocial factors in rehabilitation*. Baltimore: Williams & Wilkins.

CATALANO, E.M. (1987). *The chronic pain control workbook: A step-by-step guide for coping with and overcoming your pain*. Oakland, California: New Harbinger Publications, Inc.

CAUTELA, J.R. (1977). The use of covert conditioning in modifying pain behavior. *Journal of Behavior Therapy and Experimental Psychiatry, 8*, 45-52.

CINCIRIPINI, P.M. & Floreen, A (1983). Assessment of chronic pain behavior in a structured interview. *Journal of Psychosomatic Research, 27*, 117-123.

EDELSTIEN, M.G. (1981). *Trauma, trance, and transformation*. New York: Brunner/Mazel.

ELLIS, A. & Grieger, R. (1977) (Eds.), *Handbook of rational-emotive therapy*. New York: Springer Publishing Company.

ENGEL. G.L. (1959). Psychogenic pain and the pain prone patient. *American Journal of Medicine, 26*, 899-918.

ERIKSON, E.H. (1950). *Childhood and society*. New York: W.W. Norton.

FORDYCE, W.E. (1976). *Behavioral methods for chronic pain and illness*. St. Louis: C.V. Mosby.

FREEMAN, A. (1987). *Cognitive therapy: An overview. In A. Freeman and V. Greenwood (Eds.), Cognitive therapy: Applications in psychiatric and medical settings*. New York: Human Sciences Press, Inc.

GALLAGHER, E.B. & Wrobel, S. (1982). The sick role and chronic pain. In R. Roy & E. Tunks (Eds.), *Chronic Pain: Psychosocial factors in rehabilitation*. Baltimore: Williams & Wilkins.

GETTO, C.J. & Heaton, R.K. (1985). Assessment of patients with chronic pain. In D.P. Swiercinsky (Ed.), *Testing adults: A reference guide for special psychodiagnostic assessments*. Kansas City, MO: Test Corporation of America.

GOLDEN, W.L. & Friedberg, F. (1986). Cognitive-behavioral hypnotherapy. In W. Dryden and W. Golden (Eds.), *Cognitive-behavioral approaches to psychotherapy*. London: Harper & Row, Publishers.

GOLDFRIED, M.R. & Davison, G.C. (1976). *Clinical behavior therapy*. New York: Holt, Rinehart and Winston.

HENDLER, N. (1984). The chronic pain patient. In F.G. Guggenheim and M.F. Weiner (Eds.), *Manual of psychiatric consultation and emergency care*. New York: Jason Aronson, Inc.

HILGARD, E.R. & Hilgard, J.R. (1983). *Hypnosis in the relief of pain*. Los Altos, California: William Kaufmann, Inc.

HOLZMAN, A.D. & Turk, D.C. (1986). (Eds.), *Pain management: A handbook of psychological treatment approaches*. New York: Pergamon Press.

HORNEY, K. (1950). *Neurosis and human growth: The struggle toward self-realization*. New York: W.W. Norton.

JACOBSON, E. (1977). The origins and development of progressive relaxation. *Journal of Behavioral Therapy and Experimental Psychiatry, 8*.

KALL, R.A. (1987). *Heartwarming: The happiness response*. Manuscript in preparation. Bensalem, Pennsylvania: Futurehealth, Inc.

KELLY, G.A. (1955). *The psychology of personal constructs (Vol. 1): A theory of personality*. New York: W.W. Norton.

LANGE, A.J. & Jakubowski, P. (1976). *Responsible assertive behavior: Cognitive/behavior procedures for trainers*. Champaign, Illinois: Research Press.

LAZARUS, A.A. (1981). *The practice of multimodal therapy: Systematic, comprehensive, and effective psychotherapy*. New York: McGraw-Hill Book Company.

LAZARUS, A.A. (1984). *In the mind's eye: The power of imagery for personal enrichment*. New York: Guilford Press.

LAZARUS, A.A. (1985a). A brief overview of multimodal therapy. In A.A. Lazarus (Ed.), *Casebook of multimodal therapy*. New York: The Guilford Press.

LAZARUS, A.A. (1985b). The specificity factor in psychotherapy. In A.A. Lazarus (Ed.), *Casebook of multimodal therapy*. New York: The Guilford Press.

LEFEBVRE, M.F. (1981). *Cognitive distortion and cognitive errors in depressed psychiatric and low back pain patients. Journal of Consulting and Clinical Psychology, 49*, 512-525.

MARUTA, T., Osborne, D., Swenson, D.W., & Holling, J.M. (1981). Chronic pain patients and spouses: Marital and sexual adjustment. *Mayo Clinic Procedures, 56*, 307-310.

MAULTSBY, M.C. (1984). *Rational behavior therapy*. Englewood Cliffs, New Jersey: Prentice-Hall, Inc.

MCKAY, M., Davis, M. & Eshelman, E. (1982). *The relaxation and stress reduction workbook*. Oakland, California: New Harbinger Publications, Inc.

MEICHENBAUM, D.J. (1977). *Cognitive-behavior modification: An integrative approach*. New York: Plenum Press.

MELZACK, R. (1975). The McGill Pain Questionnaire: Major properties and scoring methods. *Pain, 1*, 277-299.

MELZACK, R. & Wall, P. (1970). Psychophysiology of pain. *International Anesthesiology Clinic, 8*, 3-34.

MERSKEY, H. (1982). Body-mind dilemma in chronic pain. In R. Roy & E. Tunks (Eds.), *Chronic Pain: Psychosocial factors in rehabilitation*. Baltimore: Williams & Wilkins.

ROY, R. (1982). Marital and family issues in chronic pain. *Psychotherapy and Psychosomatics, 37*, 1-12.

ROY, R. (1986). A problem-centered family systems approach in treating chronic pain. In A.D. Holzman & D.C. Turk (Eds.), *Pain management: A handbook of psychological treatment approaches*. New York: Pergamon Press.

SCHWARTZ, M.S. (1987). *Biofeedback: A practitioner's guide*. New York: The Guilford Press.

SHANFIELD, S.B., Heinman, E.M., Cope, D.N., & Jones, J.R. (1978). Pain and marital relationship: Psychiatric distress. *Pain, 7*, 343-351.

SIMONTON, O.C., Matthews-Simonton, S. & Creighton, J.L. (1978). *Getting well again*. New York: Bantam Books.

SPIVACK, G., Platt, J.J., & Shure, M.B. (1976). *The problem-solving approach to adjustment*. San Francisco: Jersey-Bass Publishers.

STERNBACH, R.A. (1974). *Pain patients: Traits and treatment*. New York: Academic Press.

STROEBEL, C.F. (1982). *QR: The quieting reflex*. New York: Berkley Books.

TOLLISON, C.D. (1986). *Managing chronic pain: A patient's guide*. New York: Sterling Publishing Co., Inc.

TURK, D.C., Meichenbaum, D., & Genest, M. (1983). *Pain and behavioral medicine: A cognitive-behavioral perspective. New York: Guilford Press.*

VIOLIN, A. (1982). The process involved in becoming a chronic pain patient. In R. Roy and E. Tunks (Eds.), *Chronic Pain: Psychosocial factors in rehabilitation*. Baltimore: Williams & Wilkins.

ZILBERGELD, B. & Lazarus, A.A. (1987). *Mind Power: Getting what you want through mental training*. Boston: Little, Brown and Company.

Medical Psychotherapy
1988, Volume 1, pp. 41-50

© 1988 by
Hans Huber Publishers, Toronto

Millon Clinical Multiaxial Inventory (MCMI) Clusters for Alcohol Abusers: Further Evidence of Validity and Implications for Medical Psychotherapy

DENNIS C. DONAT
Western State Hospital
and
University of Virginia School of Medicine

A cluster analysis of Millon Clinical Multiaxial Inventory (MCMI) profiles for a sample of alcohol abusers was performed to provide a comparison with previous research. The results indicate substantial correspondence of the clusters obtained across different samples and clustering methods. The data are supportive of the MCMI as a useful measure for assessing personality pathology among alcohol abusers and for planning medical psychotherapy. Characteristics of patients within each cluster and implications for treatment based on the underlying theory of the MCMI, as well as suggestions for further research, are discussed.

Introduction

Research employing objective tests of personality has failed to identify a single "alcoholic personality" or "addictive personality" (Gaines & Connors, 1982; Neuringer, 1982). Consequently, researchers have attempted to identify reliable personality subtypes of alcohol abusers either through clinical experience (Jellinek, 1960), or through the use of cluster analytic procedures on data from objective personality inventories (Conley & Prioleau, 1983; Filstead, Drachman, Kossi, & Getsinger, 1983; Nerviano &

Inquiries or reprint requests should be directed to Dennis C. Donat, Western State Hospital, Box 2500, Staunton, VA 24401.

Gross, 1983). The majority of studies using objective personality inventories have employed the Minnesota Multiphasic Personality Inventory (MMPI). In a comprehensive review of this research, Nerviano & Gross (1983) identified several MMPI clusters that reliably emerge across different subject samples of alcohol abusers from diverse treatment settings. MMPI clusters have also been found to be consistent across the sexes (Kline & Snyder, 1985).

While these data are useful in understanding the traits and symptoms of substance abusers, their utility is limited by problems inherent in the MMPI. Many fundamental psychometric problems exist, such as the coexistence of scales that are primarily trait oriented with those that are primarily state oriented (Donovan, 1986). The MMPI evolved almost independently of existing research and theories of personality development, and was developed approximately forty years ago during a period when psychiatric nosology was considerably different from today (Widiger, Williams, Spitzer, & Frances, 1985). Considerable changes have occurred in the process of psychiatric diagnosis (Spitzer, Williams, & Skodol, 1980), and it is unclear to what extent it can be helpful in understanding and diagnosing DSM III disorders (Walters, 1983).

The proper assessment of personality pathology can be crucial in adequately planning treatment for alcohol and other substance abuse. Several studies have documented the frequent presence of personality pathology in alcohol-abusing populations (Koenigsberg, Kaplan, Gilmore, & Cooper, 1985; Mendelson, Babor, Mello, & Pratt, 1986), with estimates of the presence of an Axis II diagnosis ranging from 46% (Koenigsberg et al., 1985) to 81% of alcoholic inpatients (Vaglum & Vaglum, 1985). Donovan (1986), in a review of etiological factors in alcohol abuse, concluded that a wide range of psychostructural adaptations underlie alcoholism, which will significantly affect the course and prognosis of treatment interventions. He concluded that an Axis I diagnosis of alcohol abuse or dependence is therefore insufficient and proposed that the DSM-III be modified to make the careful consideration of an Axis II diagnosis mandatory in each case of alcoholism.

To facilitate such an assessment, the Millon Clinical Multiaxial Inventory (MCMI) may offer a useful alternative to the MMPI. This inventory was developed from a comprehensive clinical theory of personality pathology (Millon, 1969, 1981) and is consistent with the DSM-III nosological system. For example, it was developed to separate scales that reflect patients' more enduring personality characteristics from scales that gauge the more acute and florid symptomatology that is displayed. This parallels the multiaxial system of DSM-III. Having both a basis in research and a theory of personality pathology (Millon, 1969), the MCMI may be more useful in understanding factors important in the development of personality pathology and in providing guidelines for medical psychotherapy. Several other potential advantages of the MCMI are outlined in the test manual (Millon, 1983). Despite its promise as an alternative to the MMPI, the MCMI is a relatively recent instrument and requires additional research to demonstrate its clinical usefulness (Widiger et al., 1985) and to provide additional convergent and discriminant validation data by researchers other than the author of the test (Frances & Widiger, 1986; Choca, Peterson & Stanley, 1986).

To provide such data, Bartsch and Hoffman (1985) administered both the MCMI and the MMPI to male patients admitted to a public alcohol treatment program. In this study, the MMPI scores of clusters derived through a cluster analysis of MCMI profiles were consistent with five subtypes that Nerviano & Gross (1983) identified from previous MMPI research, providing some evidence of concurrent validity. To examine for additional evidence of validity, this study employed cluster analytic procedures to develop MCMI clusters of alcohol-abusing patients of both sexes from a private treatment setting to provide a comparison with the results obtained by Bartsch & Hoffman (1985), and to examine for possible differences across the sexes.

Method

Subjects

The sample for this study consisted of 150 admissions to a private psychiatric hospital in Central Virginia for the treatment of alcohol and/or substance abuse. The subjects were chosen from 166 consecutive admissions. Patients who were eliminated were considered too cognitively impaired to provide valid responses, or declined to complete the inventory. All subjects had a principal diagnosis of alcohol abuse, alcohol dependence, or mixed substance abuse which included the abuse of alcohol. Diagnoses were made according to the criteria outlined in the third edition of the Diagnostic and Statistical Manual of Mental Disorders (American Psychiatric Association, 1980). Chronologic age ranged from 18 to 77 years (mean = 40.7, SD = 15.1). Mean education was 11.3 years (SD = 3.2). The sample was of average intelligence as indicated by scores on verbal and performance sections of the Wechsler Adult Intelligence Scale-Revised (WAIS-R) (Verbal IQ = 93.0, SD = 13.6; Performance IQ = 93.0; SD = 14.5; Full Scale IQ = 92.6, SD = 13.5). A total of 109 males and 41 females were included in the study.

Procedure

The subjects were administered the MCMI approximately seven to ten days after admission to the substance abuse program. This procedure was followed due to evidence that transitory alcohol withdrawal effects may bias psychometric results (Freund, 1976) and that stability coefficients for the MCMI scales are higher if not administered directly upon intake (McMahon, Flynn, & Davidson, 1985). Treatment during this period focused on physical detoxification and/or on a review of the individual's abuse history. Such treatment is unlikely to alter significantly scores on the personality scales of the MCMI. The MCMI was administered and scored for the 20 clinical scales and the correction indices (Millon, 1983). It is a 175-item true-false questionnaire that provides a measure of eight mildly pathological personality styles, three more severe pathological personality styles, and nine reactive symptom clusters. The theory underlying the test development, reliability and validity data, and detailed descriptions of these scales are outlined in the test manual (Millon, 1983). The subjects were administered the MCMI as part of a comprehensive psychological evaluation provided to all patients. All profiles met validity requirements as outlined in the test manual.

Table 1
MCMI Mean Personality Scale Scores Across Clustering Methods

		Personality Scale											
												P	ρ
Cluster	Clustering Method	1	2	3	4	5	6	7	8	S	C	52	n.s.
I	Complete	55	47	44	38	56	62	69	47	57	55	49	
	K-Means	55	51	43	42	57	60	68	42	53	53		
												62	n.s.
II	Complete	22	27	34	68	89	81	68	36	32	26	57	
	K-Means	22	23	46	74	80	71	63	39	31	41		
												66	n.s.
III	Complete	56	69	80	60	64	65	37	84	55	72	64	
	K-Means	49	60	75	64	66	65	48	76	51	65		
												46	.01
IV	Complete	29	25	52	71	68	65	59	32	36	51	63	
	K-Means	48	59	74	64	66	66	48	75	50	65		
												56	n.s.
V	Complete	79	86	89	31	36	41	50	79	69	80	65	
	K-Means	79	93	88	53	47	61	21	85	67	84		

NOTE: MCMI scales are defined as follows: 1 = Schizoid, 2 = Avoidant, 3 = Dependent, 4 = Histronic, 5 = Narcissistic, 6 = Anti-social, 7 = Compulsive, 8 = Passive-Aggressive, S = Schizotypal, C = Borderline, P = Paranoid.

Results

In order to parallel the analysis reported by Bartsch & Hoffman (1985), the scores for the 20 scales of the MCMI were hierarchically clustered employing the maximum (complete) linkage procedure (Johnson, 1967), using the euclidian measure of distance, with five clusters generated. The algorithm for the clustering procedure is available on the System for Statistics (SYSTAT) collection of statistical software programs (Wilkinson, 1986). To provide an assessment of the validity of the resulting clusters, a non-hierarchical clustering of the data for five clusters, using the k-means iterative procedure, was also performed. The algorithm for this procedure was developed by Hartigan and Wong (1979) and is also available on the SYSTAT software package. The clusters resulting from these procedures are outlined in Table 1. Of the five clusters, only cluster IV was found to differ across the clustering procedures in a MANOVA comparison. A graphic comparison of the clusters attained in this study with the clusters attained by Bartsch and Hoffman (1985) is provided in Figure 1. To provide a quantitative measure of the correspondence of profiles across studies, a Pearson correlation coefficient was calculated for each cluster. The coefficients ranged from .50 (ρ = .02) for cluster IV to .96 (ρ < .001) for cluster V. The mean of the coefficients was .82. The age, numerical distribution, and sexual composition of the clusters obtained through the maximum linkage procedure are outlined in Table 2. The sexes were unevenly distributed among the five clusters ($\chi^2(4) = 12.97, \rho < .001$), with greater representation of males in cluster three and greater representation of females in cluster five. With females excluded from the sample, the distribution of males among the five clusters did not differ from distribution of patients in the Bartsch and Hoffman (1985) study.

Table 2

Mean Age, Distribution of Subjects and Sexual Composition of MCMI Clusters

Group	N	Male	Female	Age
I	23	18	5	42.6
II	9	6	3	37.0
III	60	51	9	38.1
IV	14	10	4	46.0
V	44	24	20	42.2
Total	150	109	41	41.2

Discussion

To avoid confusion in the following discussion, the DSM-III categories that complement the labels of the MCMI personality disorder scales will be employed. The initial

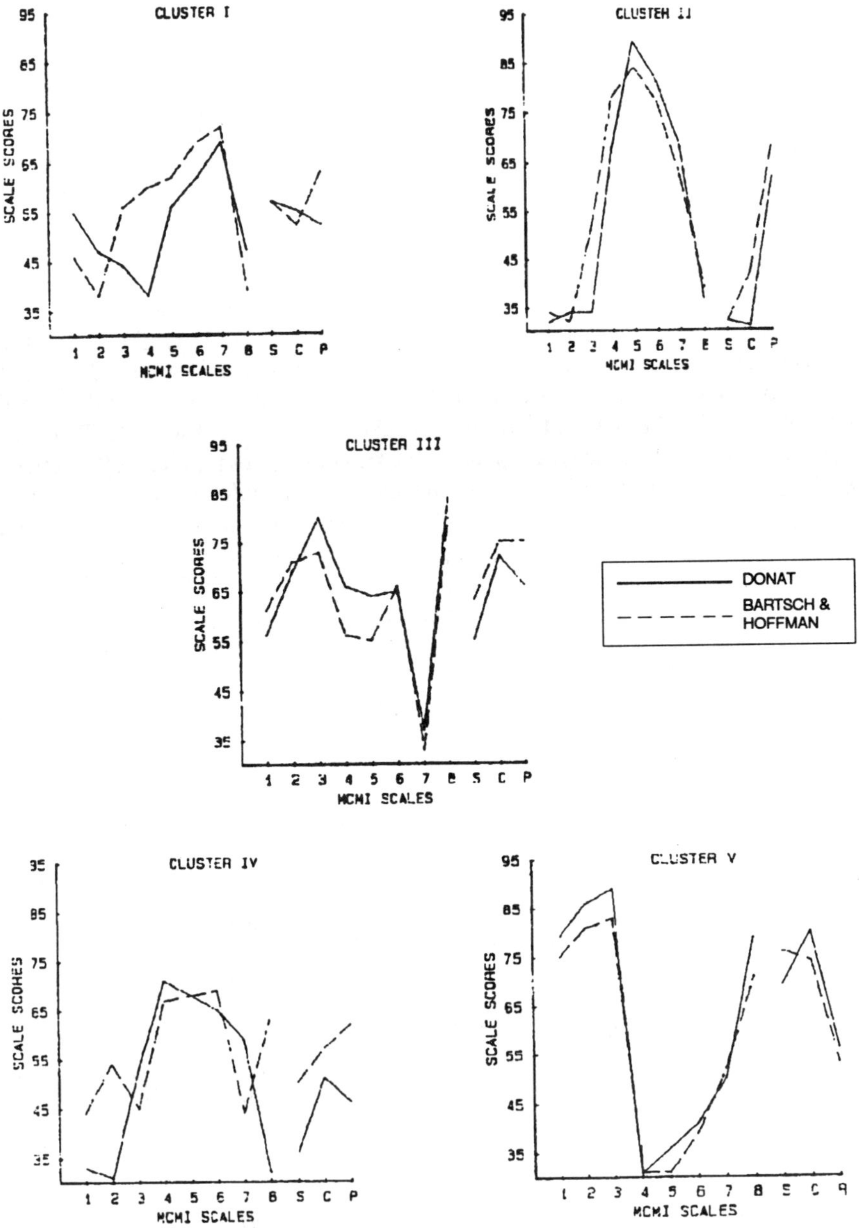

Figure 1
MCMI mean personality scales scores across studies

(MCMI scales are defined as follows: 1 = Schizoid, 2 = Avoidant, 3 = Dependent, 4 = Histronic, 5 = Narcissistic, 6 = Anti-social, 7 = Compulsive, 8 = Passive-Aggressive, S = Schizotypal, C = Borderline, P = Paranoid.)

part of this discussion will be directed toward delineating characteristics of patients within each cluster, and providing guidelines for therapeutically interacting with them.

Patients in the first cluster exhibit an elevation on the compulsive personality scale. Such individuals present as superficially cooperative and compliant to rules and authority figures, but are guarded and defensive regarding personal problem areas. Discordant emotions and behavior are strongly denied or minimized. They will quickly seek to demonstrate to staff that their problem, if they admit to it, is adequately under control. Such patients have extreme difficulty in accurately identifying and discussing emotions with the therapist and support group members, and actively avoid attempts to promote self-exploration and self-awareness. Therapists must be supportive but repeatedly present such individuals with the objective evidence of the deleterious effects of alcohol and other substance abuse on their lives, ideally with the cooperation of significant others, and how this is disrupting their home and work relationships.

The second cluster exhibits elevations on the narcissism and anti-social scales. Patients represented by this profile often present as superficially affable but have a history of impulsive, self-centered, and unreliable behavior. Interpersonal relationships tend to be shallow and temporary. Episodes of violent or dangerous behavior are frequently found in their histories. The numerous problems that their behavior arouses for them is rationalized and blame is projected toward others. These individuals actively reject the subordinate role of being a patient. They require frequent confrontation with evidence of the association between substance abuse and episodes of aberrant behavior, and respond best to therapists who project an image of strength and fair-mindedness. Therapists must remain firm and objective regarding such effects, and not allow the patient's affable and/or controlling demeanor to motivate avoidance of the topic of substance abuse.

The third cluster exhibits elevations on the passive-aggressive and dependent scales for personality pathology. This profile indicates intense interpersonal ambivalence, which motivates inconsistent and moody behavior with others. Such individuals are very sensitive to indications of censure or criticism, will frequently misinterpret others' behavior as critical, often act in a negativistic fashion, and are prone to exhibiting sudden outbursts of anger during which impulsive and dangerous behavior may occur. Embarrassment after such outbursts motivates periods of dysphoric withdrawal from social contact. A wide variety of reactive emotional symptomatology is likely to be noted. Therapists must be extremely sensitive and patient with such individuals. The principles of anger management and assertion training are particularly relevant for this group. While these patients often feel mistreated by family and significant others, the reestablishment of such relationships is, in most cases, an extremely important reinforcer for continued involvement in treatment.

Cluster number four exhibits elevations on the histrionic, narcissistic, and anti-social scales. Patients in this group share many of the same characteristics of those in the second cluster but at a milder level of severity. They may make superficially good impressions but, over time, will be self-centered and undependable. Social relationships will be shallow. They are unlikely to accept responsibility for problems that their behavior has aroused and, instead, project blame toward others. They value self-reliance in dealing with problems and eschew the idea of entering into a therapeutic relationship with another person. They must frequently be confronted with objective evidence of how their past abuse of chemicals is jeopardizing their continued access to alternative reinforcers such as their family and job. Therapists must take caution to provide such confrontation without seriously arousing the patient's strong defenses and arousing violent impulses.

The fifth cluster evinces elevations on the dependent, avoidant, schizoid, borderline, and passive-aggressive scales of personality pathology. There are many similarities here to patients in the third cluster. These individuals also experience intense interpersonal ambivalence and are sensitive to criticism by others. There is a stronger inclination to become self-critical, anxiously withdrawn, and experience periods of severe depression, during which suicidal gestures (sometimes involving a combination of alcohol and other drugs or medications) will frequently occur. These individuals require considerable emotional support to counter guilt for past behavior, self-critical attitudes, and a desire to behaviorally withdraw from interpersonal relationships. The therapist must help the patient to begin identifying and building on objective areas of strength. Anxiety management and cognitive restructuring techniques are critical for this group.

These results indicate substantial correspondence between the MCMI clusters identified in this sample and those previously identified by Bartsch and Hoffman (1985), despite differences in the setting of the research and sexual composition of the sample. In the current study, however, patients in cluster IV exhibit a much stronger tendency to restrain impulsive tendencies and exhibit a suppression and denial of discordant emotions. Because this group failed to replicate across the different clustering methods employed on the current data, it must be considered the least supported of the five clusters.

There were no differences across studies in the distribution of males among the five clusters. For subjects in the current study, however, males were overly represented in cluster III, with the associated symptomatology of behavior that is dangerous toward others, while females were overly represented in cluster V, with a greater likelihood of suicidal or self-mutilative behavior. This is likely due to differences in socialization practices regarding the expression of anger and frustration.

The data support assertions made by Donovan (1986) of the relevance of personality pathology in the assessment of alcohol abuse and dependence. While there is some similarity in the emotional and behavioral characteristics of several of these clusters, there also are important differences that must be considered in devising effective treatment strategies. The variation in the emotional and behavioral characteristics of the different clusters supports the conclusion of Vaglum and Vaglum (1985) that alcoholics are a heterogeneous group and should not be offered a uniform therapeutic approach. A more detailed delineation of the characteristics of the clusters attained in this study and suggestions for medical psychotherapists to enhance the probability that recovering alcoholics will begin and sustain involvement in recovery activities is currently being devised.

The results also add to the developing consensus that a taxonomy of alcohol abusers can be outlined, which will exhibit considerable consistency across samples with varying demographic characteristics, statistical methods, and independent investigations. These data provide additional evidence of the validity and utility of the MCMI for assessing personality pathology in a population of alcohol abusers. The results support the contention that the MCMI, having been based on a comprehensive theory of personality pathology, may be more helpful in understanding the etiology of the various clusters and in planning the treatment components of a comprehensive medical psychotherapy program. Future research should be directed toward validating the behavioral and emotional descriptions of the five clusters and toward delineating treatment approaches that most appropriately address those characteristics.

References

AMERICAN PSYCHIATRIC ASSOCIATION (APA) (1980). *Diagnostic and statistical manual of mental disorders (3rd ed.)*. Washington, D.C.: Author.

BARTSCH, T.W. & Hoffman, J.J. (1985). A cluster analysis of Millon Clinical Multiaxial Inventory (MCMI) profiles: More about a taxonomy of alcoholic subtypes. *Journal of Clinical Psychology, 41*, 707-713.

CHOCA, J.P., Peterson, C.A. & Stanley, L.A. (1986). Factor analysis of the Millon Clinical Multiaxial Inventory. *Journal of Consulting and Clinical Psychology, 54*, 253-255.

CONLEY, J. & Prioleau, L. (1983). Personality typology of men and women alcoholics in relation to etiology and prognosis. *Journal of Studies on Alcohol, 44*, 996-1010.

DONOVAN, J.M. (1986). An etiologic model of alcoholism. *American Journal of Psychiatry, 143*, 1-11

FILSTEAD, W., Drachman, D., Kossi, J. & Getsinger, S. (1983). The relationship of MMPI subtype membership to demographic variables and treatment outcome among substance misusers. *Journal of Studies on Alcohol, 44*, 917-922.

FRANCES, A. & Widiger, T.A. (1986). Methodological issues in personality disorder diagnosis. In T. Millon & G.L. Klerman (Eds.), *Contemporary directions in psychopathology*. New York: Guilford.

FREUND, G. (1976). Diseases of the nervous system associated with alcoholism. In R. Tarter & A.A. Sugarman (Eds.), *Alcoholism: Interdisciplinary approaches to an enduring problem*. Reading, MA: Addison-Wesley.

GAINES, L.S. & Connors, G.S. (1982). Drinking and personality. *NIAAA Alcohol and Health Monograph, 1*, 331-346.

HARTIGAN, J.A. & Wong, M.A. (1979). A K means clustering algorithm: Algorithm As 136. *Applied Statistics, 28*, 126-130.

JELLINEK, E.M. (1960). *The disease concept of alcoholism*. New Haven, CT: Hillhouse Press.

JOHNSON, S.C. (1967). Hierarchical clustering schemes. *Psychometrika, 32*, 241-254.

KLINE, R.B. & Snyder, D.K. (1985). Replicated MMPI subtypes for alcoholic men and women: Relationship to self-reported drinking behaviors. *Journal of Consulting and Clinical Psychology, 53*, 70-79.

KOENIGSBERG, H. W., Kaplan, R.D., Gilmore, M. M. & Cooper, A.M. (1985). The relationship between syndrome and personality disorder in DSM-III: Experience with 2,462 patients. *American Journal of Psychiatry, 142*, 207-212.

MCMAHON, R.C., Flynn, P.M. & Davidson, R.S. (1985). Stability of the personality and symptom scales of the Millon Clinical Multiaxial Inventory. *Journal of Personality Assessment, 49*, 231-234.

MENDELSON, J.H., Babor, T.F., Mello, N.K. & Pratt, H. (1986). Alcoholism and the prevalence of medical and psychiatric disorders. *Journal of Studies on Alcohol, 47*, 361-366.

MILLON, T. (1969). *Modern Psychopathology: A biosocial approach to maladaptive learning and functioning*. Philadelphia, PA: W.B. Saunders.

MILLON, T. (1981). *Disorders of personality*. DSM III: Axis II. New York: Wiley.

MILLON, T. (1983). *Millon Clinical Multiaxial Inventory manual (3rd ed)*. Minneapolis, MN: National Computer Systems.

NERVIANO, V. & Gross, W. (1983) Personality types of alcoholics on objective inventories. *Journal of Studies on Alcohol. 44*, 837-851.

NEURINGER, C. (1982). Alcohol addiction: Psychological tests and measurements. In E.M. Pattison & E. Kaufman (Eds.), *Encyclopedic handbook of alcoholism*. New York: Gardner Press.

SPITZER, R., Williams, J. & Skodol, A. (1980). DSM-III: The major achievements and an overview. *American Journal of Psychiatry, 138*, 1198-1202.

VAGLUM, S. & Vaglum, P. (1985). Borderline and other mental disorders in alcoholic female psychiatric patients: A case control study. *Psychopathology, 18*, 50-60.

WALTERS, G. (1983). The MMPI and schizophrenia: A review. *Schizophrenia Bulletin, 9*, 226-246.

WIDIGER, T.A., Williams, J.B.W., Spitzer, R.L. & Frances, A. (1985). The MCMI as a measure of DSM-III. *Journal of Personality Assessment, 49*, 366-378.

WILKINSON, L. (1986). *SYSTAT: The system for statistics*. Evanston, IL: SYSTAT, Inc.

Medical Psychotherapy
1988, Volume 1, pp. 51-63

© 1988 by
Hans Huber Publishers, Toronto

The Relationship Between Absorption Capacity And Electromyographic Biofeedback Relaxation Training with a Male Clinical Sample

HAROLD KELSO
The Pain Center, The Jewish Hospital of Cincinnati

KENNETH ANCHOR
Vanderbilt University

MICHAEL MCELROY
Alvin C. York Veterans Administration Medical Center

Biofeedback treatment has been criticized because stringently controlled research has not yet demonstrated significant clinical benefit in comparison studies done with less costly procedures. Individuals differ substantially in their capacity for physiological self-control.Controlled group outcome studies have obscured the contribution of individual differences as well as important interactions between these variables and the procedures being compared. The purposes of the present study were to replicate and extend the findings of Qualls and Sheehan (1981b) using a clinical sample, and to test the utility of the absorption capacity by treatment interaction for developing a prescriptive approach to biofeedback treatment.The obtained results support their findings of marked differences in response to biofeedback treatment between individuals who are high-and low-absorbers, and the utility of absorption capacity as a treatment relevant variable in developing a prescriptive approach for clinical biofeedback.

Inquiries or reprint requests should be directed to Dr. Harold Kelso, The Jewish Hospital of Cincinnati, 3200 Burnett Ave., Cincinnati, Ohio 45229.

Introduction

Biofeedback research appears to have reached a watershed in its development. There is growing evidence in the literature to suggest that the nomothetic approach is giving way to an idiographic focus (Blanchard, 1982; K.A. Holroyd & Lazarus, 1982; Qualls & Sheehan, 1981a). Unless researchers continue to pursue this approach, the widespread acceptance of biofeedback procedures will be in jeopardy of being disregarded before they have had ample opportunity to mature (Qualls & Sheehan, 1981a).

The initial enthusiasm for biofeedback as a clinical tool began to reach a plateau when Silver and Blanchard (1978) asked us to consider whether or not the machines are really necessary to produce change. Serious questions about the effectiveness as well as the clinical validity of biofeedback compared with relaxation training have since been raised (Carroll, 1984; Roberts, 1985; Simkins, 1982; Turner & Chapman, 1982). These authors may have prematurely concluded their reviews by surmising that biofeedback offers no advantage over other forms of relaxation training in the treatment of most psychophysiological disorders.

Qualls and Sheehan (1981a, 1981b, 1981c, 1981d) present convincing arguments that controlled group-outcome studies comparing electromyographic (EMG) biofeedback and relaxation procedures obscure the contribution of individual differences as well as important interactions between these variables and the techniques being compared. Silver and Blanchard (1978), in the same article in which they criticized the efficacy of biofeedback in treating psychophysiological disorders, concluded: "The whole field of the direct psychological treatment of psychophysiological disorders is ripe for some good work on individual differences in response to treatment and the development of predictors as to who will respond to treatment" (p. 231).

Empirical Research on Absorption

The concept of absorption was originally described by J.R. Hilgard (1970) while investigating individual differences in hypnotizability. Hilgard considered absorption to be an individual's capacity for deep imaginative involvement combined with concentrated attention and active emotional involvement in certain areas of experience that are antithetical to an analytical, reality-oriented attitude. These imaginative-feeling areas of experience are manifest in such activities as reading a novel, watching a movie, listening to music, or engaging in the dramatic arts.

Qualls and Sheehan (1979) outlined the major basic hypotheses that follow from using the concept of absorption as an independent variable. They suggested that the biofeedback condition of listening to a feedback signal would differentially affect individuals who are either high or low scorers on the Tellegen Absorption Scale (TAS) (Tellegen, 1982). Although high-absorption subjects are good at deploying, they prefer to direct their attention effortlessly toward subjective imaginal experiences. For these people, the biofeedback signal would potentially interfere with their preferred mode of relaxing by placing an external attentional demand on them. These same conditions were hypothesized to facilitate the relaxation efforts of low-absorption subjects by keeping their attention focused on the task of relaxing.

Qualls and Sheehan (1979) initiated their program of research by investigating these hypothesized interactions between absorption capacity and relaxation conditions.

Thirty-two female undergraduates were assigned to either a high- or low-absorption group based on their scores on an abbreviated 21-item version of the TAS. The study comprised two sessions. All subjects received both the biofeedback and the no-biofeedback treatments, and were randomly assigned to their initial treatment condition at the first session. During the biofeedback condition, subjects were instructed to attend to the biofeedback signal as a measure of how relaxed they were becoming. During the no-biofeedback condition, they were simply instructed to relax.

The results of the study were not all in the predicted direction. High-absorption subjects, as expected, did relax more in the no-biofeedback condition. Unexpectedly, no significant differences were found between treatment conditions for low-absorption subjects, although there was a trend in the direction of greater relaxation in the no-biofeedback condition. High-absorption subjects who received biofeedback in the second session achieved greater muscle tension reductions than those who received this treatment in the first session. Once again, the differences for low-absorption subjects were insignificant for both treatment conditions either within or between sessions.

Data from the postexperimental interviews conducted at the close of each session were also inconclusive. High-absorption subjects reported using significantly less imagery during biofeedback than during the no-biofeedback condition. By contrast, the low-absorption subjects reported difficulties in concentrating during both sessions, but stated that the biofeedback condition made it somewhat easier for them to concentrate on relaxing.

Qualls and Sheehan (1981c) published two experiments that examined the attentional demand hypothesis in more detail. They made some important methodological refinements that render their data easier to interpret. The first experiment included three experimental conditions (biofeedback, no-biofeedback, and an attentional demand condition) and two sessions. Sixteen high- and low-absorption female subjects were assigned to each condition. In the biofeedback and no-biofeedback conditions the subjects were instructed to relax as deeply as possible. Biofeedback subjects were told that biofeedback directly related to their frontalis EMG activity levels would be provided. Subjects in the attentional demand condition were told that the experimenter would help them focus on relaxing by repeating certain relaxation phrases every few seconds in a soft voice. None of the phrases in the experimenter's relaxation patter suggested a specific relaxation strategy. In addition to the patter, the experimenter asked the subjects at irregular intervals whether they were "relaxing just then," to which they were required to answer either "yes" or "no."

As predicted, the low-absorption subjects relaxed significantly more in the two experimental conditions that provided an external attentional focus compared with the no-biofeedback condition. Although the attentional demand and biofeedback conditions were in theory supposed to be equally distracting for high-absorption subjects, only the latter conditions significantly interfered with their relaxation results. The authors reasoned that the biofeedback signal was more distracting for high-absorption subjects because it was more variable, monotonous, and less predictable than the relaxation patter used in the attentional demand condition. This account of the data served as the major hypothesis for a second experiment.

In experiment two (Qualls & Sheehan, 1981c), the procedural details of the attentional demands condition were altered. Under a revised and more stringent attentional demand condition, the high-absorption subjects did not relax as effectively as the low-absorption subjects. The remaining results from the first experiment were replicated. The questionnaire data also reflected the finding that the biofeedback and attentional demand conditions facilitated relaxation for low-absorption but not for high-absorption subjects. A compelling clinical finding was the high-absorption subjects' preference for the attentional demand condition over the biofeedback condition. Qualls and Sheehan (1981c) concluded that the biofeedback signal per se is not an essential factor in relaxation. They claimed that relaxation is a performance phenomenon dependent on an individual's attentional style and the experimental condition. Attention, not biofeedback, is the important variable in relaxing under different conditions. They therefore asserted that the assessment of absorption capacity is important for determining which attentional conditions are optimal.

Qualls and Sheehan's (1981b) third and most recent study in their research provided further evidence of the Absorption x Treatment interaction, and extended their previous findings on the kind of treatment conditions that facilitate relaxation.

Eight high- and eight low-absorption female subjects were assigned to one of three treatment conditions (N = 48). In addition to the familiar biofeedback and no-biofeedback conditions, a third treatment termed the "biofeedback-imagery encouragement" condition was added. The imagery-encouragement instructions suggested that subjects use peaceful visual images as a relaxation strategy. Subjects in this condition were given an example of a set of visual images ostensibly used by someone in a previous study. The major hypothesis was that this condition would facilitate relaxation for high-absorption subjects more than the biofeedback-only treatment. It was anticipated that the low-absorption subjects would respond equally well to the two biofeedback conditions but would have difficulty in the unstructured no-biofeedback treatment.

The results were in the predicted direction. High-absorption subjects performed equally well in the biofeedback-imagery encouragement and no-biofeedback conditions across both sessions, while those assigned to the biofeedback-only condition showed the same pattern as in the previous studies (Qualls & Sheehan, 1979, 1981a, 1981c); that is, minimal progress in the first session to nearly equal the other groups in the second session.

Subjects' responses to certain feedback questionnaire items also suggest the possibility that the impressive Absorption x Treatment interaction may be short-lived. Both high- and low-absorption subjects viewed the feedback during the second session as "more useful, less interfering, and less likely to be perceived as making relaxation 'hard work'" (Qualls & Sheehan, 1981b, p. 376). Notable differences between these groups in the way they perceived the feedback were also apparent. The low-absorption subjects were more aware of the feedback and also considered it more useful than did high-absorption subjects. High-absorption subjects assigned to the biofeedback-only condition let the feedback gradually recede into the background until it became "more akin to the no-feedback condition" (p. 378). By contrast, high-absorption subjects in the biofeedback-imagery encouragement condition tended to integrate the auditory feedback signal into their fantasies.

The results for low-absorption subjects were also in line with the hypotheses. Both biofeedback conditions were equally effective for this group, while the unstructured no-biofeedback condition impeded relaxation.

The major conclusion offered by Qualls and Sheehan (1981b) is that "biofeedback interferes with relaxation in high-absorption subjects by reducing the use of imaginal processes as a mode of relaxing" (p. 377). Support for this conclusion can be found in the subjects' self-report data.

The purpose of the present study was to replicate and extend the findings of Qualls and Sheehan (1979, 1981b, 1981c) using a clinical sample. In order to be prescriptively appealing for biofeedback therapy, the long-term effectiveness of the Absorption Capacity x Treatment interaction should be successfully demonstrated.

The present study was designed to evaluate several specific hypotheses that issue from the Absorption Capacity x Treatment interaction: (a) high-absorption subjects in the imagery-encouragement instructions condition will show greater reductions in mean muscle tension than will those in the biofeedback-only condition, (b) high-absorption subjects receiving no biofeedback will reduce their mean muscle tension levels more than those receiving biofeedback only (no imagery-encouragement instructions), (c) high-absorption subjects in the biofeedback and imagery-encouragement condition will achieve decreases similar to those in the no-biofeedback condition, (d) low-absorption subjects in the no-biofeedback condition will not be able to reduce their mean muscle tension levels as much as those in the two conditions that include biofeedback, (e) low-absorption subjects in either of the biofeedback conditions will achieve similar reductions in their mean muscle tension levels, (f) high-absorption subjects in the no-biofeedback condition will be able to achieve greater reductions in their mean muscle tension levels than low-absorption subjects in this condition, (g) low-absorption subjects exposed to the biofeedback-only condition will show greater EMG decreases than high-absorption subjects in this condition, and (h) high- and low-absorption subjects in the biofeedback and imagery-encouragement condition will achieve similar reductions in their mean muscle tension levels.

Method

Design

The present study employed a 2 x 3 x 3 (High- or Low-Absorption Capacity x Biofeedback with Imagery-Encouragement Instructions, Biofeedback Only, or No-Biofeedback x Sessions) experimental design. The primary dependent variable was percentage decrease in frontalis EMG activity across three training sessions.

Subjects

Subjects were 48 males aged 25 to 60 (M = 42) with at least some high school education. All subjects were receiving treatment at either the mental health outpatient clinic or the alcohol and drug treatment halfway house of the Alvin C. York Veterans Administration Medical Center in Murfreesboro, Tennessee. Subjects were selected from a larger set of 103 individuals who had completed a 60-item questionnaire containing the 34 items constituting the TAS and 26 "filler" items as suggested by Tellegen (personal communication, June 11, 1984). None of the subjects recommended for screening was considered to be psychotic by the psychologists or psychiatrists in charge their treatment. Subjects scoring less than or equal to 14 were designated as low-absorbers, while those scoring greater than or equal to 24 qualified as high-absorbers. These cutoff scores approximate those used in previous research. Twenty-four subjects had low absorption capacities ($M = 11.17$) and 24 had high absorption capacities ($M = 26.33$). An equal number of subjects ($n = 8$) from the absorption classifications were randomly assigned to the three experimental conditions.

Apparatus and Procedures

The Bio-Electric Information Feedback System (BIFS) Model B-2 and Preamp Model PA-2M were used in this study to record frontalis muscle activity in integral averaged microvolts (mV). The bandwidth selector was set at from 95 Hz to 1 KHz. This equipment was programmed to sample frontalis EMG continuously over 1-minute trials with 18-second intertrial intervals, and to calculate the mean for each 1-minute trial. Each 60-second mean was recorded by the experimenter. During the baseline pretraining periods, the equipment was programmed to compute the mean EMG level over 2-minute trials with 36-second intertrial intervals. The biofeedback was in the form of auditory clicks varying in speed in proportion with the frontalis EMG activity. Subjects received the biofeedback signal through a headphone set.

Training sessions for all three experimental conditions consisted of four 2-minute baseline trials and eighteen 1-minute training trials. A segment from Vivaldi's Concerto in D for Two Mandolins was played for the first 12 seconds of each intertrial interval of the training trials.

Subjects were trained in three sessions, each lasting about 45 minutes. All subjects were randomly assigned to experimental conditions and the experimenter was blind to their absorption levels.

The experiment was conducted in a softly lighted, sound-attenuated room in the outpatient biofeedback clinic. Subjects were seated in a comfortable reclining chair. They were told that the purpose of the study was to learn the extent to which people are able to relax during the process of biofeedback training. Every subject filled out the trait version of the State-Trait Anxiety Inventory (STAI) (Spielberger, Gorsuch, & Lushene, 1970).

Stainless steel surface electrodes on a velcro adjustable headband were attached using the standard bipolar frontal placement site (Olton & Noonberg, 1980). Resistance was always less than 10K ohms. The skin was cleaned and lightly abraded with an alcohol-soaked gauze pad and allowed to dry before attaching the electrodes. Electro-Sol electrode paste was used as the electrolyte.

The purpose of the baseline period was explained to the subjects at the start of each session. They were instructed to sit quietly and not to begin any relaxation efforts until the experimenter read them their instructions. As previously mentioned, and unknown to the subjects, the baseline period consisted of four 2-minute trials with 36-second intertrial intervals. The first trial was considered an adaptation time, while the final three trials together served as the overall baseline against which late performance was compared. Following baseline, instructions were given to subjects according to their experimental conditions.

At the conclusion of each session, the 13-item feedback questionnaire devised by Qualls and Sheehan (1981b) was administered to subjects in the two biofeedback conditions. In addition to this questionnaire, a postexperimental interview was conducted with all subjects at the conclusion of the final session.

RESULTS

Data Reduction

Baseline EMG data were combined into a single baseline mean for each session. Experimental session EMG data were collapsed into three trial blocks with six 1-minute trials per block. A mean EMG score was then calculated for each block.

The dependent measure for EMG activity is expressed as a percentage of baseline:

$$\frac{\text{Baseline mean} - \text{Trial block mean}}{\text{Baseline mean} \times 100}$$

This percentage score was used by Qualls and Sheehan (1979, 1981b, 1981c) and facilitates comparison with their results.

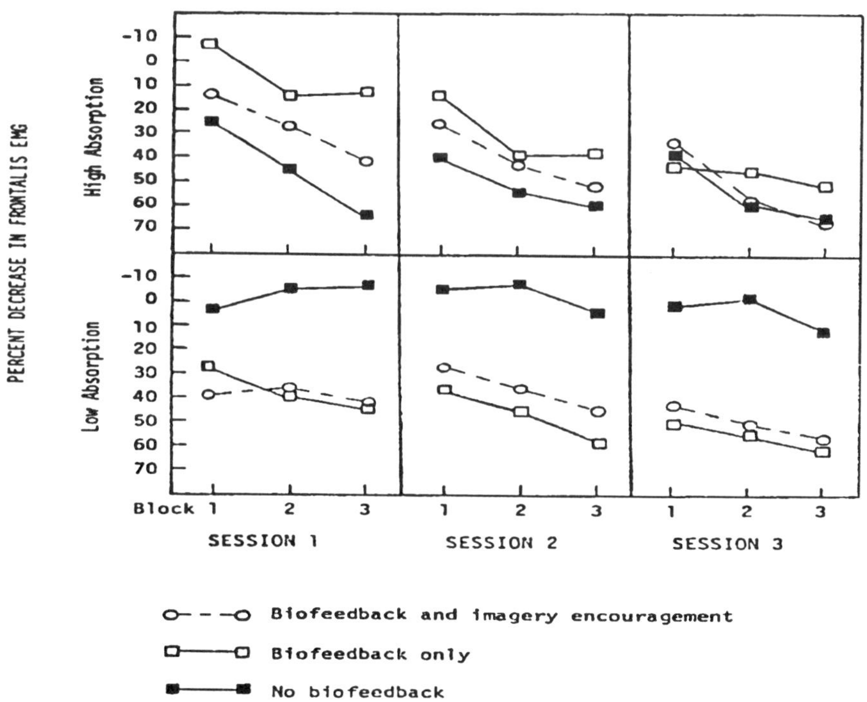

Figure 1
Mean percentage decrease in frontalis electromyograph (EMG) activity for the main effects and interaction effects of absorption capacity, experimental condition, session, and trial block.

The central hypothesis of this study, that high- and low-absorption subjects would be differentially affected by the experimental conditions, was supported by the presence of an Absorption Capacity x Experimental Condition interaction effect ($F[2, 42] = 11.92, p < .001$). The results are displayed in the Figure. The main effect for experimental conditions was significant only for the low-absorption subjects ($F[2, 21] = 14.72, p < .001$). The results of a Newman-Keuls post hoc analysis supported the predictions about the performance of low-absorption subjects. No significant difference in muscle tension reduction was found between low-absorption subjects in the biofeedback and imagery-encouragement condition and those in the biofeedback-only condition: subjects in either of these conditions made significantly greater reductions than their counterparts in the no-biofeedback condition ($p < .001$ in each case).

The Absorption Capacity x Experimental Condition interaction was further analyzed by comparing high- and low-absorption subjects in each experimental condition. Once again, the results were all in the predicted direction. High-absorption subjects responded much more favorably to the no-biofeedback condition than the low-absorption subjects. In contrast, low-absorption subjects exposed to the biofeedback-only condition relaxed more than high-absorption subjects who received this treatment ($F[1, 14] = 7.82, p < .05$). Finally, there was no significant difference between high- and low-absorption subjects assigned to the biofeedback and imagery-encouragement condition. Therefore, the Absorption Capacity x Experimental Condition interaction was due to the opposite response patterns of the high- and low-absorption subjects in the no-biofeedback and biofeedback-only conditions.

The overall analysis of the experimental session EMG data also yielded an Absorption Capacity x Trial Block interaction ($F[2, 84] = 4.53, p < .05$). Analysis of simple effects indicated no significant differences between the high- and low-absorption groups at each trial block. Further analyses revealed significant trial block main effects for both the low-absorption ($F[2, 46] = 4.11, p < .05$) and high-absorption ($F[2, 46] = 19.08, p < .05$) groups. A Newman-Keuls post hoc analysis of the low-absorption group means showed that trial block 1 was significantly different from trial block 3 ($p < .05$). A Newman-Keuls test applied to the high-absorption group means showed a significant difference between trial blocks 1 and 2 ($p < .001$) and between trial blocks 1 and 3 ($p < .001$). Therefore, this interaction can be explained by the greater decrease in mean muscle tension from trial block 1 and to trial block 3 among the high-absorption subjects.

The three within-group predictions concerning high-absorption subjects were analyzed separately using a 2 x 3 x 3 (Experimental Condition x Session x Trial Block) factorial analysis of variance with repeated measures on the last two factors. The prediction that subjects in the no-biofeedback condition would relax more than those receiving biofeedback only was supported by a significant experimental condition effect ($F[1, 14] = 7.94, p < .05$). Also as predicted, no significant difference was found between subjects in the biofeedback and imagery-encouragement and the no-biofeedback conditions. The expected difference between subjects in the two biofeedback conditions was not supported.

Feedback Questionnaire

The 13 feedback questions were each analyzed using a 2 x 2 x 3 (Absorption Capacity x Experimental Condition x Session) factorial analysis of variance with repeated measures on the last two factors.

Important differences emerged in the ways that high- and low-absorption subjects responded to the biofeedback signal. Analysis of responses to question 4 (feedback interfered) indicated that high-absorption subjects reported more interference from the biofeedback signal than low-absorption subjects ($F[1, 28] = 4.72$, $p < .05$). Related to this result was the finding that high-absorption subjects also reported in Question 10 that the biofeedback signal made relaxing hard work ($F[1, 28] = 4.54$, $p < .05$). Compared with the high-absorption subjects, the low-absorption subjects said that the biofeedback signal made it easy for them to relax (question 6; $F[1, 28] = 9.55$, $p < .01$). They also considered the biofeedback signal to be more useful (question 8; $F[1, 28] = 9.04$, $p < .01$) than did the high-absorption subjects.

Analysis of question 1, "the feedback stopped my mind from wandering," produced three effects. The main effect for experimental condition was qualified by the presence of an Absorption Capacity x Experimental Condition interaction ($F[1, 28] = 8.71$, $p < .01$) and a Session x Experimental Condition interaction ($F[2,56] = 5.92$, $p < .01$). Further analysis of the Session x Experimental Condition interaction indicated that subjects in the biofeedback-only condition reported the biofeedback signal stopped their minds from wandering more in the second and third sessions than did subjects in the biofeedback and imagery-encouragement condition. The Absorption Capacity x Experimental Condition interaction was caused by low-absorption subjects in the biofeedback-only condition reporting that the biofeedback signal served to stop their minds from wandering more than did those who received imagery-encouragement instructions.

Analysis of item 12 showed that subjects who were encouraged to use imagery to facilitate relaxation tried to block out the biofeedback signal more than those in the biofeedback-only condition ($F[1, 28] = 4.02$, $p < .05$).

DISCUSSION

The present study provides empirical support for using absorption capacity as a treatment-relevant variable in developing a prescriptive approach for clinical biofeedback. If this construct has clinical validity, then there should be marked and predictable differences between high- and low-absorption subjects' responses to the treatment conditions. There should also be a high degree of correspondence between subjects' evaluations of their experimental condition and their absorption levels. These premises were examined in terms of eight specific predictions.

The first question investigated was whether high-absorption subjects in the imagery-encouragement condition would show greater reductions in EMG activity than those in the standard biofeedback condition. Obtained results were clearly in the predicted direction but did not attain statistical significance. Close inspection of individual EMG data revealed great variability among high-absorption subjects in the imagery-encouragement condition during the first two sessions. Some differences between these two groups were revealed during the postexperimental interview that could explain this result. Four subjects in the imagery-encouragement condition had particular difficulty overcoming the distraction of the biofeedback signal and developing a relaxing visual image, especially during the first two sessions. All four subjects described a similar process of incorporating the biofeedback signal into their visual imagery before they could begin to relax. One subject, for example, discovered he could make progress by thinking of the auditory clicks of the biofeedback signal as raindrops on the tin roof of his vacation home. Qualls and Sheehan (1981b) also observed this phenomenon, and reported similar anecdotal data from high-absorption subjects encouraged to employ relaxing visual images.

The second prediction advanced in the current study was that high-absorption subjects not receiving biofeedback would relax more than those in the standard biofeedback condition. This prediction was confirmed. High-absorption subjects made the greatest reductions in EMG activity when they were simply instructed to relax and then left to their own devices. Postexperimental interview data with these subjects confirmed that their natural strategy of choice is to become involved in relaxing imagery.

The third prediction made was that high-absorption subjects in the no-biofeedback and the biofeedback and imagery-encouragement conditions would achieve similar levels of muscle tension reduction. Results indicated that the relaxation levels of subjects in the imagery-encouragement condition gradually converged with the no-biofeedback condition across sessions. This result is also consistent with the findings of Qualls and Sheehan (1981b) but, as discussed earlier, the data for these two groups did not converge until much later in the present study. Nevertheless, the imagery-encouragement instructions do appear to help high-absorption subjects overcome the interfering effects of the biofeedback signal.

The fourth hypothesis tested was that low-absorption subjects in the no-biofeedback condition would not be able to relax as effectively as their counterparts in the two biofeedback conditions. This prediction was confirmed and was the most robust result of the present study. Qualls and Sheehan (1981b) observed a deterioration in the performance of their low-absorption subjects in the no-biofeedback group toward the end of each session. In the present study, this group performed poorly in each session but made some gains only at the close of the second and third sessions. Qualls and Sheehan (1981b, p. 378) interpreted these data to support their contention that low-absorption subjects have trouble sustaining their attention to the task of relaying when the situation is highly unstructured as in the no-biofeedback condition. This explanation appears to fit the data in the present study. For example, the present low-absorption subjects in the no-biofeedback condition switched frequently and ineffectively from one strategy to another. Their lack of sustained attention in the absence of structure and their poorer imaginative and creative capacities combined to make the no-biofeedback condition a very poor fit for them.

The fifth prediction advanced was that low-absorption subjects in the two biofeedback conditions would achieve equal levels of relaxation. Implied here is the idea that imagery-encouragement instructions would neither enhance nor inhibit the performance of low-absorption subjects. Results indicated that these groups closely paralleled one another throughout the study. Although the biofeedback-only group attained somewhat larger reductions in EMG activity, the differences between these two groups were not statistically significant. The subjects appeared to comply with their experimental instructions. All subjects who were encouraged to use visual imagery appeared to try to do so throughout each session, but stated they did not generally believe this was a useful strategy to relax. Subjects in both groups reported that the biofeedback was a useful and dominant feature of their relaxation efforts.

The sixth question investigated was whether or not high-absorption subjects in the no-biofeedback condition would attain greater reductions in EMG activity than low-absorption subjects in the same condition. The results indicated a significant difference between these two groups. This was entirely expected since the no-biofeedback condition was predicted to be the best treatment for high-absorbers and the least suited to low-absorbers.

The seventh prediction was that low-absorption subjects who were exposed to the biofeedback-only condition would relax more than the high-absorption subjects assigned to this condition. This prediction also served to compare high- and low-absorption subjects on their hypothesized most and least compatible experimental conditions. Data from the feedback questionnaire provided additional support for the opposite response patterns of these two groups.

The final prediction advanced was that high- and low-absorption subjects in the biofeedback and imagery-encouragement condition would achieve similar levels of relaxation. This prediction was also confirmed. Qualls and Sheehan (1981b) concluded that imagery-encouragement instructions had very little impact on the low-absorption subjects. They did, however, note a reduction in the incidence of unpleasant and intrusive thoughts compared with low absorption subjects in the other two experimental conditions. In the present study, these groups all reported similar problems with intrusive thoughts while relaxing.

The overall pattern of obtained results suggest that there are marked differences in response to the biofeedback signal between individuals who are high- and low-absorbers. Further, the results obtained suggest that subjects with low-absorption capacities are better suited to treatment conditions that are task-oriented and structured by the biofeedback signal. In contrast, the biofeedback signal functions as an obstacle to be overcome by high-absorption subjects. Instructions designed to encourage the use of visual imagery serve to facilitate the process of relaxation by high-absorbers in spite of the apparent distraction of the biofeedback signal.

Implications for Clinical Biofeedback and the Development of a Prescriptive Approach

The absorption construct has the potential for contributing significantly to the goal of developing a prescriptive approach to biofeedback training. Until the completion of the present study, the intriguing results reported by Qualls and Sheehan (1979, 1981b, 1981c) were limited in their clinical applicability by their restriction to female undergraduate subjects, the brief training regimen involved, and data trends indicating that the Absorption x Treatment interaction might be short-lived. The present study addressed these deficiencies by expanding the number of treatment sessions and demonstrating the long-run stability of the Absorption x Treatment interaction using an adult male clinical sample. The results of this experiment lend credibility to the clinical applicability of the absorption construct, and underscore the importance of developing a reliable pretreatment screening and assessment protocol for matching persons to treatment conditions when self-regulation training procedures are indicated. The machines do indeed appear to be necessary for some people.

Implications for Future Research

Qualls and Sheehan (1981a) concluded their review of the biofeedback literature by calling for a new model capable of incorporating the full complexities of the data. They suggested that the new model should be based on a taxonomy of person-treatment interactions. The inherent shortcomings of traditional nomothetic research using controlled comparison studies have exacerbated the disaffected relationship between research and clinical practice (Barlow, Hayes, & Nelson, 1984). The group comparison studies that largely comprise the biofeedback literature have oversimplified the data by obscuring the role of key individual difference variables. The results of many of these factorial studies suggest there may be no advantages of biofeedback over more cost-effective procedures. Even in the present study, if between-subject differences in absorption capacity are not considered, it would be possible to conclude that biofeedback is less effective than simply instructing people to relax. Barlow et al. (1984) detail a similar historical process during the development of interventions for phobias. Various treatments were examined in controlled comparison studies before the mechanisms of action of these procedures were understood. In the introduction to this investigation, it was suggested that biofeedback research has reached a watershed. What may be happening is that biofeedback has reached the end of an era dominated by an ineffective research strategy in which many studies directly comparing two or more treatments have yielded inconclusive findings.

What is now needed is a research program designed to provide a detailed analysis of the variables influencing subjects' performances in the biofeedback treatment setting (Poppen, 1983). This can be accomplished by implementing a clinical replication series (Barlow et al., 1984; Kazdin, 1984) that will yield additional data on the interaction of absorption capacity and the active ingredients of biofeedback and other self-regulation treatments.

Future research should also evaluate the impact of how the treatment sessions were structured in the present study. The sessions were divided into eighteen 1-minute trial periods that were apparent to the subjects. This structure does not correspond to treatment procedures in most clinical settings. The imposition of the trial periods may have been an additional impediment to the performance of the high-absorption subjects along with the distraction of the biofeedback signal. Some preliminary evidence supports this possibility (Dekker, 1983).

The present study pushes absorption capacity another step forward as a promising treatment-relevant variable by demonstrating the generality of this variable from female college students (Qualls & Sheehan, 1979, 1981b, 1981c) to a male clinical sample. A next logical step is to is to begin the idiographic studies necessary for testing the utility of absorption capacity in a comprehensive preintervention assessment. Studies should also assess the costs and benefits of a prescriptive approach by detailing the proportion of variance in treatment outcome accounted for based on clinical significance and not solely statistical inference (Haynes, 1979).

References

BARLOW, D.H., Hayes, S.C., & Nelson, R.O. (1984). *The scientist practitioner: Research and accountability in clinical and educational settings*. New York: Pergamon.

BLANCHARD, E.R. (1982). The role of biofeedback in behavioral medicine. *American Journal of Clinical Biofeedback, 5*, 126-130.

CARROLL, D. (1984). *Biofeedback in Practice*. New York: Longman.

DEKKER, J.D. (1983). Electromyograph biofeedback with high absorption subjects: Attentional demand, mental set, and informational components (Doctoral dissertation, Ball State University, 1983). *Dissertation Abstracts International, 44*, 288B.

HAYNES, S.N. (1979). Behavioral variance, individual differences, and trait theory in a behavioral construct system: A reappraisal. *Behavioral Assessment, 1*, 41-49.

HILGARD, J.R. (1970). *Personality and hypnosis: A study of imaginative involvement.* Chicago: University of Chicago Press.

HOLROYD, K.A. & Lazarus, R.S. (1982). Stress, coping and somatic adaptation. In L. Goldberger & E. Breznitz (Eds.), *Handbook of stress* (pp. 21-35). New York: Free Press.

KAZDIN, A.E. (1984). Treatment research: The investigation and evaluation of psychotherapy. In M. Hersen, A.E. Kazdin, & A.S. Bellack (Eds.), *The clinical psychology handbook* (pp. 265-284). New York: Pergamon.

OLTON, D.S. & Noonberg, A.R. (1980). Biofeedback: *Clinical applications in behavioral medicine*. Englewood Cliffs, NJ: Prentice-Hall.

POPPEN, R. (1983). Clinical practice and biofeedback research: Are the data really necessary? *The Behavior Therapist, 6*, 145-148.

QUALLS, P.J. & Sheehan, P.W. (1979). Capacity for absorption and relaxation during electromyographic feedback and no feedback conditions. *Journal of Abnormal Psychology, 88*, 652-662.

QUALLS, P.J. & Sheehan, P.W. (1981a). Electromyographic biofeedback as a relaxation technique: A critical appraisal and reassessment. *Psychological Bulletin, 90*, 21-24.

QUALLS, P.J. & Sheehan, P.W. (1981b). Imagery encouragement, absorption capacity, and relaxation during electromyograph biofeedback. *Journal of Personality and Social Psychology, 41*, 370-379.

QUALLS, P.J. & Sheehan, P.W. (1981c). Role of the feedback signal in electromyographic feedback: The relevance of attention. *Journal of Experimental Psychology: General, 110*, 204-216.

QUALLS, P.J. & Sheehan, P.W. (1981d). Trait-treatment interactions: Reply to Tellegen. *Journal of Experimental Psychology: General, 110*, 227-231.

ROBERTS, A.H. (1985). Biofeedback: Research, training, and clinical roles. *American Psychologist, 40*, 938-941.

SILVER, B.V. & Blanchard, E.R. (1978). Biofeedback and relaxation training in the treatment of psychophysiological disorders: Or, are the machines really necessary? *Journal of Behavioral Medicine, 1*, 217-239.

SIMKINS, L. (1982). Biofeedback: Clinically valid or oversold? *Psychological Record, 32*, 3-17.

SPIELBERGER, C.D., Gorsuch, R.L., & Lushene, R.E. (1970). *STAI manual for the State-Trait Anxiety Inventory*. Palo Alto, CA: Consulting Psychologists Press.

TELLEGEN, A. (1982). *Brief manual for the Multidimensional Personality Questionnaire*. Unpublished manuscript, University of Minnesota, Minneapolis.

TURNER, J.A. & Chapman, C.R. (1982). Psychological interventions for chronic pain: A critical review. I. Relaxation training and biofeedback. *Pain, 12*, 1-21.

Medical Psychotherapy
1988, Volume 1, pp. 65-72

© 1988 by
Hans Huber Publishers, Toronto

A Clinician's Guide to Differential Diagnosis Between Physical and Psychiatric Disorders

DR. CHRIS E. STOUT
Forest Hospital and Foundation

When a patient presents with a psychiatric problem, the clinician must be aware of any possible underlying physical etiology. This article contains a concise reference guide developed from the medical literature, structured in a flow-chart fashion, that provides suggested psychiatric diagnoses for particular sets of presenting symptoms, as well as indicating which physical disorders can be ruled out and which lab tests are recommended for the purpose.

Introduction

The purpose of this work is to provide a quick and relatively unencumbered aid in considerations of physical problems masking as psychiatric disorders. The accuracy of such differential diagnosis is paramount to proper treatment and patient care. Ignorance of a physical malady in an erroneously presumed psychiatric problem can result in permanent physical, cognitive, and emotional disability, and even death in extreme cases (not to mention litigation against the erring clinician). Thus, the importance of this knowledge is marked.

The practicing clinician can expect that literally any new patient coming in for "emotional problems" may indeed be experiencing a physical disorder with emotional sequela. Patients may often have a combination of physical problems concomitant with psychological issues.

When dealing with a new patient, much information must be obtained regardless of the clinician's orientation. This can oftentimes be an overwhelming, burdensome amount of data to deal with, and this pressure increases when the clinician suspects an

Inquiries or reprint requests should be directed to Dr. Chris E. Stout, Director, Department of Clinical Research and Evaluation; Psychodiagnostics Division, Forest Hospital and Foundation, 555 Wilson Lane, Des Plaines, Illinois 60016-9990.

Presenting Psychiatric Complaint or Symptom	Suggested Psychiatric Diagnosis	If the Following Physical Sx Are Present	Rule Out This Possible Physical Disorder	Recommended Lab Tests
Anxiety Depression	Anxiety Depression	Muscle Spasms Increased Tendon Reflexes Tetany	Hypoparathyroidism	Serum Calcium, Phosphorus, & magnesium levels 24 hour urinary calcium excretion Chest or bone X-rays Renal Dye Study
Anxiety Depression	Anxiety Depression	Somnolence Irritability Muscular Weakness Gastrointestinal complaints Anorexia Nausea Constipation Renal Stones Increased urinary output Abdominal pain	Hyperparathyroidism	
Depression Negativism Apathy Suspicion	Depression	Weight loss Loss of appetite Nausea Abdominal pain Recurrent diarrhea Decrease in strength Salt craving Muscle cramps Low blood pressure Loss of sex characteristics in females Increase in skin pigment	Hypoadrenalism (Addison's Disease)	Serum Pituitary & Adrenal Hormone levels Amount of 24-hour urinary excretion of endogenous steroids Dexamethasone Suppressant Test Adrenocorticotropic Hormone (ACTH) stimulating test
Somatic Delusions Psychotic Thinking	Psychosis	Fatigue Emotional lability Incongruent weight gain with central deposits of fat & very thin limbs Acne, Impotence/amenorrhea Large purple lines on the abdomen Easy bruising	Hyperadrenalism (Cushing's Syndrome)	

		Hypertension Fragile skin Increased pigmentation Poor wound healing Increased urinary output		
Depressed Affect Lethargy Loss of Energy Delusions Hallucinations Paranoid Symptoms	Depression Schizophrenia	Weight gain Hypersomnia Cold intolerance Muscle aching Dry skin Hair loss Change in facial appearance Constipation Decrease in sexual functioning	Hypothyroidism	Thyroid Suppression Tests Tests of Thyroid Stim. Hormone Thyrotropin-Releasing Hormone Test Radioactive Iodine Uptake Test Measure levels of thyroxine, Tri Iodothyromine, & level of blood serum Protein
Episodic Anxiety Depression	Anxiety State Depression	Heat intolerance with excessive sweating Palpitations Tachycardia Fine rapid muscular tremor Weight loss Increased appetite combined with fatigue & weakness Bowel complaints Decreased menstrual flow Peculiar staring & prominence of patient's eyes	Hyperthyroidism	
Depression Lethargy Lack of energy Sense of weakness Inability to complete tasks	Depression	Bad breath Urine odor Eccentric food cravings	Diabetes Mellitus	Fasting Blood Glucose levels Blood Sugar Challenge Glucose Tolerance Test
Fear Confusion Anxiety	Hysteria Dementia Anxiety Disorder Drug Intoxication	Tremulousness Sweating Heart palpitations Faintness Weakness	Excessive Insulin levels	

Presenting Psychiatric Complaint or Symptom	Suggested Psychiatric Diagnosis	If the Following Physical Sx Are Present	Rule Out This Possible Physical Disorder	Recommended Lab Tests
Distractable Less careful about environment and personal hygiene	Personality Change Depression	Fatigue Weight loss Social Withdrawal Insidious Personality change Loss of recent memory Impaired immediate recall Inconsistent errors in calculating	Early Dementia (Chronic OBS)	Careful MSE with cognitive functioning evaluation Screening for Metabolic Abnormalities & Toxins EEG Lumbar Puncture & Lab Analysis of Cerebral Spinal Fluid CT Scan
Disorientation Auditory Hallucinations Visual Hallucinations Gait Problems	Psychosis Mania Schizophrenia	Causes: Stroke Severe hypertension Wernicke-Korsakoff Syndrome Meningitis Encephalitis Severe hyperthyroidism Acute Adrenal failure Poisoning ESP. Anticholinergics Hypoglycemia Vitamin Deficiencies Systemic Infections Renal Failure Liver failure Blood Electrolyte Imbalance Subdural Hematoma	Delirium (Acute Confusional state or acute OBS)	
Confusion Disorientation Acting Out	Psychosis Delirium Explosive Personality Disorder Drug Reaction	Automatic behavior Lip smacking Clothes picking Wandering about Unaware of environment Violent outbursts Increased with certain drugs or ETOH Visual, olfactory, or auditory hallucinations	Seizure Disorder (Psychomotor or other temporal lobe)	EEG History & a therapeutic trial with anticonvulsant medication

Personality Change Depression Vague Neurologic or Endocrine Complaints	Dementia Depression	Gradual & Progressive Development of Sx including: - Loss of social comp. - complaints of a new type of headache - Specific loss of neurological or muscular control - Development of seizures during adulthood	Brain Tumor	CAT Scan Neurological consult
Personality Change Increased Lethargy	Depression	Recent head trauma Hx of blackouts Decreased energy Decreasing activity levels (especially in elderly and alcoholics)	Subdural Hematoma	CAT Scan
Listlessness Irritability Periods of muscle weakness	Depression	Decreased muscle strength Easily fatigued	Myasthenia Gravis	Tensilon Test Electromyography or Serological Testing
Vague Complaints of neurological losses	Hysteria/conversion Reaction	Repeated episodes in which the migratory nature of Sx becomes apparent & neurological losses become more persistent	Multiple Sclerosis	Exam of Cerebral Spinal Fluid for Protein & Electrophoresis of the fluid
Complaint of numbness or pain with vague distribution Tiredness of a variable degree	Hypochondriasis	Complaints continue over time with only subtle changes in physical findings (Especially in alcoholics & Vitamin B deficiencies)	Peripheral Neuropathy	Nerve Conduction Studies Medical work-up
Dysphoric mood	Depression	Anorexia Weakness Fatigue Irritability Diffuse pain Unsteady walking gait Incoordination	Pernicious Anemia	Physical exam Blood count Shilling Test
Emotional Lability Sudden onsets of anxiety	Conversion Reaction Anxiety State	Colicky abdominal pain Vomiting Generalized weakness Seizures Rapid heart rate	Acute Porphyria	Blood Test Barbiturate Use Family History

Presenting Psychiatric Complaint or Symptom	Suggested Psychiatric Diagnosis	If the Following Physical Sx Are Present	Rule Out This Possible Physical Disorder	Recommended Lab Tests
Turmoil Adjustment Reactions Schizophrenic-like episodes	Anxiety Reaction Depression Psychosis	History of liver, renal, or neurological disease Aggressive acting-out Mood swings Intellectual impairment	Wilson's Disease	Look for Kayser-Fleischer ring in cornea Levels of serum ceruloplasmin and copper
Depression	Depression	Unexplained physical complaints & findings	Tumor in a variety of organ systems	Physical evaluation
Depression	Depression	Development of liver complaints or Jaundice Dull, aching upper abdominal pain Constipation	Pancreatic Carcinoma	Cat Scan
Episodic Attacks Extreme Anxiety	Anxiety disorder	Hypertension Panic attacks Anxiety Perspiration Headache Tremor All without signs of neurotic adaptation	Pheochromocytoma (Adrenal Tumor) or Carcinoid Tumor	24-hour collections of urine for specific metabolites
Hallucinations Delusions Agitation Difficulty in Associations Flight of Ideas Vague Symptoms of Somatic Origin	Schizophrenia Hysteria/Conversion Disorder	Labile, rather than flat affect Unexplained fever Skin Rash Arthritis Chest & abdominal complaints	Systemic Lupus Erythematous	Serologic Tests Skin & Tissue Biopsies
Agitation	Mania	Fever Other complaints compatible with viral infection	Viral Infections (influenza, Q fever, post-St. Louis type A Encephalitis)	Blood tests dependent on site & type of infection
Depression	Depression	Fever Masses Symptoms of localized infection	Bacterial Infection	

Disoriented Delusional Hallucinations	Psychosis	Post-Surgical Sx present	Magnesium Deficiency	Trial Dose of Magnesium for Sx remission
Confused Delusional	Dementia	Skin Rash Persistent Diarrhea	Pellagra (Niacin Deficiency)	Typical in chronic alcoholics & patients with unusual dietary habits Blood Tests
Depression	Depression	Fatigue Muscle Weakness Weight loss Pain Sx of Heart Disease Visual Gaze & Gait problems Dementia	Beri-Beri (Thiamine Deficiency) Wernicke's encephalopathy Korsakoff's Psychosis	
Drugs & Meds		Causal Agents		Thorough Drug History Blood & Urine Tests
Anxiety	Anxiety	Thyroid Hormone, Antihistamines, & cold preparations containing ephedrine or pseudephedrine, phenylpropanolamine, insulin, and aminophylline (for asthma). Nicotine, caffeine, alcohol, ginseng, cocaine. Withdrawal from: Opiates, sedatives (barbiturates), alcohol, nicotine, and antipsychotic, anti-anxiety, and anti-depressant meds.		
Depression	Depression	Anti-hypertensives, hormones, tranquilizers, cardiac drugs (e.g., Digitalis), Antibuse, & drugs for treatment of infections, diarrhea, & malignancy		
Psychotic Reaction	Psychosis Mania	Steroids (e.g., Cortisone), Iproniazid (Antituberculosis drug), hallucinogens, & PCP		

underlying organic etiology to the disorder. Certainly one can go to the medical library and review numerous texts, volumes, and handbooks – yet this can become impractical, tedious, and time-consuming. Other times, some disorders presented may seem to be either totally emotionally or "physically" based – and *not* be. In either scenario, diagnosis, treatment, and clinician time factors may be adversely impacted upon.

As an answer to such differential diagnostic problems, the following concise reference guide has been developed from the medical literature. It is designed to be easy to grasp and utilize. The quick reference tabular format is self-explanatory, and is structured in a flow-chart fashion of logical sequences. For example, if a patient's presenting symptoms included depression, suspicion, negativism, and apathy, one might conclude a psychiatric differential diagnosis of affective disorder, depressive type; paranoid personality disorder; and so forth. The clinician using this chart can then look at the presenting psychiatric complaint or symptoms and be provided not only with a suggested psychiatric diagnosis, but also physical signs and symptoms (in this case, weight loss, abdominal pain, salt craving, muscle cramps, low blood pressure, recurrent diarrhea, and decreased strength). At this point, if sufficient physical symptomology exists, one can then make a rule-out physical diagnosis (e.g., Addison's disease – Hypoadrenalism) with recommendations for lab tests to verify (e.g., serum pituitary and adrenal hormone levels, ACTH Stimulating Test, D.S.T.). Towards the end, a special addition of medication and drug effects is also incorporated.

References

HALL, R.C. (Ed.) (1980). *Psychiatric Presentations of Medical Illness: Somato-psychic Disorders*. New York: SP Medical and Scientific Books.

HALL, R.C., Popkin, M.K., Devaul, R.A., Faillale, L.A., & Stickney, S.K. (1978). Physical Illness Presenting as Psychiatric Disease. *Archives of General Psychiatry, 35*, 1315-1320.

KATERNDAH, D.A. (1982). Nonpsychiatric Disorders Associated with Depression. *Journal of Family Practice, 13*, 619-624.

LOSCHEN, E.L. (1984). Psychiatric Syndromes with Physical Causes. In P.A. Keller & L.G. Ritt (Eds.) *Innovations in Clinical Practice*. Sarasota, Fl.: Professional Resource Exchange, Inc.

Medical Psychotherapy
1988, Volume 1, pp. 73-81

© 1988 by
Hans Huber Publishers, Toronto

Body Symptoms and the Medical Psychotherapist

THOMAS G. PAUTLER, M.D.
Lakeview Immediate Care Clinic

Psychosomatic factors are increasingly being seen as playing a role in many common physical ailments and disorders. This paper discusses how such factors can lead to illness; describes techniques that psychotherapists can use to obtain information from patients regarding their body symptoms; and proposes a "relationship" approach to physical illness. Six case histories are presented.

The role that psychological factors play in the leading causes of death in the United States – coronary artery disease, accidents, cirrhosis, cancer, and of course, suicide – is gaining firm acceptance. With recent advances in the understanding of mind-body interactions, there is renewed interest in the illnesses thought of as psychosomatic. These common health problems of functional bowel disorders, abnormalities of eating, hypertension, headaches, skin disorders, fatigue states, autoimmune disorders such as rheumatoid arthritis, and being accident-prone, are beginning to be seen as disturbances in psychobiology: that is, the delicate interaction between mind-brain and body. This paper will discuss disturbances in psychobiology leading to illness; ways of working with body symptoms to obtain information; a systems or relationship approach to illness; and case histories.

In order to understand disturbances in mind-body interaction, it is first necessary to review briefly the usual process where mind is stimulated by a new situation. Novel stimuli are first recognized by norepinephrine-containing cells in the locus coeruleus of the pontine area in the brain stem (Reiser, 1984). From here, via the reticular activating system, stimuli are received by higher cortical centers and from there are sent

Inquiries or reprint requests should be directed to Thomas Pautler, M.D., Lakeview Immediate Care Clinic, 3216 N.E. 45th Place, Seattle, WA 98105.

to the limbic-hypothalamic system, where the memory is integrated and processed emotionally. In the hypothalamus a phenomenon known as transduction occurs, where neural impulses of mind are transformed into hormones of body via the formation of various neuropeptides (Rossi, 1986, pp. 20-35). These neuropeptides are messenger molecules, which cause the formation and secretion of hormones that engage the autonomic nervous system, endocrine, and immune systems in an organized physiological fashion (Figure 1).

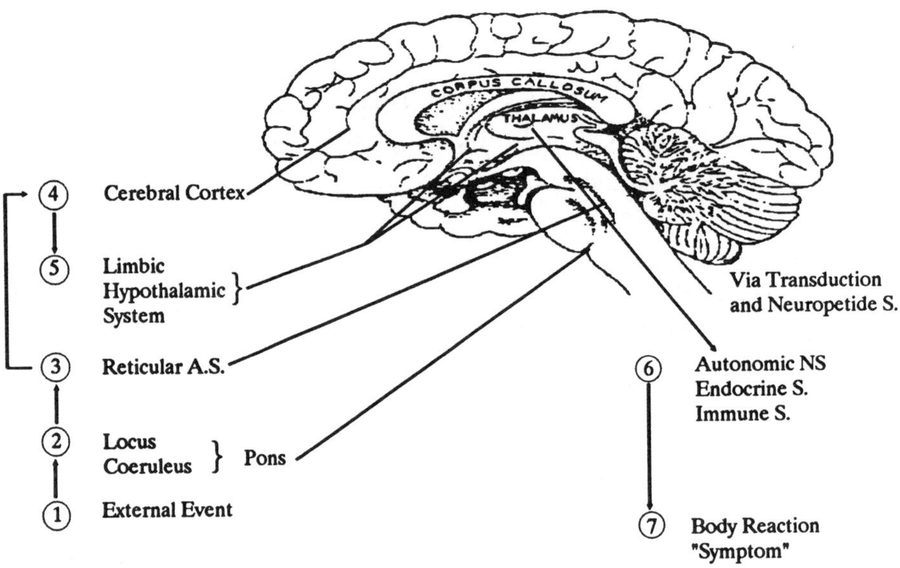

Figure 1

But what of the situation that is a shock to the consciousness – such as sexual abuse to a child or severe physical injury? Life experiences that have traumatic power are in some ways not processed as our previously described format. Here, the individual may lapse into a hypnotic or altered state of consciousness. The subsequent memory of the event is known as *state-bound*, as it is state-bound to the different level of consciousness it was originally conceived in (Rossi, 1986, pp. 36-56). The memory of the traumatic incident does not have free recall by the individual. This psychophysiological event accounts for the disassociation, repression, complexes, and amnesia that are the roots of psychoanalytical theory.

The vital link with higher cortical centers seems to be absent for traumatic events. Most of the memory storage in this condition seems to occur in the limbic-hypothalamic system, also known as the emotional or animal brain.

The memory of the traumatic experience, in its state-bound form along with the various neuropeptides produced in the hypothalamus via transduction, becomes a unique psychobiological pattern. This pattern is capable of being activated and producing various physiologic sequelae and body symptoms when the individual is exposed to similar or related traumatic events (Rossi, 1986, pp. 59-60). Any period of great stress may cause this sort of physiological regression giving rise to a previously coded mind-body reaction pattern.

This described situation has obvious relevance to our topic of physical symptoms and the medical psychotherapist. Are physical symptoms actually related to the intermittent firing off of these state-bound unconscious memories into body? Do illnesses and chronic disease states result from continued activation of these processes? Is it possible to backtrack from body symptoms into the state-dependent memory of their origin, and reprocess, recode, or reframe them in such a way as to actually change the psychophysiology that has previously been established? (Rossi, 1986, pp. 68-70). Answers to these questions are in the affirmative, and are the cornerstone of this paper.

Before going on to some techniques on working with body symptoms, I would like to discuss some other situations where state-dependent memories or complexes may be formed other than being caused by traumatic events. It seems as though any constant double message that is given to a child may be enough to induce a trance-like state and form a state-dependent memory. Imagine the effect on the child when the parent presents one message vocally, "I am doing this because I love you," but an entirely different message with facial expression and body language saying "I hate you and will hurt and destroy you." This situation seems to produce a splitting of the right and left cerebral hemispheres, the left attending to the verbal cues, and the right to the facial gestalt and body language (Bakal, 1979). The event is unable to be processed by higher cortical centers and remains state-bound in the limbic system, to be retriggered perhaps by similar muddled communications in the future.

There may also be circumstances in traditional medical care that, if unrecognized, may result in the formation of state-dependent memories capable of producing symptoms in the future. As an example, let us consider a 40-year-old woman who presented to my clinic with a laceration of her lip secondary to a dog bite. After explanation of the need for suturing, her wound was cleaned and her face was covered with a drape. A local injection of Novocain was given. During this time, she began to hyperventilate, and was obviously in severe distress. Initially, it was felt that this was all related to the trauma of the incident and that sedation was going to be necessary. It was noted, however, that despite her struggle, her hands tightly grasped the operating table, preventing her from sitting up. When I asked her what her hands were doing, she was able to stop her hyperventilation and tell me she had been reliving a previous experience ten years earlier, when at the time of a caesarean section, her arms were tied down prior to the administration of anesthesia for surgery. Any situation involving a critical illness, childbirth, general anesthesia, surgery, accidents, or even witnessing these in another, may be capable of eliciting an altered state and state-bound memories. The more I look for these conditions, especially with regard to childhood illnesses and surgery, the more clues I find that early traumatic experiences with medical care often seem to be factors in subsequent illnesses in the adult.

I would like to leave theory for the present and discuss more practical applications. If we begin to consider physical symptoms as representing somatic clues to inner memory-locked events, what are some available methods the medical psychotherapist may use with these symptoms?

For some time, body workers such as massage therapists and Rolfers have noted the occurrence of spontaneous altered states when certain chronic, painful areas of the skeletal muscular system are worked on. These altered states may range from varied levels of trance to a marked emotional catharsis with anger, crying, and subjective increase in pain. This phenomenon may be explained in a similar manner to the limbic system – state dependent memory – and neuropeptide cascade as previously described. There is, however, reason to believe that proprioceptive nerve endings, in particular around joints and muscle insertions, have a sort of "cellular memory" of their own, which can be actively stimulated.

Old injuries that occurred at a pre-verbal level of development in the individual may be recalled when a seemingly uncaused area of pain around a joint is worked on. "Trigger points" – areas of local tenderness in the neck, interscapular areas and lumbar spine, when amplified by direct pressure, can often produce a memory, image, or emotion which can be explored for further information.

Subtle changes in body posturing can be exaggerated, yielding substantial information. For example, increasing the slightly stooped shoulder position of a young woman brought out memories of cowering necessary in early childhood because of a physically abusive father.

These stored somatic memory bank phenomena can be actively pursued by the therapist. This interaction implies that touch becomes a part of the therapist-client exchange and needs prior explanation and agreement. Potential patient responses, such as an increase in pain, altered states of consciousness, and deep emotions, also should be explained to any client before this type of work is attempted. The therapist requires considerable skill and confidence in handling the various aspects of this type of work before it is conducted.

Less direct methods of dealing with body symptoms include imagery or active imagination around the areas of discomfort. A 24-year-old woman with four years of chronic abdominal pain was invited to become her own endoscopist. With minimal coaching, she imagined swallowing a tube with a light and viewing her own stomach. There, she visualized a scene from a ghetto, with an alley, trash cans, a drunk, garbage, and laundry hanging between buildings. Following her experience, various areas of emotional poverty in her life began to surface, areas that had been felt to be insignificant before.

Drawing a picture of one's body symptom or modeling it in clay often gives excellent clues to be explored, as well as reviewing the individual's perception of his or her total body image. This body image is often somehow distorted by the primary symptom.

A careful review of the individual's life circumstances at the time of the original onset of symptoms may give quite revealing information (Breuer & Freud, 1893-1895). For instance, a 60-year-old woman with chronic functional bowel disease traced her initial onset of symptoms back to a rather tragic lunch some 35 years before. At this time, her one true love had announced to her his decision, which he later regretted, to marry another. Recalling this event produced an attack of abdominal pain in the office.

Recurrent dreams, especially those dating to childhood, are also rich sources of clues to subsequent body problems (Mindell, 1985). The bogeyman, being chased by monsters, or other frightening situations of a childhood dream often end up as a chronic body symptom in the adult. If a recurrent dream cannot be recalled, then an early memory can also be explored for information.

It is also of interest to work with body symptoms as representing changes that individuals won't or cannot make themselves, even though they may be aware they should. This viewpoint sees a person's life as consisting of a variety of ongoing processes. When major processes are blocked or thwarted, either consciously or unconsciously, the "energy" of the process may drop down to a somatic level and be expressed there as symptoms or illness. For example, a myocardial infarction in a 45-year-old man was seen in retrospect by him as "the only way" he could legitimately leave his corporate position. It is probably pertinent to look for such "hidden agendas" in any major illness. Other useful techniques include the therapist noting the way symptoms are described by the patient, such as speech patterns, voice tonality changes, and repetitive words and phrases.

The therapist can even be aware of discomfort in his or her own body as signals for what is going on or not going on in the client. This phenomenon raises speculation that there is a field of energy existing between the therapist and patient, the somatic equivalent of transference and countertransference. Common examples would be a tendency of the therapist to fatigue, or to become restless. Occasionally, the therapist may actually experience the affect the client is not connecting with: deeper somatic symptoms such as "post-session headache" or various other fleeting body complaints are not uncommon. Although these reactions may initially be considered a nuisance, they can be homed in on and used as a guide in therapy. Exercises may be productively created when psychotherapists follow their own body symptoms to obtain additional information (Schwartz-Salant, 1982)

In general, working with body symptoms can become a creative ongoing experience for both therapist and client. Body symptoms can be trusted on a level not reached by the usual intellectual, verbalized dialogue.

Before presenting some cases, I would like to spend some moments on the differences between traditional medical data gathering, and the historical interview that honors both psyche and soma.

Medicine falls into the category of a reductive science (Capra, 1982, pp. 127-129). In a sort of "smaller is better" logic, causation is pursued from larger to smaller, ending with the molecular theory of disease. The physician, in a certain way, is an archetypal Dick Tracy, chasing down the etiology of illness from germ to chromosome to DNA strand.

A psyche-soma approach to illness, however, uses much more of a systems or a relationship approach between the individual and illness (Capra, 1982, pp. 265-304). A 40-year-old man, after extensive evaluation, is found to have chest pain on a psychosomatic basis. On acquiring a medical history, it would be of importance to know that his father died of a heart attack in his forties. But other related areas of concern are of equal importance. How old was the client when his father died? What time of the day and month of the year did his father die? What were the circumstances of death? Was the client present or absent? If present, did he participate in resuscitation techniques? If absent, is there guilt over that factor? Were there dreams, fantasies, fears, or other disturbances secondary to his father's death? Investigating all these areas and information obtained can turn a psychosomatic symptom from an onerous nuisance into a wealth of meaning for the individual and therapist, as well as relieving the complaint.

In some ways, what is *not* said in taking the psyche-soma history becomes as important as what is stated. The individual who can deliver a rendition of a horribly traumatic illness or event in a smiling, matter-of-fact way often is giving a gigantic double message that suggests that much more is to be uncovered, including the seemingly lost affect.

The case histories that follow will illustrate various points previously described.

Case I: A 40-year-old woman came to see me with complaints over the last ten years of recurring blanching and pain in her fingers and toes related to cold exposure. She described these attacks in some detail and admitted that they panicked her. They were severe enough to cause small ulcers on her fingers and toes in the winter. Medically speaking, the patient had previously been diagnosed as having Raynaud's disease. She had been told that the disease has an unknown cause, and varying medical treatments had been unsuccessful. Her other complaints consisted of long-term infertility and sexual unresponsiveness. I asked her for a memory of a recurrent childhood dream. She had none. However, asking her for her first memory proved interesting. She stated in a somewhat slow, timid, child-like voice, that her earliest life recollection had been of her father reading her a bedtime story when she was about three, concerning a duck named Shingebis who lived in the Arctic. The patient managed to retrieve the story. It is an old Chippewa legend called "The North Wind's Defeat" (Judd, 1929):

> Shingebis, the great loon-bird, lived in a lodge alone. It was by a great lake over which thick ice had come.
> He had only four logs of wood for his fire for the whole winter. But each log would burn a whole moon, and as but four moons were cold, there was wood enough. Shingebis cared for no one. He liked the cold. When the wind blew the coldest, he would go out to where the reeds grew through the ice, and pulling them up, dive down into the holes for fish.
> Kabibonokka, the cold north wind, felt ashamed that there lived anything which did not fear him.
> "Why, this is wonderful. Here is one who cares no more for me than I do for him. I will try once more to see if he will give up to me."
> Then came the wind from the north ten times colder than ever. Great drifts of snow were heaped everywhere. Still, the fire burned in the lodge of Shingebis. Every day, he went out as before and pulled up the rushes and reeds from the ice, and dived down for fish which were always there.
> "I will go to his lodge and visit him," said the North Wind one day as he saw Shingebis dragging home a fish.
> He went that night to a lodge by the water.
> Shingebis did not know he was coming. He did not care. He cooked the great fish and ate his supper, then lay on his side before the burning log and sang a mocking song about the North Wind.
> Shingebis may have known that the one he was singing about stood outside his door, for he sang the song many times.
> The North Wind could endure it no longer. He would see the creature that did not care for his hurting. He came in and sat down opposite the loon bird, the great Shingebis.
> This did not frighten Shingebis. He simply rose and stirred the coals of the fire about the log until they blazed and sent out a great heat.
> "You are but my fellow creature," kept singing the brave Shingebis, and he sat down again in his place.
> Very soon, the icy tears began to flow down the cheeks of Kabibonokka. He said nothing aloud, but whispered to himself, "I cannot endure this; I must leave." As he slipped out of the door, not saying a word, he flew as straight as he could to the places where the reeds and rushes grew. He froze the roots very tightly into the ice. "Shingebis shall have no more fish," said the ice cold wind.
> Yet, Shingebis found fish all that cold winter. He was brave, and

> laughed at his trials.
> At last, the great North Wind gave up trying to conquer the great Shingebis. "Some Manitou is helping him. I can neither freeze him nor starve him. I will let him alone."
> When the four logs were burned and the four cold moons had passed, Shingebis still laughed and sang in his lodge by the water.

It becomes apparent from a review of the story that Shingebis is no ordinary duck. The patient experienced no attacks of her Raynaud's disease this last winter. It is my feeling that there was a direct correlation between the reemergence of her childhood memory to her consciousness, some work with negative father issues, and the resolution of her symptoms. Interestingly enough, the patient attributed her cure to being completely listened to.

Case 2: This patient was a 60-year-old woman with a past history of multiple surgeries, including two lower back operations in the last five years.Her visit was prompted by her orthopedist, who had told her that her neck was now "full of arthritis." At her second mind-body session, she brought in a dream in which a voice had asked her a question, "Are you lithic?" She had looked up lithic, and finding the word meant stone, was concerned that the dream had a bad prognostic significance for her condition, i.e., she would become more stiff and stone-like. An involuntary muscular process took over her body, with helpless motion of her hands and marked rigidity of her trunk, arms, lower extremities, neck, and facial musculature. At one point, she screamed out in Serbian, her native tongue, a phrase that meant, "Don't monkey with me." Eventually, there was a violent shaking of her head, gagging, and spitting. Later, memories were recalled of a mysterious boarder who had lived in her family's home during the time she was three to five years of age, and who had undoubtedly molested her. When asked to draw a picture of herself and her various body complaints, she brought in a drawing of a softball with the cover coming off, saying that this represented herself having been beaten and injured, but still having a good core.

Case 3: This patient was a 38-year-old woman with chief complaints of chronic depression and painful relationships with men. She often had the feeling that there was a veil over her, separating her from life in some way. She described her family life at home when she was a child as existing with a mother who periodically shut down and had to be admitted to various mental hospitals; a father who was emotionally absent; and a rebellious older brother. The patient felt that her role in the family was to be nice and to help people, and she had, indeed, become a physical therapist. Her recurrent childhood dream was that of viewing a TV screen with a wavy line going across it, and then the line suddenly going flat. At this point, she would wake up in a state of fear. Her significant illness pattern had been three retinal detachments involving her left eye, causing various visual distortions and requiring surgery. Working with her consisted of efforts to separate her from a negative mother complex. Seeing with her vision-impaired left eye when her normal right eye was temporarily covered brought up childhood memories and feelings that have been valuable in terms of her progress.

Case 4: The patient was a 31-year-old woman who had presented to another physician with nausea and a general sick feeling. The illness had first come on during her menstrual period. A blood sugar indicated definite diabetes, and she was placed on oral agents to lower her serum glucose. Her diabetes was quickly and easily controlled with medication. She saw me approximately two weeks after diagnosis, stating that she was in a panic over all the grim things in life that could happen with diabetes.

The patient had been raised by her grandparents until she was 2-1/2, and then returned to her father and abusive stepmother. Her earliest childhood memory was of her stepmother threatening to call the "Indians," and then putting her outside in the snow dressed in a pink snowsuit. This type of intimidation was done on numerous occasions, and in one instance the patient recalled seeing the "Indians." Her adult illnesses included various groin abscesses, premenstrual syndrome, and recurrent yeast infections. Her ongoing fears were those of being dependent, helpless, fear of violence, and "death before I am ready." The patient was asked to draw a picture of herself and her illness as she saw it. Her initial drawing showed her encased in a womb-like structure with pink skin reminiscent of her pink snowsuit. She received no therapy, but returned in approximately a month, having learned much more about her diabetes and complying in every way with traditional management, which had been encouraged. She expressed considerable resolution of her panic feelings, and stated that "It's in my hands now." She drew a second picture, which showed a much more integrated drawing of her sitting on the beach, and reflects her progress.

Case 5: This patient was a 42-year-old woman with progressive multiple sclerosis over the last ten years. Her symptoms consisted of varying degrees of spasticity and rigidity of her arms and legs, decreasing vision, loss of sensation from the waist down, and an inability to walk. In her recurring childhood dream, she is a small rabbit, hiding in a thicket of grass. Circling her is a larger animal, an unknown predator. Her feeling is that she will be safe if she is absolutely still and does not move. Work with her on the dream has consisted of having her take roles of both rabbit and predator. Other areas of concern have been her repression of sexuality, stemming from a sexually repressive, puritanical mother. The patient had had no formal explanation of the facts of life until she looked up information in a book at age 20. There was a traumatic exposure to an exhibitionist at age 19, when she was a car hop. She is in a marriage where her husband is an alcoholic, and her multiple sclerosis has occasionally worsened after periods of his heavy drinking. During various sessions, we noted how her condition causes symptoms of staggering, falling, slurring of words and on occasion, accusations by other people that she was drunk. This precipitated work with a character we call her "inner drunk," and allowing her some contact with her own needs to "lighten up." In the most recent work with this patient, I have shared her care with a physical therapist. The patient has started walking, and we have allowed her to fall safely forward or backwards, experiencing her natural tendency to do so. This seems to be of value to her in terms of bringing up issues centering around trust, in particular with men. She has made slow, gradual improvement in her multiple sclerosis over the last year.

Case 6: The patient was a 38-year-old man with an 18-year history of chronic migraine headaches following his return from Vietnam, where he had served in-country as a Marine. He describes his childhood as being one where he felt comfortable only outside the family environment. He suffered from a negative father, who forced him to box with him starting at age 5, and a frightened, dependent mother who would not intervene on his behalf. His recurrent childhood dream is one of being chased by the devil. He was asked to draw pictures of himself during different phases of his migraine: no headache; early headache; and severe headache. In the drawings, there was a progressive distortion of his self-image going from a fairly normal to an almost Mr. Hyde-werewolf kind of change. Various other techniques have included amplifications of his head pain while he was having an actual headache, resulting in images of a birth experience and recalling that he had been told that his mother actually had a 72-

hour labor. Careful word and sentence evaluation is another technique used with this individual in terms of gaining meaning, as it was noted after a number of sessions that his response to, "How have your headaches been?" would be, "I've been bad." Other work has centered around his fundamental Christian beliefs, working with karate movements, and analysis of various plays and songs that he has written.

In closing, we have reviewed a theory for a psychobiological approach to illness, where a traumatic, confusing event is capable of subsequent expression as a physical symptom. Various techniques of working with body symptoms have been reviewed. The importance of data gathering from a systems or a relationship point of view, honoring both psyche and soma, has been elaborated on. It is my feeling that in the near future, the medical psychotherapist will not only be a consultant in many physical illnesses, but may indeed be the primary caregiver in those conditions we have called psychosomatic, offering a non-pharmacologic approach in a true mind-body healing.

References

BAKAL, D.A. (1979). *Psychology and Medicine*. New York: Springer Publishing Co., p. 29.

BREUER, J. & Freud, S. (1983-1985). *Studies on Hysteria*. New York: Basic Books Inc., 1957, p. 268.

CAPRA, F. (1982). *The Turning Point*. New York: Bantam Books, pp. 127-129.

JUDD, M.C. (1929). *Wigwam Stories Told by North American Indians*. Boston: Athenum Press, pp. 189-191.

MINDELL, A. (1985). *Working with the Dreaming Body*. Boston: Routledge and Kegan Paul, pp. 67-70.

RIESER, M.F. (1984). *Mind, Brain, Body*. New York: Basic Books Inc., pp. 145-152.

ROSSI, E.L. (1986). *The Psychobiology of Mind-Body Healing*. New York: W.W. Norton and Company.

SCHWARTZ-SALANT, N. (1982). *Narcissism and Character Transformation*. Toronto: Inner City Books, pp. 114-116.

Medical Psychotherapy
1988, Volume 1, pp. 83-86

© 1988 by
Hans Huber Publishers, Toronto

Stress and Headache in the Workplace: The Role of Caffeine

JOSEPH SARGENT, M.D.
PATRICIA SOLBACH, Ph.D.
The Menninger Foundation

Caffeine is both a cause and a treatment for headache. To appreciate caffeine's unique effect on headache, one must understand the role stress plays in this process.

Many people assume that stress in the workplace is bad and that when possible, exposure to it should be reduced to a minimum. Few realize that it is not stress itself but one's reaction to it that causes problems. The extent to which a person's psychological and physiological responses are activated depends on his or her perception of the stress.

The Effects of Stress

Meeting crucial deadlines and handling work overload are common occurrences in the workplace. In responding, the body slows down digestion so that blood can be sent to the muscles and brain. Heart rate increases, blood pressure rises, breathing becomes faster. Perspiration increases to cool the body. Muscles tense.

When frequently called into action, the body's response to stress can cause adverse reactions. Headaches, ulcers, and irritable bowel syndrome are just a few of the somatic manifestations of acute and chronic stress.

Stress is an inevitable component of the workplace environment, but it has a positive as well as a negative aspect. Hans Selye (1974), a leading authority on stress, points out that it can motivate and spur one on to do creative work. However, many working people, both men and women, sometimes have difficulty handling stress on the job. In the United States, the estimated yearly cost to industry caused by stress-related absenteeism is as much as fifteen billion dollars (Charlesworth & Nathan, 1984).

Inquiries or reprint requests should be directed to Joseph Sargent, Headache and Internal Medicine Research Center, The Menninger Foundation, Topeka, Kansas 66601.

Events in the workplace exclusive of work demands can also trigger the body's stress response. Physical irritants such as air pollution, noise, or temperature changes may contribute; unrealistic self-expectations or a competitive desire to always be the best are often at play. In this milieu, headaches frequently occur.

Tension Headache in the Workplace

The most frequent cause of head pain is tension headache. Whereas migraine headache is thought to occur in 10,000 per 100,000 population, the incidence of non-migrainous headache without structural cause is 15,000 per 100,000 population (Kurtzke, 1982). Clinical manifestations that help distinguish tension headache from other types of headache are its variability in location and its characteristic bilateral pattern of discomfort. It can present as pain in the occipital, sub-occipital, bitemporal, or bifrontotemporal regions, and it is often described as a tightness or pressure sensation without significant gastrointestinal symptoms. The onset of such headaches is often related to stress.

Tension headaches often occur at work. The symptoms may not be initially noted, but as they build up to a certain level of intensity, the worker may suddenly realize their presence. Often the pain builds gradually, resulting in a tense, tired, and irritable person by the end of the day. The headache can become severe enough to send some people home, while others remain at work but at the expense of impaired performance. Tension headaches cause difficulty in reading and thinking, poor concentration, and decreased energy, all of which contribute to poor work output.

Although research studies have found that few people have never experienced a headache, there is nevertheless prejudice against its sufferers (Ziegler, Hassanein, & Couch, 1977). Those afflicted are often forced to endure in silence, as the initial concern and sympathy of co-workers and superiors quickly disappear after multiple episodes of decreased productivity.

Effects of Caffeine on Headache

Caffeine is used in the treatment of headache because of its vasoconstrictor action on the cerebral blood vessels. This physiological effect has been demonstrated in cerebral blood flow studies (Mathew & Wilson, 1985). Ergotamine tartrate, a chemical substance commonly used in aborting migraine, is often combined with caffeine because of caffeine's alleged ability to enhance its absorption. This action, of course, has no relevance to the treatment of tension headache but is of interest to those involved in the medical care of headaches.

Some sufferers may find that a cup of hot coffee ingested in the headache's early stages can provide relief. However, others find that *eliminating* caffeine is a significant step toward reducing headache activity. Greden et al. (1980) have questioned whether caffeine is a useful ingredient in over-the-counter analgesic medications.

Withdrawal from caffeine can also produce headache: a mean intake of slightly over 600 mg of caffeine per day for a group withdrawn from caffeine led to "withdrawal headache" (Greden, Victor, Fontaine, & Lubetsky, 1980). In spite of this disadvantage, caffeine is a common ingredient in many headache-relieving compounds (Pennington & Church, 1985).

Sources of Caffeine

The greatest source of caffeine is coffee, which has approximately 50-150 mg per cup, depending on cup size and brand. Other beverages such as tea, cocoa, and cola-flavored drinks are also important sources. Some soft drinks other than colas have considerable amounts of caffeine added to them, and chocolate contains it in sizable quantities. Sources other than food, beverages, and headache medications are prescription and non-prescription drugs for insomnia, fluid retention, and upper-respiratory symptoms.

In the U.S., the estimated daily per capita intake of caffeine is 200 mg (Council on Scientific Affairs, 1984). Much of this is consumed in the workplace, where coffee makers and vending machines are in frequent use.

Effects of Caffeine on Existing Medical Conditions

Caffeine is a powerful stimulant to the central nervous system, which explains the popularity of caffeine-containing beverages at work. Its use in excess amounts or by individuals sensitive to it can result in a physiological reaction with significant adverse effects. Greden (1974) described a syndrome called "caffeinism," with features difficult to distinguish from anxiety attacks. Boulenger and colleagues (Boulenger, Uhde, Wolff, & Post, 1984) presented preliminary evidence that persons with panic disorders have increased sensitivity to caffeine, and it would seem prudent for these individuals to drastically reduce their intake. The question of how much is too much for other people is difficult to answer, because of considerable variability in sensitivity from individual to individual.

Caffeine, along with other members of the xanthine group, acts directly on the myocardium to produce increased heart rate and increased force of contraction by the cardiac muscle. If the stimulation to the heart is great enough, cardiac arrhythmias can develop; this side effect has been demonstrated in research studies (Dobmeyer, Stine, Leier, Greenberg, & Schall, 1983). The lay press has reported that heavy coffee users run a greater risk for heart attack than non-coffee drinkers, but the scientific data for this conclusion are contradictory. Land (1983) has shown that ingestion of caffeine potentiates cardiovascular responses to stress.

Caffeine also strengthens contractions of skeletal muscle; thus, individuals who ingest it in excess may experience tremulousness. It also increases urinary output through a diuretic action on the kidneys. Another effect is gastric irritation, brought on because of its ability to stimulate gastric secretion. Because of this effect, caffeine intake has been suggested as a method for testing gastric secretion.

Clinically, the elimination of caffeine from the diet seems beneficial in ameliorating breast discomfort in women with fibrocystic mastitis, but this assertion has not been scientifically proven (Heyden & Muhlbaier, 1984). In patients who are prone to irritation of the lower urinary tract, the elimination of caffeine-containing beverages, as well as of alcohol and spices, aids in providing symptomatic relief. Those who suffer from irritable bowel syndrome may also obtain relief of symptoms by abstaining from these items.

Finally, caffeine has been implicated as a cause of cancer and birth defects, but no attempt will be made here to discuss these topics since they are very controversial. For further details, readers may consult a report by Barone and Grice (1985).

Conclusions

Since a considerable number of people may have conditions that are adversely affected by caffeine, the availability of headache-relieving medications that do not contain caffeine is a welcome addition to the clinician's armamentarium. The ingestion of caffeine can reach significant levels if headache analgesics are taken frequently. To have alternative drugs without caffeine allows more flexibility in prescribing for headache sufferers.

Further, patients who are asked to eliminate caffeine from their diets must become aware of the numerous food products, beverages, and medications presently available that contain caffeine. Caffeine is an amazing chemical compound that has many physiological actions that can, at times, have adverse effects. How important it is in provoking or relieving headache will depend on each individual's response. To assess its contribution, clinicians must carefully evaluate and follow up each patient individually.

References

BARONE, J. & Grice, H.D. (1985). Report of Fifth International Caffeine Workshop, Cancun, 1984. *Chemical Toxicology, 231*, 389-399.

BOULENGER, J., Uhde, T.W., Wolff, E.A., & Post, R.M. (1984). Increased sensitivity to caffeine in patients with panic disorders. *Archives of General Psychiatry, 41, 1067-1071.*

CHARLESWORTH, E.A. & Nathan, R.G. (1984). *Stress Management*. New York: Atheneum.

COUNCIL ON SCIENTIFIC AFFAIRS (1984). Caffeine labeling. *Journal of the American Medical Association, 252*, 803-806.

DOBMEYER, D.J., Stine, R.A., Leier, C.V., Greenberg, R. & Schall, S.F. (1983). The arrhythmogenic effects of caffeine in human beings. *The New England Journal of Medicine, 308*, 814-816.

GREDEN, J.F. (1974). Anxiety or caffeinism: A diagnostic dilemma. *The American Journal of Psychiatry, 131*,1089-1092.

GREDEN, J.F., Victor, B.S., Fontaine, P. & Lubetsky, M. (1980). Caffeine-withdrawal headache: A clinical profile. *Psychosomatics, 21*, 411-418.

HEYDEN, S. & Muhlbaier, L.H. (1984). Prospective study of "fibrocystic breast disease" and caffeine consumption. *Surgery, 96*, 4379-4384.

KURTZKE, J.F. (1982). The current neurologic burden of illness and injury in the United States. *Neurology, 32*, 1207-1214.

LANE, J.D. (1983). Caffeine and cardiovascular responses to stress. *Psychosomatic Medicine, 45*, 447-451.

MATHEW, R.J. & Wilson, W.H. (1985). Caffeine consumption, withdrawal and cerebral blood flow. *Headache, 25*, 305-309.

PENNINGTON, J.A. & Church, H.N. (1985). *Bowes and Church's Food Values of Portions Commonly Used*. Philadelphia: J.B. Lippincott.

SELYE, H. (1974). *Stress Without Distress*. New York: Signet Books.

ZIEGLER, D.K., Hassanein, R.S. & Couch, J.R. (1977). Characteristics of life headache histories in a nonclinic population. *Neurology, 27*, 265-279.

Medical Psychotherapy
1988, Volume 1, pp. 87-93

© 1988 by
Hans Huber Publishers, Toronto

Medical Psychotherapy With Elderly Psychiatric Inpatients: Uses of Paraprofessionals in Treatment

PETER A. LICHTENBERG, Ph.D.
GARY C. HECK, M.A.
AUDREY B. TURNER
Western State Hospital

Medical psychotherapy has only recently been applied to the elderly inpatient suffering from mental illness. In the past, psychologists served primarily as behavioral consultants when they treated this population. This role is a valuable one; however, the lack of any programmatic focus greatly limits its usefulness. Current professional training prepares the psychologist to offer a wide range of services to the elderly, and extensive upgrading of paraprofessional services can be used to supplement this. This paper highlights the role of paraprofessionals, and presents three in-depth case studies to demonstrate the varied types of effective interventions that a program utilizing paraprofessionals can have.

Introduction

The application of medical psychotherapy to elderly inpatients being treated for mental illness has been limited. Typically, psychologists have served this group in the role of behavioral consultants, which enables the application of general medical psychotherapy techniques to a specialized population. This has led to many treatment successes (see Hussian & Davis, 1985; Macurik, 1985; Sanavio, 1981; Journal of Applied Behavior Analysis, 1986). However, despite the value of these efforts, there are severe limitations with such an approach.

Inquiries or reprint requests should be directed to Peter A. Lichtenberg, Ph.D., Box 2500, Western State Hospital, Staunton, Virginia 24401-1405.

As behavioral consultants, psychologists limit the nature of the problems they treat and the methodology used in treating them. In behaviorally treating incontinence, for example, emotional reactions to a stroke are not addressed. Psychologists are now being trained to work directly with the elderly, and have much more to offer (Eisenberg & Jansen, 1983).

The field of applied geropsychology has become recognized as an important area for which specific training is needed (Santos & Vandenbos, 1982). This includes knowledge from developmental, rehabilitation, and medical psychology, as well as cognitive and behavioral therapies. The roles of geropsychologists are now described for nursing home consultation (Hyerstay, 1979; Sbordone & Sterman, 1983) and for outpatient services (Lewinsohn, Teri, & Hautzinger, 1984). Despite these advances, no descriptions are available for the practice of medical psychotherapy with elderly inpatients being treated for mental illness. What follows is a brief overview of an inpatient program and three case studies.

Background of the Service

The Shenandoah Geriatric Treatment Center in Virginia is a state hospital Intermediate Care Facility. At the time of this study, 96% of the patients were over 60 years old, with the average age being 75. Fifty-seven percent were women. Using the DSM-III-R, 48% of the patients had been diagnosed as having organic mental disorders and syndromes, the most common being Alzheimer's, multi-infarct dementia, and organic mood or personality disorder. Most of these patients were wheelchair-bound. The remaining diagnoses were as follows: schizophrenic illness (31%); affective disorders (12%); and other (9%). Most of these patients were ambulatory.

The psychology service staff included a PhD psychologist and four paraprofessionals whose education ranged from a high school graduate to a master's degree. The paraprofessionals were state employees. These positions were created to improve the quality of interpersonal services the patients received.

In order to achieve a programmatic focus and to offer a wider range of psychological services, paraprofessional input was extensively upgraded. Past research has demonstrated that paraprofessionals can be highly effective, especially in the delivery of structured tasks (Durlak, 1979). This was thus a good match, since working with elderly psychiatric inpatients requires highly structured interventions. Two areas were zeroed in on to prepare the paraprofessionals: training and support.

Training consisted of individual and group sessions. Weekly group lectures and films included talks on listening skills, counseling techniques, brain-behavior relationships, depression, dementia, group treatment, grief, caregiving, and behavioral treatment. (A manual for this training is available from the authors.) Weekly individual supervisory sessions focused upon the influence of psychopathology, medical conditions, and neuropsychological deficits. Detailed treatment plans and goals were also established and thereafter monitored.

A supportive effort was initiated to help manage job stress and burnout, by allowing the paraprofessionals to ventilate frustrations, discuss concerns, and obtain group support. Moracco (1983) specifically addressed burnout in clinical gerontology, and we agree that varying job tasks and experiencing increased decision-making authority helps maintain satisfaction.

Case Studies

The following case studies demonstrate the effective interface between the psychologist and paraprofessional in assessment and treatment. In the first case, the history, formal assessment and treatment approach are the work of the psychologist, while the paraprofessional provides supportive treatment and carries out the structured intervention. The second study describes a psychoeducational group in which the paraprofessionals spent considerable time researching topics and arranging the group. They acted as the primary therapists while the psychologist performed in-vivo supervision and guided their interventions. The third case is an example of improved coping with a manic-depressive illness, in which the paraprofessional employed a daily structured intervention and the patient responded with improved coping.

Comprehensive Psychosocial Approach for Yelling Behavior

Mr. G., a 63-year-old, single, white male was referred to psychological services because of his frequent yelling. Previous interventions had included a response-cost approach in which he lost privileges if he yelled, but this plan was ineffective. Mr. G. had an extensive history of medical and psychiatric illness. He was diagnosed in childhood as having juvenile onset diabetes and seizure activity. In his early twenties, he had been forced to leave university due to "schizoid" and "paranoid" behaviors. He believed that his life was being controlled by an elderly gentleman he had met while in college. From 1956 to 1974, Mr. G. lived with his older brother. He was noncompliant with his diet, and almost died once from a diabetic coma. Eventually, he was placed in a nursing home. He had been in several homes before admission to the state hospital, which was necessitated by his combativeness and loud yelling. At the time of the referral, he was an insulin-dependent diabetic with an amputation below his right knee and was wheelchair-bound. He continued to be treated for seizures and also had hypothyroidism.

Clinical interview, behavioral observations, the Dementia Rating Scale (DRS), and the Minnesota Multiphasic Personality Inventory (MMPI) were used in psychological assessment. Results from the DRS revealed the following cognitive strengths: orientation, naming, following commands, and excellent recall of well-learned verbal information. Deficits included abstract reasoning, attention span, and verbal memory for new information.

On the MMPI, Mr. G. endorsed items reflective of ongoing delusions and ideas of reference. Interpretation of the profile indicated a distinct lack of interpersonal trust, coupled with intense feelings of hostility and aggression. He attempted to use isolation as a defense, but due to his loneliness could not keep his feelings to himself.

Behavioral observations and clinical interview suggested that Mr. G. yelled out primarily out of frustration in meeting his own needs (e.g., going to the bathroom, turning on a radio, personal privacy). He was also extremely bored and begged to be taken off the ward.

Mr. G. thought of himself as an autonomous, capable man, but had serious physical and cognitive limitations and suffered from severe psychopathology. An intensive treatment plan was recommended, and a paraprofessional was designated to carry it out.

A multiple baseline design was used to implement treatment. The first goal was to address Mr. G.'s feelings of isolation and lack of stimulation by providing him with a close ongoing relationship and new activities. Prior to this intervention, Mr. G. had been involved in less than an hour of off-ward activities a week, due to his "perpetual yelling." One of the paraprofessionals was assigned to coordinate ten hours of off-ward activities a week for Mr. G., and take him to these activities and monitor him. She was also instructed to monitor his on-ward behavior for three 90-minute sessions a week. If he yelled during the off-ward activities, she was to warn him to be quiet two times, and if he continued, to remove him.

As can be seen in Figure 1, Mr. G. responded well to this plan. Throughout the first baseline of nine weeks, he averaged being quiet 87% of the time. He became particularly attached to the paraprofessional during this time, and his favorite activity was watching a film each week with her. On the ward, however, Mr. G. maintained quiet behavior an average of only 31% of the time.

A second treatment component was introduced during week 10: 4.5 hours a week of on-ward training. During these three weekly training sessions, the paraprofessional provided rewards for each 10 consecutive minutes that Mr. G. remained quiet. The rewards consisted of four ounces of juice or a diabetic cookie. Off-ward activities continued to be offered. As can be seen in Figure 1, Mr.G. responded well to this treatment, increasing his on-ward quiet time to 69% (a 38% increase), and maintaining quiet behavior while on off-ward activities. At the end of the 18 weeks, his on-ward program was suspended and he maintained on-ward quiet at a 70% level for the month following treatment. He remained attached to the paraprofessional and often asked for her when he was feeling upset, confused, or lonely.

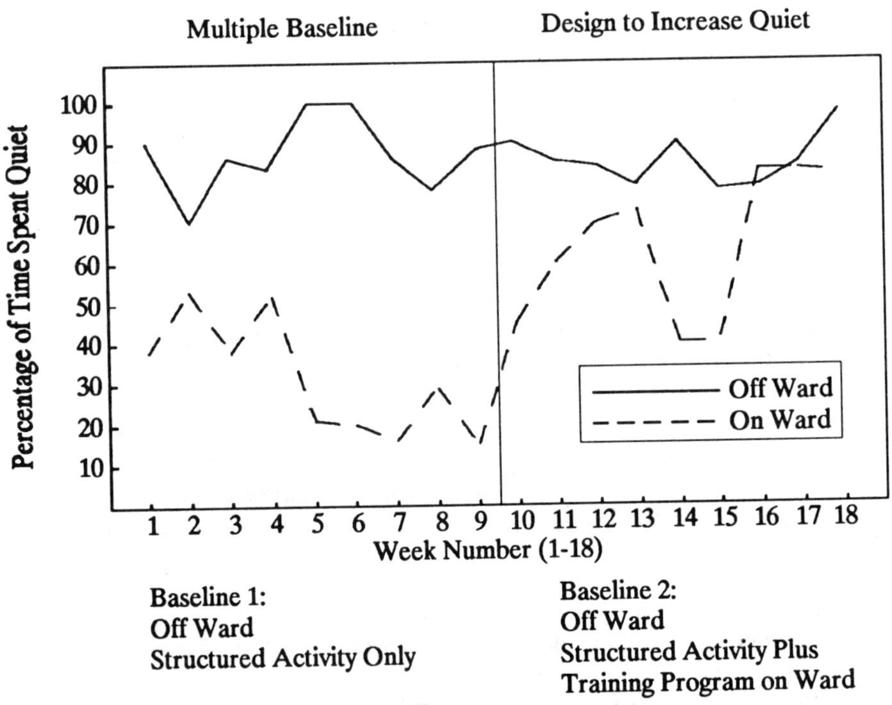

A Psychoeducational Group to Develop Social Interactions

During our work with geriatric inpatients, it became evident that the patients displayed deficits in the ability to interact well with one another. They were not able, for instance, to talk ideas out with one another, to solicit opinions, or to obtain emotional support. Rather, they were often observed talking at one another, or more typically, sitting silently. Under the supervision of the psychologist, a paraprofessional and a master's level nursing student began to prepare to lead a psychoeducational group. Group members were chosen by the therapists and interviewed individually prior to the first session. Criteria for selection included adequate verbal skills and no current psychotic symptoms. Structure was provided for the patients in that topics were pre-determined, but the sessions were organized to provide for maximum patient involvement. Supervision was provided by the psychologist in 75% of the sessions. The following topics were chosen: self-disclosure, self-esteem, loss, anger, assertiveness, empathy, and personal change. The typical sequence of events was as follows: the group met once a week for 45 minutes, and topics were introduced and defined through lecture and discussion, followed up by exercises to promote group sharing. For example, during the self-disclosure session, patients brought in magazine pictures that were meaningful to them.

The psychologist determined and monitored the goals for both the patients and the therapists. Patients goals were as follows: a) attendance, b) dialogue with the therapists, c) sharing of personal concerns, and d) giving feedback and emotional support to other group members. Goals for the therapists included: a) presenting the group in a positive fashion, b) using follow-up questions, c) using examples, d) labeling emotions, and e) generating discussion between group members.

Overall, the group was successful in commanding the patients' interest and enthusiasm. Of the five group members, three attended all twelve sessions, one attended eleven, and one, due to a recurrence of hallucinations, attended only six. The patients were prompt and prepared. It was clear in the early sessions, however, that their dialogues with the therapists were superficial. During one exercise, for example, when they were asked to choose a picture that represented their emotions, one woman chose a fry pan because she said she liked to cook. Another problem was that the therapists were initially too didactic and presented the group in a threatening way. With experience, instead of stating that the group would "help" the patients, they learned to say, "you were chosen for this group because you have a lot to offer and will do well."

By the fourth session, patients were beginning to disclose personal concerns. In a discussion of self-esteem, one woman described being told years ago that she had six months to live: "I believed I was being punished and I prayed for forgiveness." The therapist began to use examples and to label emotions the patients described. For instance, in discussing guilt as a part of grief, one therapist asked, "do you remember times that you were mean to your mother, and how that feels now?"

The patients began interacting more with one another. One woman told a second group member that earlier she had observed her glowering at another patient. This, she went on, was an aggressive posture and not an assertive one, and she wondered what message she had wanted to deliver. In another instance, the group encouraged a patient to ask for help when she began to feel depressed. The therapists learned the art of using follow-up questions. One patient revealed, "I asked God to take my mother because I hated her, and that night she died." The therapist asked what feelings she had, and then labeled the guilt as normal, while also supporting the notion that the patient had had no control over the matter.

These above examples illustrate the potential for effective intervention by a psychoeducational group. During the final session, the patients expressed the importance of the group to them and their sadness at seeing it end. (A training packet outlining each group session is available.)

Behavior Change in Manic-Depression

Ms. F. is a 66-year-old woman carrying a diagnosis of Bipolar Affective Disorder, Manic, with psychotic features. She was reviewed by the treatment team for targeting current behavior problems.

One noted difficulty was Ms. F.'s disregard for the condition of her bedroom, often resulting in loss or damage to her personal items. Her difficulty/inability to clean and maintain a neat room was especially evident during her periods of extreme mood swings. A plan was developed in order to encourage her role in performing this task. Previous interventions had involved letting staff do it, thus disregarding the patient's part in the behavioral resolution. The new plan included a paraprofessional meeting with Ms. F. each morning, and supervising her completion of at least one task, such as making the bed, hanging up clean clothes, rearranging the dresser top, picking up soiled clothing, etc. During periods of depression, Ms. F. typically needed to make her bed and rearrange her dresser top. During periods of mania, she needed to sort out soiled clothing and hang up her clean ones.

Ms. F.'s elevated or depressed mood was a major variable in the type of task to be completed every morning. When her mood was extremely elevated, she readily accepted this plan, but she required increased supervision. During her periods of depression, she also willingly accepted her responsibility in the plan, but needed a great amount of support regarding her feelings of hopelessness and helplessness.

Consistency played a crucial role in this approach. Ms. F. began to regularly seek out the paraprofessional each morning in order to show what tasks she had already completed, as well as for further instructions. Throughout the documented period, her physical health neither improved or deteriorated and her typical medical regimen did not change.

This intervention allowed the paraprofessional to gain a deeper understanding of how Ms. F.'s manic-depressive illness affected her. Furthermore, using this intervening approach the patient's moods were noted as becoming less extreme. Prior to intervention, when her mood was manic her behavior was typically loud and disruptive to the entire ward. She scattered her personal belongings everywhere and was careless in her smoking, frequently burning her clothing as well as herself. Following consistent implementation of the plan she was increasingly able to stay on task with supervision, and was more careful with regard to her smoking habits. Pre-intervention, during depressed states she had been fearful, isolated, frequently refused meals, and was unwilling to participate in any on/off ward functions. Post-intervention observation noted that during periods of depression she was now able to seek out help and encouragement more appropriately. A review of all written notes during the period revealed that Ms. F. became a more willing participant in group activities, missed fewer meals, and overall complied with the plan.

Summary

The purpose of this paper was to describe the role of a geropsychologist working with psychiatric inpatients. In the past, the behavioral approach has been the only method of treatment applied to this population. Here, we describe a program that involves varied assessment and treatment techniques and includes collaboration among professional and paraprofessional staff. In the first case, a treatment intervention based on considerations from both personality and neuropsychological assessment was successful in meeting the social needs of the patient and improving his behavior. The second case study described a group technique that was used to help the patients explore their lives and themselves. They experienced a supportive environment while confronting emotional issues. The last case study described how a simple intervention, applied consistently, aided a patient in coping with her manic-depressive illness. Many psychotherapeutic approaches need to be used with the elderly psychiatric inpatient, and with creative use of personnel these needs can be better met.

References

DURLAK, J.A. (1979). Comparative effectiveness of paraprofessional and professional helpers. *Psychology Bulletin, 86*, 80-92.

EISENBERG, M. & Jansen, M. (1983). "Rehabilitation psychology: State of the art". *Annual Review of Rehabilitation, 3*, 1-31.

HUSSIAN, R.T. & Davis, R. (1985). *Responsive Care: Behavioral Interventions with Elderly Persons*. Research Press: Illinois.

HYERSTAY, B. (1979). "The role of a psychologist in a nursing home". *Professional Psychology, 101*, 36-41.

JOURNAL OF APPLIED BEHAVIOR ANALYSIS (1986). *19*, 4.

LEWINSOHN, P., Teri, L.T. & Hautzinger, M. (1984). "Training clinical psychologists for work with older adults: A working model". *Professional Psychology: Research and Practice, 15*, 187-202.

MORACCO, J. (1983). "Managing stress and burnout in clinical gerontology". *Clinical Gerontologist, 2*, 30-51.

MACURIK, K. (1985). *Behavior Management With Elderly Persons*. Piedmont Geriatric Institute.

SANAVIO, E. (1981). "Toilet training psychogeriatric resident". *Behavior Modification, 5*, 417-427.

SANTOS, J. & Vandenbos, R. (1982). *Psychology and the Older Adult*. Washington D.C.; American Psychological Association.

SBORDONE, R. & Sterman, L. (1983). The psychologist as consultant in a nursing home: Effect on staff morale and turnover. *Professional Psychology; Research and Practice, 14*, 240-250.

Medical Psychotherapy
1988, Volume 1, pp. 95-111

© 1988 by
Hans Huber Publishers, Toronto

Somatic Communications: Interpersonal Theory and Therapy of Psychosomatic Disorders[1]

ROBERT SANDERS, Ph.D.
Private Practice

Psychosomatic diseases may be viewed as disorders in interpersonal communication. The approach taken here is that the therapist should treat every somatic development that significantly affects the sufferer's interpersonal relationships as if it were an intentional communication, and try to explore its adaptive purposes.

Introduction

Contemporary thinking about psychosomatic disease appears to be based on a picture of something *bad* in a person's thoughts or feelings; responsible, almost as a demon would be, for a morbid condition in that person's body. Few authorities are drawn instead to an anthropological perspective on psychosomatic complaints, which would presume hidden relationships among the members of a group, the understanding of which would actually reveal the observed "illnesses" to be orderly contributions to group life. Field anthropologists often have the experience of re-defining behaviors over and over again as they learn more and more of the social relationships that determine the rationality of these behaviors. Psychotherapists probably would do well to think of themselves as anthropologists of a sort, at least to the extent of valuing this reframing experience in connection with what they call psychosomatic diseases.

Terms such as *illness, abnormality*, and *dysfunction* have only analogic applications in the mental sphere. True, we have long known that the brain, evidently a structure of cellular tissues like other organs in the body, mediates thought and action. Surely, then, we might reasonably say that it does its job normally or abnormally, just as we can say that kidneys filter blood well or ill. But for all we really know (by the stand-

Inquiries or reprint requests should be directed to Robert Sanders, 4528 Main St., Suite 200, Kansas City, Missouri, 64111.

ards of biological knowledge), psychiatric disorders may not be diseases at all, nor even extraordinary modes of nervous function. They might, just as probably, be extraordinary modes of communication, exploiting quite ordinary physiology and data-processing, like extraordinary books composed of ordinary words on ordinary typewriters.

Against the prejudice that only psychological pathology can cause psychosomatic problems, I want to articulate the idea that certain interpersonal processes (pathological or not) require the participants to develop special methods of communication, some of which involve the use of somatic disturbances in ways that cannot reasonably be called "sick."

This perspective contrasts with the received view that only hysterical conversion symptoms serve a communicative purpose. Alexander (1950), for example, has no difficulty with the idea that vegetative functions respond to chronic, unrelieved emotional tensions with remarkable derangement, but cannot believe that the vegetative derangements called "organ neuroses" could possibly express complex ideas the way hysterical conversions do. He dismisses this notion with the remark that the nervous centers responsible for the function of these internal organs have no functional access to the centers where complex ideation occurs. "Symbolic expression of psychological content," he writes, "is known only in the field of voluntary innervations, such as speech, or expressive movement, such as facial grimacing, gesticulation, laughter, weeping, etc. Possibly blushing could be included in this group. It is most improbable, however, that internal organs such as the liver or the small arterioles of the kidney can symbolically express ideas."

But in fact, we can always propose a plausible mechanism that gives psychological significance to any somatic development, problematic or otherwise. These linking mechanisms need not be confined to neuronal pathways between the brain ganglia we like to think of as the bright villas of thought and the "lower" centers presumed to be the dull sweatshops of vegetative function. If autonomic processes are not under voluntary control, they still seem to be under the control of imagination or fantasy (Green & Green, 1977), which is itself undoubtedly subject in certain ways to voluntary control. This would place the vegetative functions within reach of any mental content whatever, for purposes of its expression to another person. Should we put it past anyone to have a fantasy in order to induce a vegetative condition that communicates an intended proposition? And even when the somatic problem has evidently come into being as a pure accident, what is to prevent its subject from using it communicatively?

The psychotherapeutic stance that I have adopted toward psychosomatic problems is to treat every somatic development that significantly affects the sufferer's interpersonal relations as if it were an intentional communication, to be understood as an orderly contribution to an ongoing "dialogue" with his or her intimates.

Treating every somatic development with impact on the person's relationships as if it were intended to have that impact, and thereby communicate something, must from time to time lead to what is called in statistical decision theory a type I error, or false positive (Snedecor & Cochran, 1967). In this context, a type I error would be deciding that a somatic development encoded an intentional communication, when in fact it did not. A type II error would be deciding that a somatic development encoded no intentional communication when in fact it did. No matter how frequent somatic developments without communicative purpose may be, we are going to make more type I errors than type II errors if we adopt the strategy of treating every somatic event as if it had such a purpose. The strategy recommended here of refusing to risk any type

II error is reasonable only if the expected cost of type I errors is offset by the expected benefit of avoiding type II errors.

A bit of reflection makes it clear that type I errors seldom have significant cost, since responding to an event as a communication rarely interferes with other things that one must do about it. After all, the only thing one *must* do with something one believes to be a communication is to think about what it communicates. Suppose that the somatic event in question is, to take an example from Minuchin, Rosman, and Baker (1978), severe ketoacidosis. To commence medical treatment of the ketoacidosis while at the same time wondering aloud about its communicative import, seems not only feasible but downright easy. Likewise, should heroic measures become necessary to save the life of an anorexic, need any of them prevent one from the kind of thinking, listening, and talking that might uncover a message in the person's starvation? Believing that an event is a communication entails no particular course of action, except to think about that event in a certain way. The only course of action it absolutely forbids is treating people as if they were not a communicating kind of thing. Certain quite communicative gestures make us want very much to do exactly that, and then we might wish that the melodramas of Mr. Charles Bronson, rather than being psychological reflection, were an acceptable guide to our conduct. And maybe it is latent scenarios of this type that we appeal to when we suppose that treating some behavior or somatic development as messages is impossible. But even in cases where the person uses an intolerable communicative medium, such as violence (severe anorexia can be viewed as a form of violence), which we must eliminate as quickly as possible, the effort to understand the content is not necessarily aborted by what we do to restore order. So long as we do not destroy the communicating person in the process, we leave open the possibility of understanding later what must be brought to an abrupt halt now.

Having convinced ourselves that type I errors are costless, let us consider the expected cost of a type II error, in which we decide that a somatic development has no communicative purpose when in fact it does. As with type I errors, a type II error can generate a cost only through the material consequences of the decision. Deciding that an event is *not* a communication is likely to have very destructive consequences. If you seek to communicate with me, and I refuse to classify your behavior as a vehicle of communication, then I effectively classify you as something outside the human world. If our relationship forces you to take that classification seriously (as all but the most casual relationships do), then my stance toward you is equivalent to the worst mischief imaginable, whether I intend you any harm or not, and whether you are conscious of the harm or not. Failure to classify a human being as a human being is a biological calamity as well as a moral one, as I shall attempt to show in the following digression on the role of communication in human survival.

Human Beings and Their Instrumental Communities

Communication touches all human relations, and in fact totally constitutes the great majority of them. Indeed, because it is the passage of information from brain to brain that effects human survival, we can say – with no intention whatever of speaking metaphorically – that the actual locus of adaptive human intelligence is not only inside individual brains, but also in the network of communication links throughout the community of individual brains. Social organizations with cultures, what we might call *instrumental communities*, are the real medium of human intelligence. If (as would be most exact) we think of a person's instrumental community as all of the necessary conditions of his or her survival that originate in human activity, the boundaries of this or that instrumental community would be virtually ungraspable. For all we know, the instrumental community of a contemporary citizen of the western industrial societies extends throughout the whole human population and all of human history. (Instrumental communities are *not* the same as corporations, societies, or nation-states. In fact, such organizations as these often impede the individual's access to the power of the instrumental community.)

It is an ideologically embarrassing but nonetheless biological fact that individual human beings cannot engage any terrestrial environment successfully without the aid of an instrumental community. Be they corporate managers in Japan or hunter-gatherers in Brazil, individuals must bring more intelligence to every task of survival than fits in a single head.

The relationships of the individual to instrumental community and environment are modeled in a certain kind of parallel-processing computer, called the "Connection Machine" (Hillis, 1987). The Connection Machine links a great many relatively weak processing units, each with a small memory, into an arrangement that allows each processor to work on a small part of a computational problem, with the assistance of outputs generated by the other processors working on their own small parts. The work that each processor can actually accomplish thus exceeds its individual capacity. The additional power at its disposal is not the capacity of any one other processor, but what that other processor creates with the help of outputs from still others, and so on. There is no *a priori* constraint on how much of the total network the input from any one processor to any other represents.

We cannot predict what an individual processor can do from knowledge of its intrinsic properties. We must understand not only those properties but the network within which it operates.

As human individuals at work on any task, we are like individual processors in the Connection Machine, each focusing the power of an instrumental community, of arbitrarily large systems of information in flux and information congealed in artifacts, onto our own small part of the problem of human survival. As with the Connection Machine, it is through our interpersonal contact of the moment that the whole instrumental community speaks to each of us.

Because the Connection Machine is wholly external to us as an object of perception, it can easily be conceived as an integral thing, and the individual processors as integral parts of that thing. Because the instrumental community is both an object of perception and part of the means whereby we perceive all objects, we must accomplish a difficult "Copernican turn" (Kant, 1787) to conceive of the instrumental community as a *thing*, a biotic system in which individuals participate as components. Nevertheless, every detailed consideration of how human beings actually survive points to such biotic systems as the real units of human ecology.

Instrumental communities and relations of individuals to them are not only communicative affairs, they are life-and-death matters. For human beings, reliable communicative relations outside the body are as relevant to physical survival as are reliable supplies of enzymes inside the body.

Now let us go back to our discussion of the cost of a type II error, to set it in our current context. When I classify your communicative acts as nothing that I should even try to understand, then I exclude you from the communicative net that makes up the instrumental community. If you and I are in a serious dialogue relationship at that moment, then I represent the instrumental community to you, and I speak with its authority when I effectively dismiss you from the human world.

Calling this an assault with intent to kill would be extravagant; nevertheless, to threaten people with disconnection from their instrumental community offers them no less harm than threatening them with disconnection from their central nervous systems. The cost of a type II error is, indeed, the psychological damage attendant on threatening someone with death. To the people of ancient city-states, exile was a capital sentence (Fustel de Coulanges, 1873); this kind of exile still is.

If, as I think we have shown, the cost of type II errors is incomparably greater than the cost of type I errors, then we should give complete priority to avoiding the former over avoiding the latter. The only rational way to minimize type II errors, when we cannot readily distinguish communications from non-communications (and of course in the cases of somatic events we cannot) is to eliminate type II errors completely by having *no criterion at all* for communicative intents; that is, to accept every somatic development with an impact on relationships as an intentional communication to the other members of the relationships.

Fundamental Anxiety

Our sense of vulnerability to expulsion from the human world is at the root of what Freud called, in the title of one of his later works, *Das Unbehagen in der Kultur*, famously translated as *Civilization and its Discontents* (Freud, 1961). This translation, completely unfaithful to the syntax of the original, quite fails to capture the *immanence* of uneasiness in social life. Freud's phrase suggests an inherent and profoundly anxiogenic tension between our instinctual nature and our vital dependence of interpersonal relations. While he believed this tension to be an unavoidable feature of civilized life, he also believed that many people suffer from more of it than is necessary, and that they can be helped to an easier life. What follows is my view of how this universal minimum of social malaise comes about.

The adaptation and survival of many nonhuman social species depend on stable communicative relations within communities, but, unlike human beings, their communicative links are guaranteed by genetically inherited mechanisms. Human beings cannot afford genetic dedication to a given pattern of social communication, which is what would result from having genetic guarantees. They can survive only by *technology*, that is, by discovering ways to operate on any environment they happen to occupy, so as to bring its physical properties within the competence of their physiological homeostatic mechanisms. The necessary conditions of such discoveries, and of their implementation, are invariably distributed throughout an instrumental community. The instrumental community, as much as any individual in it, must respond creatively and flexibly to the ecological circumstances of its members. This flexibility of response to environmental variation requires flexibility of communicative patterns among individuals. To return to our Connection Machine analogy: it is because the individual processors can be connected to one another in any of all possible communicative arrangements that the machine can serve as a general purpose computer. Likewise, it is because human communities can be organized in virtually any conceivable way that the human species is a completely general adaptor/survivor. Of all species, only the human can survive habitat destruction, for it is not genetically bound to any habitat.

The stable communicative relations upon which human life depends are created and maintained by what individuals say and do as they deal with one another every day. Consequently, they are, at least in principle, vulnerable to disruption by what others say and do. We must "safely inspect" our every action to make sure that it will not interact with the circumstances (as far as these can be known) so as to derange our fundamental communicative relations. We consult our deepest convictions about the nature of the instrumental community, about what its members expect of us, and about what they cannot tolerate in us, to assess each thought and feeling and impulse for its potential to ruin our very humanity.

Thus do we guard against errors of *commission*, but we must be just as vigilant against errors of omission. Every activity has in the mind of the agent some connection to interpersonal relations. There are, to be sure, physically solitary activities, but even these are carried out in a penumbra of considerations of how they fit into the agent's relations with other people. Often, it is not so much that one considers, say, how brushing one's teeth should be materially integrated into an encounter with another person as it is that one must consider how one's toothbrushing might have to be represented in dialogue with another person. Our fundamental condition as technological creatures denies us the luxury of any *a priori* decision that something need never be talked about. Human beings cannot be human beings together unless they leave open their every dialogue to any content. This is not a pleasant ethical ornament, but dire necessity: if we exclude beforehand any content from our communicative networks, it is as if we injected a toxin into our vital tissues. The vital tissue of communicative relations cannot maintain its integrity if individuals have to keep information from one another. Here, then, is the fundamental conflict that pervades human life and touches every human moment with a measure of anxiety: we dare not leave anything out of our dialogues with one another; we dare not bring anything into such dialogues that would break them down.

The Presuppositions of Communicative Relations

Interpersonal relations are maintained by interpersonal encounters, and these are essentially communicative. Communications *presuppose* shared information, shared expectations, shared values, and a shared general theory of the world. If two entities are to communicate, the sender must construct messages on assumptions about information the receiver possesses or lacks. Humans have put messages on space vehicles that are supposed to leave the solar system, on the slight chance that some "intelligence" will retrieve them. The designers do not of course presuppose specific knowledge, such as of English or Mandarin, on the part of whatever might retrieve the vehicles, but they presuppose quite a bit (e.g., that whatever picks the vehicle up will count as we do, that it allows two-dimensional distributions of texture or albedo to encode messages, and that it will have no strong prejudices about what part of the vehicle might bear a message). The point is, these guesses can never be part of the communicative content that they make possible. The NASA engineers cannot send out a preliminary plaque asking the folks of Barnard's Star what should be assumed about them for purposes of communicating with them. Likewise, we cannot ask one another what it takes to begin talking with one another. That would be to articulate the presuppositions of a message in the message itself, a logical impossibility. We have personal theories of what it takes to have one another's company, theories we have developed privately and which we have never articulated in words. To do that, we would have to bring them into a dialogue, but being in a dialogue versus not being allowed into a dialogue is what these theories are about.

One's personal theory of human affairs is *presuppositional* to one's participation in them. The presuppositional status of these beliefs makes them almost impossible to test. For a belief to be tested it must be articulated in some way – but articulating a belief can take place only in some kind of dialogue, an interpersonal encounter. If the belief in question is one about what it takes to be a person in an encounter, how can it be articulated *in* such an encounter?

Because one's experience actually takes place in the net of communicative links with others, these presuppositional matters cannot enter one's awareness, any more than they can enter conversation. One's presuppositional system concerning all human encounters and relations can never be articulated in any of them, and therefore cannot be formed as propositions. This presuppositional system is one's *unconscious*. A substantial fraction of it comprises presuppositions that cause the discomfort Freud considered avoidable or reducible; these are the *neurotic* presuppositions.

A neurotic presupposition says, contrary to reality, that some unavoidable, unsuppressible affective process is incompatible with human company. It *presupposes* people's intolerance of this or that instinctual development. These false beliefs are "neurotic" because of the peculiar behavioral distortions they induce. These distortions keep the instinctual affective material from entering the person's dialogues as content. There is not merely a taboo against discussion of these instinctual matters; honest dialogue about them would require articulating one's presuppositions concerning dialogue itself, and that is *in principle* impossible. If we neurotically presuppose that we can be in dialogue with another human being only if the other perceives us as devoid of sexual instincts, then it is *logically* impossible for us to say, authentically and while truly engaged in the dialogue: "I must not allow you to see my sexuality." Hunger, sexual drive, defensive fear, and aggression are the threats to each person's world, not as private events but as visible properties, perceived by others.

Two Channels of Communication: Language and Action

The presuppositions of human encounter are denied expression in language, but this does not mean that they are entirely mute. If you believe others must see you to have this or that property in order for you to interact with them, then you will behave in ways that urge them to see you that way, even though you cannot use words to tell them of this need. In effect, you communicate about your presuppositions by impact rather than by symbolic representation. Nonverbal communication seems to be the designated channel for communicating about presuppositions, and what we have been talking about are the presuppositions of verbal communications exclusively. You cannot articulate the presuppositions of what you are saying *in* what you are saying, but if you have a second communicative medium at your disposal and can operate it simultaneously with the first, then you can transmit in one channel the presuppositions of messages in the other. The second channel does not relieve the first of an excessive burden; it merely is free to inform the partner in dialogue of facts *about* the content of the first channel, something that the first channel cannot do simply because messages cannot talk about themselves.[2] There is a special way in which language relates people, a very different kind of relation than that formed by communicative action. When I describe an object to you I actually integrate our minds with respect to it. You and I then constitute a single intelligence apprehending the object. It may be my sense organs that take data directly from the object, but we both apply our stores of general knowledge, combining them by language, to our comprehension of the object through these data. Language is a wonderfully specialized medium of connection for this purpose, this welding of brains into bigger brains for the adequate mental representation of things in the shared world. Speech, the essential form of language, occupies "small," low-inertia compartments of the alimentary and respiratory functions; it is capable of running in parallel with every praxic, locomotory, or vegetative operation required of a living animal. It does not disengage the individual from the very involvement with objects that is necessary for their adequate description.[3] Only speech can bring data from the experience of individuals to the kind of interpersonal cognition that makes for adequate representation of the environment. While written language is not merely a visual transcription of speech, it derives all of its essential features from speech. This state of affairs dedicates all verbal expression especially to the representation of extra-psychic objects.

On the other hand, nothing intrinsic to language disallows descriptions of one's own psychic processes. It would be likely, then, that neurotic presuppositions tell us not to present our psychic processes in the medium that is most likely to bring communal attention to them, namely, the verbal medium.

Actions, illnesses, styles, forms of the body (Lowen, 1975): these can legitimately represent our neurotic presuppositions to other persons, for such forms of representation do not "call out the community" as does articulation in language.

Intimacy as Natural Psychotherapy

Just possessing nonverbal means of communication does not rescue us from our neurotic dilemma: we need to retain *all* possibilities of verbal communication, if we are to have full access to the instrumental community. But if we put no constraints on the verbal channel, then in effect we allow anything that happens inside us to find expression in the channels that weld us into the instrumental community. Among the things that happen inside us are emotions that (we are convinced) can only destroy those channels if they find expression in them.

The need to relieve this tension, this pervasive murmur of anguish beneath humdrum business, confers great value on *intimate relationships*. For they provide human contact apart from the world of ordinary relationships (which is why "private" and "intimate" are so closely related in usage), in a setting where the presuppositions that conflict with the need to communicate can be suspended. In an intimate relationship, emotional communication takes precedence over all pragmatic concerns. Here, partners reveal to one another the affective business that their neurotic presuppositions forbid them to reveal in any other interpersonal relationship. The difference between participating in pragmatic social relations and participating in intimate ones is that in the former one's deportment has no other purpose than to keep him or her in the relation, while in the latter one's deportment has the additional purpose of "betraying" the secret nature that one believes would get him or her kicked out of the human world.

Intimacy is a kind of psychotherapy, discovered, for all we know, in prehistory as an extraordinarily effective solution to the basic problems of neurotic presuppositions. It works very nearly as Weiss and Sampson (1986) believe the psychoanalytic process to work. What those authors call "pathogenic beliefs" are much like our "neurotic presuppositions." In their conception of therapy, patients actively test and disconfirm their pathogenic beliefs in the transference to the therapist. When things go well in an intimate relationship, the partners' presuppositions, at first nonverbally expressed as in any other kind of relationship, eventually come into the relationship as verbal contents. This is all that needs to be done in order to strip them of their presuppositional status. Intimate partners remain connected despite the revelation of affective reality, and the neurotic presuppositions are disconfirmed. But now the problem is whether or not these things that are dialogic contents in the intimate relationship are still presuppositional in pragmatic relationships. Corresponding to a positive transference stage in analysis, there is a phase of intimacy when one sees one's partner almost as an imaginary playmate of childhood, a special being not at all representative of the world at large.

Here it is necessary to focus on the fact that it is the relationship that is special, and not the person to whom one relates. This is not an easy step to take, this countenancing of the ordinariness of one's intimate. But at some point, one realizes that this intimate accepts one's secret emotional nature not because of some special capacity, but just because he or she has made a commitment to do so.

Experiencing the tolerance of one's intimate thus better resembles one's encounters with the human world than might have been supposed. In fact, it often seems that partner selection is based on some sense that the partner will afford a particularly strict test of the hypothesis that one's inner nature can be accommodated by human company. If one's preeminently understanding partner tolerates one's emotional interior, then one is better assured that the toleration one experiences in the intimate relationship is *not* the kind one has always sought in the pragmatic world, namely, toleration obtained by concealing one's inner reality.

Thus the curative status of intimacy depends on its character apart from the individual properties of the partner. The distinguishing feature of intimacy is that it subordinates everything to emotional revelation; it is constituted of the promise of relationship after any such revelation. Nothing in one's secret nature can break an intimate relationship.

Malignant Conflict in Intimate Relationships

Things certainly do go wrong in intimate relationships, but they are not pathologies of communication, of thought, of feeling, or neurotic business of any kind. Intimate relationships get into trouble because they, like so many other things in this world needful of social attention, are socially isolated.

The commitment to maintain connection without regard to what might emerge as dialogic content is almost invariably honored in intimate relationships. What destroys intimacy is not a reneging on this fundamental contract, but a malignant process that breeds in the intimacy itself.

Partners in intimate relationships make appeal after appeal to one another for understanding and toleration of their emotional inner natures. When such appeals are simultaneous, either partner's appeal looks to the other like a rebuff. An appeal for understanding of one's affective reality is made nonverbally, of course, since that is the only way people are allowed to communicate their neurotic presuppositions. A nonverbal communication of one's own presuppositions is at best a worthless response to such a communication from one's partner. More likely, it will appear to the partner as a dreadful confirmation of the presupposition.

When an appeal for understanding and toleration is rebuffed, or felt to be rebuffed by the appellant, there is a renewed, intensified effort to obtain them. Because the situation is symmetrical between the partners, this renewed effort is likely to be met again with what seems to be a rebuff. Actually, the partner has simultaneously launched a second, intensified effort to obtain the appellant's understanding and toleration. One can see that, even if there is at first no temporal correlation at all between the partners' appeals to one another, the first chance coincidence will make it very likely that all subsequent appeals will collide. Indeed, unless some other process combats this tendency, absolute synchrony of appeals will set in directly. If other people outside the intimate relationship were available to provide one partner enough psychological support to suspend his or her appeals just long enough to permit the other partner's appeals to register, the machine-like collisions would halt. Were this a custom, the malignant synchrony of appeals would be broken up every time it threatened. But that would be in a very different world than ours.

Repeated frustration of appeals for care (of any kind) promotes the *talionic* reaction. This is the desire to cause suffering in a care-giver who is failing. It never occurs outside the context of care-begging, no matter how much the vengeful appellant may strive to make it look like the orderly business of magistracy. Talion is derived from the aggression spontaneously recruited to care-begging action patterns, and its bitter enmity and sadism cannot arise except when the injured party was counting on some kind of parental care from the "villain." The care-eliciting actions of young animals are of a kind with predatory actions of adult animals; they recruit the same aggression to keep them going in the face of frustration. The appeal for care by human and other babies may appear sweet to us, but it is not driven by a sweet mood in the baby. In the respect of needing understanding from one another, we remain forever infantile: we pursue this form of care with increasingly violent aggression when it is frustrated, whether we are dependent children trying to get it from adults, or, as happens invariably in families, we are adults seeking the understanding of our children.

Because our society confines the utterly pragmatic business of childrearing to households formed around sexual pairs or single parents, childrearing is socially isolated. We are supposed to engage our children alone; our dealings with them are "private" matters, to which we are not encouraged to recruit community help. Other adults may give us physical help, or a certain kind of "professional advice" that mostly disguises criticism of what we are doing, but the affective business of our relations with our children in sealed off from the instrumental community. The social isolation of childrearing is more thorough than the social isolation of intimate adult relationships: in the early phases, we encourage mothers to do it without the help of their husbands. During the period romanticized by Winnicott (1953) and others, the mother actually loses all adult intimacy, and her natural psychotherapy is suspended. In such a circumstance, people will attempt to form intimate relationships with anything that has even the nominal status of human being, quite without regard to its real fitness for such a relationship. One would think that a mother would have better sense than to turn to her child for representation of the instrumental community, saying, "Be my human company," to a little animal a few hours old. But appealing for human company – which is appealing for understanding – is not a matter entirely governed by good sense. It is an overwhelming instinctual compulsion; when one is deprived of customary contact with real representatives of the instrumental community, the nearest thing that looks like a human being will receive appeals for understanding. On the one hand, no mother is so silly as to think that her child can understand her; on the other hand, she is in a remarkably silly situation, and should not be judged by intellectual standards.

So, adult and adult, adult and child rage at one another for failure of care, and guarantee the failure in the raging, and domestic life becomes hard, bitter, and sad.

The Psychosomatic Family and the Clinic

Children do not begin life in need of intimacy, but given the misfortune just described, this need is acquired rapidly. They then find themselves in a remarkable position: their families are simultaneously their pragmatic social world and their intimate world. This suggests that in the child, psychosomatic problems have a dual function: the ordinary social one of controlling others' perceptions of oneself, and the intimate one of correcting one's own presuppositions regarding other's expectations of one.

The psychosomatic problem comes to the clinic as part of a malignant process, or as a corrective effort against such a process, that has developed in a normal intimate relationship. The observable part of this malignancy happens to include communications through the somatic channel, a fact that in itself is not even extraordinary, let alone pathological. Somatic methods of communication are probably most useful in family structures with narrow distributions of formal authority, along with monopoly by one member of the verbal domain. The history of our recognition of conversion (Ellenberger, 1970) suggests that, as a method of communication, it originated in just such circumstances. Women and children developed it in a more enthusiastically patriarchal time than our own. It continues to be accessible and useful to every kind of person who finds him or herself in a "benevolent authoritarian" system.

We blandly assume that such systems are pathological and pathogenic, and conclude that the election of the somatic channel is one of the "disorders" that they cause. It is true that the material impact of certain somatic complaints amounts to a serious problem, requiring interventions that do not essentially acknowledge the communicative need behind them. The need for these interventions is a "side-effect," and the accidental property of physical seriousness bears no consistent relation from case to case to the import of the communicative intent.

If we blame the nature of the family system as the "cause" of a psychosomatic illness, we are refusing to understand the collective intention of the family. We are then not fostering the family's welfare so much as we are redesigning the family to suit our prejudices.[4]

Of course, the whole family therapy movement is formed around an implicit set of prejudices concerning families, so that one of the most glaring instances of this "doctor knows best" attitude is Minuchin et al.'s (1978) approach to psychosomatic problems. Minuchin and his associates use plainly pejorative and honorific language in characterizing interpersonal processes; plainly espouse and defend values of autonomy as if these were under attack by the "dysfunctional" family; and express norms of family organization and process as against the "pathogenic" processes they discover in the families of patients. They refer to the *proper* relation of spousal business to parental business, the *right* degree of involvement of family member with one another, *normal* rates of interpersonal differentiation, and so on, as if these were physiological parameters. For example, they talk of "rigid" families who fail to "... alter rules and transactional patterns in periods when change and growth are necessary." The decision as to when such things are necessary is not to be derived from some platonic image of human life; promoting a clinical norm in the matter is just prejudice disguised as science.

Seltzer (1985a, 1985b), studying the families of adolescents with conversion-hysterical problems, exhibits a much more anthropologically sophisticated attitude toward the family context of a presenting problem. She is aware that families are cultural systems and that "...culture, familial or otherwise, is not something that individuals are free to choose, nor something that individuals can be for or against." (Seltzer, 1985b). She describes the culture of a family as existing in two planes: (1) a material plane consisting of observable behavior patterns, and (2) an ideational plane containing myths, thematic beliefs, secrets, and pseudosecrets. The material plane is like an organismic phenotype; the ideational plane is like the genotype. The material plane contains the somatic problem; the ideational plane is largely hidden.

"Conversion families" (families with conversion-hysterical members) have a belief system on the ideational plane that resist articulation of any psychological distress. Conversion families present themselves as "supernormal units" showing no mental or affective disorder, only physical discomfort. The corporate entity claims to be free of all difficulty, except for the ill child. Conversion families exhibit deep suspicion of psychiatry (Seltzer, 1985b).

When the members of a family collectively believe that the integrity of the family and its world-position are jeopardized by admission of psychological disturbance, then the therapist's very profession places him or her in a potential dispute with them. The premise of psychotherapy is that admission of a disturbance helps with alleviation of the disturbance. Both therapist and family can be right in what they believe, while they look wrong indeed to one another. What warrant does the therapist have to assume that the disturbance concerning the family is the one he or she knows to be tractable with insight? There is a great deal of arrogance in our presuming to have a service of use to everyone in every situation.

Maybe these families do what they do always to preserve themselves from the breach of discipline that they know will hurl them into the proletariat. One of Seltzer's most important findings concerning these families is that they have within a generation or two escaped from poverty into the middle class, by intense industry and discipline.

Conversion families morbidly fear loss of class. The subjective probabilities of such an event, conditional on relaxation of family discipline and ideology, are probably not grossly inflated above objective frequencies. At any rate, we are in no position to pass judgement on their realism. The discipline and ideology of the conversion family could well be quite practical. Any defect connected to the spirit in any way might actually threaten to return the family to the class from which it has escaped, and out of which it so precariously manages to remain from hour to hour.

Seltzer's therapeutic approach to these families reflects an anthropological sensitivity to their values. She puts much emphasis on making sure that members of the family save face, and in fact much of her technique is designed to get change started without getting caught at it. She incessantly acknowledges, in a variety of direct and indirect ways, the family's belief that they must be exemplars of the class they wish to join.

And yet Seltzer's therapy is essentially at odds with the family as an intimate system. She depicts the culture of the conversion family as a pathogen and works on it, albeit subtly and respectfully, with the intention of transforming it into something better.

That the therapist has come upon a natural therapeutic system at work on the correction of neurotic presuppositions is not considered. But if we do believe that families are natural therapeutic systems, then we should assume that the family is already at work on the problem they have brought to the clinic. We should assume that they seek help with the correction of neurotic presuppositions (perhaps, in the case of conversion families, with presuppositions about aggression and dependence in human relations), and that our task is to provide *only* the help they need.

Some General Remarks About Communication-Oriented Therapy

(In the following discussion, the term *Patient* refers to the bearer of the somatic complaint; and the term *Intimate* refers either to a partner in an intimate dyadic relationship or to a representative member of the Patient's family.)

The greatest professional service we can render in most of these cases is to facilitate the family's understanding of the Patient's somatic communication. We are then promoting a "natural" process rather than intervening disruptively. We are adjusting a system to which the Patient will belong long after therapy has ceased. There is much to be said in favor of modest, adjustive interventions that enable systems already in place to rectify problems over time, according to their own ecologies. There is much to criticize in invasive interventions that take the family structure apart and attempt to put it back together again in "better" shape.

It is overwhelmingly important to bear in mind that somatic communications are addressed to family members; they were in place before the Patient or the family members ever set eyes on the first doctor in the case. Thus, even if it is recognized that the Patient's complaint has a communicative function, it can also be ruinous of that function for the Patient to be taken out of the family context and given to a stranger who is to understand the complaint. In such a case, one might be saying in effect, "Whatever your message is, we don't deem it proper for transmission to your family." In the majority of psychosomatic cases, the Patient and family had long been at work together on the therapeutic issue when their medium of communication finally accumulated sufficient material impact to bring in the doctors. To extricate someone from the family system and bring him or her to individual therapy under such conditions raises questions of the reasons for denying patients communicative access to the people they have been dealing with up to this point. Generally speaking, such an intervention must have the impact of saying to the Patient that his or her efforts are more part of the natural world than the human world. Thus we should always work with the Patient and the Intimates present in the same session. In what follows, I shall speak of "the Intimate" as a single individual, with the understanding that more than one Intimate might be present with the Patient in a family therapy session.

The kind of therapy I am talking about enables Patient and Intimate to continue working within the expressive idioms they have developed. This approach presumes that these families come to the clinic *not* because one of their members is using a somatic form of communication, but because *a malignant blockade of communications* has set in. Thus, this therapy does not try to remove somatic communications, but to remove the blockade, the miserable cycle of rebuffed appeals and talionic gestures.

This therapy is premised on the belief that there is no therapeutic value to correcting a communication. Correcting the form of communication runs the risk of suppressing part of the content to be transmitted. Form and content cannot be separated *a priori* by any context-independent formula. Systems of therapy that assign an invariant pathological status to somatizing, acting out, etc. are based on prior evaluation of communicative forms.

The injunction against correcting communications applies to those of Patient and Intimate with the same force. Encouraging the family to modify the behavior presumed to have caused the somatic problem rides roughshod over their communicative efforts, for the behavior of the family is as communicative in intent as the Patient's somatic problem.

The therapist's moment-to-moment labor is largely a matter of helping the Intimate to a non-transferential attitude toward the somatic problem, usually called "listening through" it. The final product of listening through the somatic problem is a story about the Patient's subjectivity without reference to the Interpreter. We want the Patient to appear as a whole object to the Intimate, and we want this appearance reflected in the Intimate's conversation during the session. Ordinarily, family members are not entire, free-standing objects in one another's phenomenal field; rather they are partly thus and partly the medium through which each member's phenomenal field is generated. In a sense, they are simultaneously *objects* of perception to one another and *organs* of perception to one another.

The therapist should remember at all times that the Intimate bears a transferential relation to the Patient, no matter what customary or normative relation between the two appears to obtain. There is no particular reason to suppose that the Intimate has ever had an objective experience of the Patient, even when the Patient was newborn. Likewise, the Patient may be assumed never to have had an objective experience of the Intimate. Without objective experience of one another, Patient and Intimate cannot experience one another's appeals as what they are; each can only experience his or her own failure to obtain understanding as it seems to result from the activity of the other.

The somatic complaint is talked about just as if it were a piece of voluntary behavior. The principal difference between the psychosomatic and the behavioral case is that in the former the Intimate is usually reluctant to take a blameful stance toward the problem, while in the latter case a blameful stance is more or less expected. The therapist should not be impressed at all by this difference. Whatever stance the Intimate standardly takes toward the somatic problem in the Patient, we should construe it as the former's way of escalating appeals for understanding in the face of rebuff. We should assume, therefore, that it prevents the Intimate from listening to the Patient in a helpful way.

The therapist must break this vicious cycle by helping one of the parties to suspend his or her appeals long enough to get a glimpse of the objective reality of the other party. We have assumed that the first one to suspend should be the Intimate, because we have been focusing on the problem that was brought to the clinic. But in fact from this theoretical perspective it makes no difference whether the Patient is listened to or does the listening, to start with.

Because collision of appeals initiates and promotes the malignant negativity of intimate relationships, part of the remedy sought by this method is to establish turn-taking in the making and receiving of appeals for understanding. Thus, when the therapist turns to the one who ought to be listening at the moment, all the support possible should be given to the "receiver" for suspending his or her own appeal to the sender. The therapist seeks to provide the partners with the experience, *during the session*, of the collisions halting and the appeals slipping past one another.

A common prejudice in dealing with a Patient who is a dependent child and an Intimate who is the parent, is assuming that the Intimate's appeal to the Patient is inappropriate, and that if we countenance it we are somehow doing to the Patient what the parent did to "cause" the neurosis. But the kind of therapeutic procedure described here blatantly advocates treating children as if they were capable of having objective experiences of their parents. It would probably be a fine thing if parents did not have to make appeals to their children for understanding, but the situation of families in the world at present is such that it is impossible for them to refrain from it, and the best must be made of it as an irreducible fact of family life. That the parent once made transferential appeals to the child, with the result of the child's neurotic presuppositions, hardly takes away the parent's current right to understanding from the child. As they come to the therapist now, parent and child are an intimate couple with neurotic presuppositions individually held and capable of correction in the one by the other. We must assume that they are already at work on this mutual correction, and that they have come to the therapist because this work has run into difficulty. The remedy for this situation is not necessarily a therapist-gratifying drama of protecting a child from a pathogenic parent.

We might be seized by the sentimental fantasy that the Patient is still being formed, now by the therapist as much as by the parents, and that the therapist is under the criterion of the "good enough mother," with his or her own self-esteem at stake. Careful protection of the child-Patient from parental demands for understanding in that case, mainly by never calling on the Patient to understand his or her parental Intimates, can be a subtle appeal to the Patient to take care of the therapist by allowing the latter to be a "good enough mother." If the Patient is never called upon to do what the Intimate is called upon to do every session, the message will quickly become clear to Patients that they are expected not to understand their Intimates. What can this mean to them but that they are not expected to grow up?

But whatever the therapist's ideology concerning justice between parents and children, it should be seen that parental Intimates will not cease their appeals to the Patient until the Patient acknowledges them, and until the Intimates can leave off those appeals, they will not understand the Patient.

We are not after either person's objective experience of the other as a permanent revision of his or her mode of experiencing people. The idea that one's normal working attitude toward others should or even could be non-transferential is unrealistic. An important basis of the therapy under discussion here is that people are biologically incapable of material or psychological independence. The nature of human dependence is such that most of the time our experiences of one another will be dominated by transference. *Episodes* of non-transferential, objective experience of the Patient by the Intimate, and vice versa, are entirely on a reliable, "turn-taking" basis.

Therapist and Intimate talk about the possible meanings of the somatic problem in the presence of the Patient, but not *to* the Patient, so that the Patient always *overhears* what is said. Of course, the Patient is not forbidden to talk, and typically will soon begin to inject comments. As these comments enter the field, the therapist incorporates them into the overall communication of the Patient, and talks with the Intimate about them just as the somatic problem is talked about.

I have observed, in almost every case, a considerable difference in outcome between letting Patient and Intimate talk *to one another*, and requiring them to talk to me *about one another*. When they talk to one another, they repeatedly enact the malignant blockade of communication, with its machine-like collision of appeals for understanding.

When they talk to me about one another, they begin to understand each other. The phenomenology of being talked to versus overhearing is crucial to this method of therapy. We might not at first appreciate what radically different kinds of experience these two encounters with language are. When someone talks *to* you, your neurotic presuppositions are intensely activated; you are being challenged at the gates of human company. To overhear, affords you the opportunity to relax your presuppositions. To overhear long enough is to undergo a kind of hypnotic process that transplants you from the customary social framework to an internal framework in which you have almost no social presence. (You would liken yourself, perhaps, to a fly on the wall.) While you have psychic continuity between this special mode of experience and the rest of your life, in this overhearing mode you can be temporarily liberated from virtually all of your presuppositions. A patient recently illustrated this to me when, after hearing her husband and me talking about certain dreadful events in her early life, she expressed astonishment at how she contained herself better than she would have thought herself capable of doing. With another patient, I made the error of telling her something that I should have told her husband, for her to overhear. What I had to say to her did not help her at all, but was only painful.

In all these proceedings, therapists should subordinate their own understanding of the Patient's communications to the Intimate's understanding. It is a good idea to offer very few interpretations of somatic processes, behavior, or any other forms of communication. Instead, the therapist should work to make the Intimate's discovery of the Patient's meanings more likely. The therapeutic function is something like an auxiliary ego, in that it consists to such a great extent of pointing things out: resources of contextual data, alternative perspectives, the Intimate's own need for psychological support. As a therapist, one represents an informed, friendly body of constructive opinion about the relationship in the dyad one is working with at the moment. One represents the community interest in the family process that is ordinarily suppressed by the customs of our society – interest that, had it been allowed expression, would have prevented the malignant process that brought the family to therapy.

Notes

1 This paper received the considerable benefit of editorial and substantive input from Michael Lacy, PhD and C.L. Sheridan, PhD, to both of whom the author is deeply indebted.

2 The only way that a *materially interesting* message can say anything about itself is by way of tacit presuppositions, as when we say such things as, "This book is about. . . ." We know what such sentences mean because of presuppositions, set up by the context, that rule out alternative interpretations, such as, "This book [that my aunt has asked me to describe] is about..." The artificial "self-referring" sentences, à la Goedel (Nagel & Newman, 1958), quite fail to represent language in any interesting way.

3 People who for excellent reasons use sign languages instead of speech might wish to interject here that sign languages can say anything that speech can say, as if to defend their medium of communication from imputations of inferiority. Visible gesture is not inferior to speech in what it can encode, but in its interactions with other behavior. It cannot be used as a simultaneous running commentary on one's manual activities, and it cannot be processed simultaneously with visual observation of an ongoing process. It is, relative to such functions, a *prosthesis*.

4 A particularly intense and widespread prejudice concerning families – and all multipersonal entities – is that they have no collective psychological properties. Thus, authors such as Vetere and Gale (1987) would find my reference to the family's collective intention almost self-evidently fallacious. It is easy to demolish the notion of a transpersonal spook (a "collective mind," perhaps) who has the family's collective intention for them, but this is not the same as dismissing the idea of collective psychological processes, such as having an intention. Vetere and Gale suppose it to be as much nonsense to consider the latter as the former.

References

ALEXANDER, F. (1950). *Psychosomatic Medicine*. New York: Norton.

ELLENBERGER, H.F. (1970). *The Discovery of the Unconscious*. New York: Basic Books.

FREUD, S. (1911). "Formulations regarding the two principles in mental functioning". In *General Psychological Theory*. New York: Collier Books, 1963.

FREUD, S. (1961). *Civilization and its Discontents*. (J. Strachey, trans.) New York: Norton.

FUSTEL DE COULANGES, N.D. (1873). *The Ancient City*, translated by Willard Small; reprinted without date or citation of original English publisher, Garden City, New York: Doubleday.

GREEN, E. & Green, A. (1977). *Beyond Biofeedback*. New York: Dell.

HILLIS, W.D. (1987). The connection machine. *Scientific American*, June, *256*, 108-115.

KANT, I. (1787). *The Critique of Pure Reason, Second Edition*, translated by N.K. Smith, London: MacMillan and Co. Ltd., 1923.

LOWEN, A. (1975). *Bioenergetics*. New York: Coward McCann and Geoghegan.

MINUCHIN, S., Rosman, B., & Baker, L. (1978). *Psychosomatic Families: Anorexia Nervosa in Context*. Cambridge: Harvard University Press.

NAGEL, E. & Newman, J.R. (1958). *Goedel's Proof*. New York: New York University Press.

SELTZER, W.J. (1985a). Conversion disorder in childhood and adolescence, Part I: a familial-cultural approach. *Family Systems Medicine, 3*, No. 3, 261-280.

SELTZER, W.J. (1985b). Conversion disorder in childhood and adolescence, Part II: therapeutic issues. *Family Systems Medicine, 3*, No. 4, 397-416.

SNEDECOR, G.W. & Cochran, W.G. (1967). *Statistical Methods, 6th Edition*. Ames, Iowa: The Iowa State University Press.

VETERE, A. & Gale, A. (1987). *Ecological Studies of Family Life*. Chichester: John Wiley and Sons.

WEISS, J. & Sampson, H. (1986). *The Psychoanalytic Process*. New York: Guilford Press.

WINNICOTT, D.W. (1953). Transitional objects and transitional phenomena. *International Journal of Psychoanalysis, 34*, 89-97.

Medical Psychotherapy
1988, Volume 1, pp. 113-118

© 1988 by
Hans Huber Publishers, Toronto

Understanding Learning Disabilities: A Primer for the Psychotherapist

MARIJANET DOONAN, Ph.D.
ROY E. EHRLICH, M.D.
Thomas Aquina College

In many cases encountered by the psychotherapist, the presenting problems may stem from an underlying learning disability. Learning disabilities may affect individuals throughout childhood and continue into adulthood, causing difficulties in numerous areas of successful life functioning. This article discusses the scope and types of such disabilities, evaluates the major issues indicated for therapy, and discusses prescriptive approaches that psychotherapists should be aware of when dealing with learning disabled clients.

For more than two and a half decades, professionals in education, medicine, and psychology have been aware that large numbers of students have specific difficulties in learning. In recent years, educators, psychologists, physicians, and learning disabled adults themselves have recognized that these difficulties can interfere with many areas of life functioning and have a causal relationship with significant psychological problems. Thus, there has been an increasing demand for psychotherapeutic intervention for the "learning disabled" population.

In most cases, mental health professionals have not recognized nor had extensive experience with learning disabled clients. They may have worked with patients with presenting difficulties such as "school phobia," or "management concerns" related to families, schools, and the community, but may not have been aware of the possibility of an underlying learning disability as a causative factor in the presenting problem. Since the learning disabled population differs in significant ways from others who may seek therapy, the psychotherapist must be aware of the probable cause. Understand-

Inquiries or reprint requests should be directed to Marijanet Doonan, Thomas Aquina College, Route 340, Sparkhill, N.Y. 10976.

ing the problem and its invasive ramifications, as well as developing competencies in providing appropriate and effective therapeutic approaches, are essential.

It is estimated that between 10 and 15 percent of the student population in the United States is learning disabled (Brown, 1978). The educational model most commonly used with this population has been basically remedial, implying the promise of a cure, which we now know does not exist (Cohen, 1985). These young people have spent endless hours focusing on their inabilities. They have been identified and often isolated in special classes. They have been removed from substantive education and subjected to watered down academic programs that are considerably below their intellectual capabilities. This creates significant psychological overlays such as insecurity, depression, anxiety, and acting-out behaviors.

Eventually, this population grows to adulthood and recognizes that the promise of a "cure" implied by these remedial approaches has not materialized (Johnston, 1984). Their disabilities have continued into adulthood and provided significant impediments to successful life functioning in areas beyond academics, most notably in interpersonal interactions and psychological adjustment. Psychotherapy thus may be indicated both for the child and the adult. In addition, the psychotherapist is a vital part of the interdisciplinary team advocated by our improved educational approach. These factors indicate that mental health professionals will be sought out by increasing numbers of people with learning disabilities. In order to assist this population, psychotherapists must have a better knowledge, understanding, and acceptance of this disorder.

In this paper we will consider the scope of learning disabilities among the student population of the United States. We will provide information on specific types of disabilities, evaluate the major issues indicated for psychotherapy, and discuss prescriptive multidisciplinary approaches. The hope is that this will result in increased awareness of the learning disabled population by psychotherapists. In addition, it will document some of the unique aspects of this population and the resulting need for effective therapy.

From a psychological point of view, the scope of the problem these patients present is extensive and pervasive. Learning disabilities and their concomitant effects are particularly evident on a day-to-day basis in elementary and secondary schools. In school situations, these young people are vulnerable to constant assaults on their self-confidence. In the past, and unfortunately still today, most educational interventions for them have focused on a deficit model (Poplin, 1984). This constant emphasis on disability has allowed for little recognition of strengths in either intellectual or personal areas and has resulted in decreased self-confidence.

As the psychotherapeutic community prepares to work intensively with this population, new information and considerations must be reviewed. Psychotherapists already understand that medical conditions can affect psychological states, and include a medical history in their initial patient interview. They must now also be aware that educational factors can significantly affect psychological states. The necessity for taking an educational history as part of the initial interview becomes apparent for all patients, and essential for those who may be learning disabled.

In working with this population, some basic philosophical concepts must be considered. The term "learning disabled" itself has a negative, defeatist connotation and presents a disabling concept. In our work, we have adopted the terminology "learning process dysfunction" (Doonan & Ehrlich, 1986a), which presents a more accurate description of the way in which the learning process is affected. This population is not truly "disabled" in learning; rather, one or more of the processes by which they learn may be affected or dysfunctional. What must happen is that they must be taught how to use other learning processes to compensate for the dysfunctional areas.

In the population under discussion, learning process dysfunctions exist from the time of birth. These people have average to above average intelligence and do not have serious emotional pathology. We are not including those who may have dysfunctions resulting from some type of postnatal trauma, although psychotherapeutic issues may be similar.

Traditionally, learning process dysfunction is defined as a

> disorder in one or more of the central nervous system processes involved in perceiving, understanding, and/or using concepts through verbal (spoken or written) language or non-verbal means. This disorder manifests itself with a deficit in one or more of the following areas: attention, reasoning, processing, memory, communication, reading, writing, spelling, calculation, coordination, social competence and emotional maturity (U.S. Rehabilitation Services Administration, 1985). This is not primarily due to severe mental retardation, sensory handicaps, emotional problems, or lack of opportunity to learn (Kirk & Gallagher, 1979).

In discussing learning process dysfunction, it would be impossible to present all of the individual types. However, the chart in Table 1 gives a brief overview of some of the major areas that can be affected.

Table 1

Major Areas Affected by Learning Disabilities

Perception	Processing	Expression
auditory	memory	written
visual	organizing	verbal
kinesthetic	reasoning	non-verbal
spatial	evaluation	
temporal	extrapolation	

For our purposes here, we will present examples of one type of dysfunction commonly noticed in young children, in the area of visual processing. By discussing this dysfunction, we can begin to understand how insidious this difficulty can be. Problems in this area can affect the way one perceives things that are seen. In education, this can seriously affect reading and can result in one seeing written materials in one or more distorted ways. Two examples of these distortions are shown in Table 2.

Consider the effects of facing twelve or more years of educational experiences when reading materials are perceived in formats similar to these. For the person *without* difficulties, deciphering this type of material is tedious and frustrating but possible. For a person *with* this type of difficulty, deciphering often is impossible. Due to problems inherent in the dysfunction and the type of remedial approaches used in schools, ac-

Table 2

Example	Translation
Tobay I was Dat. He sat dy the deuch which si on wy street. He is a doog doy wost of the tiwe dut sowetiwes he is verq dab. Once he stole sowe dreab anb once he stole sowe dooks.	Today I saw Tad. He sat by the bench which is on my street. He is a good boy most of the time but sometimes he is very bad. Once he stole some bread and once he stole some books.
Th enob elpri zesw er efi rs taw ard edi n19 0lj us tfi veye ar saft eral fr edno be ldie dac cord in gtoh isw ill the yar egi venf orp hysic schem istryphy siolog yorm edic in elite rat urean dfo rtheb est wor kfo rfra ternit ybe twe enna tions.	The Nobel Prizes were first awarded in 1901 just five years after Alfred Nobel died. According to his will, they are given for physics, chemistry, physiology or medicine, literature, and for the best work for fraternity between nations.

tual subject area knowledge obtained by this population is marginal. They have tremendous gaps in all areas of academic learning.

Along with the educational limits and frustrating attempts to correct this inability, there is the continuous risk of "public" discovery of the true extent of the disability by peers, teachers, and family. The inability to keep pace with age cohorts in reading (as well as in other subject areas) places a student in continuous jeopardy of exposure, ridicule, and assaults to self-image. Learning disabled individuals often view themselves as stupid and inept. They often question self-worth and feel unable to interact equally and acceptably with peers. Their views of the world, and of probable life happiness, can be flawed. Career options are often perceived as limited. A sense of control over learning and the environment has been removed as a result of a bewildering array of inaccurate perceptions and faulty interactions with the environment. Thus, life adaptation can be impaired.

Change is needed in our approach in order to provide a more ego-syntonic method of working with this population in educational settings, but change is a slow process. Therefore, psychotherapists who work with the learning disabled must strive to put in place multidisciplinary, strength-based, enabling atmospheres in order for therapeutic interventions to be effective.

The therapist has several responsibilities. First, there must be an evaluation and understanding of the patient's learning strengths and specific learning style. This must then be communicated to the patient, and the effects of the learning process dysfunction on his or her academic and psychosocial experiences explained. As part of this, the patient needs to understand that success can be achieved by re-ordering learning in a way that utilizes strengths and develops compensatory strategies. In some cases, the therapist may need to teach or provide opportunities for the patient to develop specific learning strategies, such as "pre-reading" and "outlining" (Doonan & Ehrlich, 1986b). In other cases, utilizing technology may be an effective compensatory strategy. Technology can include using taped textbooks to circumvent reading difficulties; word processors and taping of classes or meetings to deal with some types of writing problems; and calculators to assist with math dysfunctions. These are but a few of the many possible compensatory strategies that can be used. In general, the therapist must see that the student has access to information and the means for acquiring and utilizing it.

Second, the psychotherapist must address the psychosocial aspects of the dysfunction. This involves identifying areas of interpersonal strengths and weaknesses and directly helping the patient recognize and circumvent those difficulties. Interpersonal communication dysfunctions can impede social interactions. Language difficulties, such as in the perception and discrimination of sound, may preclude the ability to perceive conversations accurately. Processing of information may be accurate but slow, which may cause difficulties in conversation. Patients may not recognize non-verbal cues, often major determinants of communication situations. The difference between vocal inflections indicating sarcasm and anger may not be discriminated; a smile may be interpreted as a grimace. The unwritten rules regulating personal space and territory may not be understood. Furthermore, an ongoing educational focus on remediation may have resulted in educational gaps that fail to provide sufficient information to enable ease in everyday conversation.

Third, on a psychological level, constant focus on deficits and dysfunctional areas may affect the patient's identity and self-evaluation. Issues of dependency, learned helplessness, mild to moderate depression, fear, anxiety and stress, self-depreciation, and vulnerability may be evident. Also present may be issues of relationships and the use of inappropriate, maladaptive strategies for coping such as defensiveness, masking, flight, rigidity, deception, and overcompetitiveness. The far-reaching effects of dysfunctions in the learning process can influence psychological development and adjustment in significant ways. This must be recognized as a lifelong assault on a person's psyche.

Fourth, the therapist must recognize the need for extended time to effect desired change. Often, working with this population requires more patience, more insight, and more tenaciousness than with other populations. Many people with learning disabilities have little, if any, understanding of what their dysfunction actually involves or how it directly affects their lives outside of the classroom. Thus, education is an important task.

As we have noted, the therapist may have a multifaceted role with learning disabled patients. He or she must help them to understand themselves, the extent of their dysfunction, and how it affects their life functioning as well as school learning. Once this is achieved, a level of acceptance of self is more likely to occur. Then, the patient and the therapist must work together to recognize, accept, and adjust to whatever realistic limitations these learning process dysfunctions place on life expectations. Without this, the concomitant issues in therapy may not have adequate resolution.

We hope that it has become evident that when working with a patient who has a learning process dysfunction, one's role must be not only that of therapist, but also that of educator and ombudsman. It may include providing supportive intervention with the patient's family, seeking supportive educational programming, and providing ways to enhance the patient's interpersonal skills that can lead to improved peer interactions. The professional abilities necessary for working with this population are similar to those utilized with other patients, but differ in significant enough ways to provide a direct, ongoing, professional challenge. The task is arduous but interesting, for this population is both frustrating and challenging. The results can be extremely rewarding professionally, as well as meaningful and vital.

References

BROWN, B.S., (1978). Forward. In A.L. Benton and D. Pearl (Eds.), *Dyslexia: An appraisal of current knowledge*. New York: Oxford University Press.

COHEN, J. (1985). *Adolescent Psychiatry: Developmental and Clinical Studies*. Chicago: University of Chicago Press, 1985, 177.

DOONAN, M. & Ehrlich, R. (1986a). "Ability not Disability: A Better Focus for the Learning Disabled." *Strategies for Academic Independence Newsletter*. Chappaqua, New York: SAI Press, I, 1.

DOONAN, M. & Erlich, R. (1986b). "Learning strategies for the student with learning process dysfunction." Presentation at the New Jersey Professional Counselors Association Conference, Princeton, New Jersey, May 1986.

JOHNSTON, C.L. (1984). The learning disabled adolescent and young adult: An overview and critique of current practices. *Journal of Learning Disabilities, 17*(7), 386-391.

KIRK, S.A. & Gallagher, J.J. (1979). *Educating Exceptional Children*. Boston: Houghton Mifflin, 285.

POPLIN, Mary. (1984). Summary rationalizations, apologies and farewell: What we don't know about the learning disabled. *Learning Disability Quarterly*, 7(2), 130-134.

UNITED STATES DEPARTMENT OF EDUCATION OFFICE OF SPECIAL EDUCATION AND REHABILITATIVE SERVICES (1985). *Specific Learning Disability for VR Purposes, Program Policy Directive*. Washington, D.C.: Rehabilitation Services Administration, RSA-PPD-85-7.

Medical Psychotherapy
1988, Volume 1, pp. 119-129

© 1988 by
Hans Huber Publishers, Toronto

Brief Versus Extended Relaxation: Relationship to Improvement at Follow-Up in Mixed Headache Patients

ALVIN E. LAKE III
JEFFREY D. PINGEL
Michigan Headache and Neurological Institute, P.C.

There has been little systematic study of the relationship between the use of brief versus extended relaxation techniques and headache improvement at follow-up. One hundred and two randomly selected fee-for-service patients with mixed migraine-muscle contraction headache (67% with daily pain) completed a follow-up survey between 3 months to 4 years after treatment. Fifty-six percent of the patients met a clinical criterion of 50% improvement in headache, with 69% of the improved patients reporting the continued daily use of brief relaxation in contrast to only 39% of those with less improvement ($\rho < .005$). Fifty-three percent of the improved patients continued to practice extended relaxation at least once per week, in contrast to 32% of those with less improvement ($\rho < .05$). The frequency of brief relaxation was significantly correlated with eight specific parameters of both migraine and muscle contraction headache control, whereas the frequency of extended relaxation was only associated with "coping more effectively" with muscle-contraction headache and reducing the duration of migraine. Use of brief relaxation on a daily basis was also associated with reductions in preventive medication ($\rho < .01$), while there was no relationship between extended relaxation and preventive medication reduction.

The frequent use of brief relaxation was maintained over time, while the percentage of patients continuing to practice extended relaxation as little as once a week declined significantly after one year ($\rho < .01$). When asked to identify what was of most help in controlling headache, 66% identified either brief relaxation or "awareness of thoughts and feelings related to headache," while only eight percent identified extended relaxation. Clinically improved patients were much more likely to identify a change in behavior as the most helpful aspect of treatment than less improved patients (66% versus 31%, $\rho < .025$). Sex, age, pretreatment headache frequency, number of sessions, and years

Inquiries or reprint requests should be addressed to Alvin E. Lake III at Michigan Headache and Neurological Institute, P.C., 3120 Professional Drive, Ann Arbor, Michigan, 48104.

since completing treatment were all unrelated to improvement. These results provide empirical support for the frequent use of brief relaxation in the self-regulation of headache, and underscore the importance of systematic assessment of this variable in future studies.

Introduction

Comprehensive biofeedback programs for headache typically encourage the participant to employ two modes of relaxation or biofeedback practice: (a) extended periods of 15 to 20 minutes duration, usually twice a day, and (b) brief periods of possibly only a few seconds in duration, frequently integrated into the person's ongoing activities (Blanchard & Andrasik, 1985; Fuller, 1977; Schwartz, 1987; Shellenberger & Green, 1986). How important is the frequency of either type of relaxation to continued symptom improvement? Although there now exists a large body of research that examines the relationship between treatment outcome and the level of physiological control achieved during training (Chapman, 1986), there has been less attention to the role of relaxation in maintaining headache control, and very little if any analysis of brief relaxation.

Some studies have found a significant statistical relationship between relaxation practice and headache improvement during treatment (Blanchard et al., 1983), and at follow-up (Libo & Arnold, 1983; Sargent, Solbach, & Coyne, 1980). Other reports provide data suggesting such a relationship, but without supporting statistical analysis, in some cases due to the small number of subjects involved (Budzynski, Stoyva, Adler, & Mullaney, 1973; Ford, Stroebel, Strong, & Szarek, 1983; Reinking & Hutchings, 1981; Steger & Harper, 1980). On the other hand, some studies have failed to find any relationship between relaxation practice and headache control during the course of the treatment (Attanasio, Andrasik, & Blanchard, 1987; Martin & Mathews, 1978), or at follow-up (Andrasik, Blanchard, Neff, & Rodichok, 1984). Lake, Rainey, and Papsdorf (1979) found a strong relationship between both the frequency and duration of home practice as recorded on daily records during the third month of follow-up and the subject's global estimates of improvement, but failed to find a relationship with improvement as measured by the daily record.

Continued relaxation practice may be important for some headache sufferers to maintain improvement, but not for others (Silver, Blanchard, Williamson, Theobald, & Brown, 1979). Although Libo and Arnold (1983) found a significant association between continued relaxation practice and long-term improvement, a few patients managed to improve without it, while others continued to practice but lost symptom control. They also found that patients who were practicing only "occasionally," "as needed," or "when stressed" improved as much or more than those who practiced regularly and frequently. However, in our review of the literature, we were unable to find any direct comparison of the relationship between brief versus extended relaxation techniques and headache improvement.

We addressed the following questions in a long-term follow-up study of medically referred mixed migraine-muscle contraction headache patients who had completed a comprehensive biofeedback program:

1. How important is the frequency of brief versus extended relaxation to the maintenance of headache control and medication reduction?
2. To what extent do patients who completed treatment over a year ago at

the time of the follow-up continue to practice both types of relaxation, in comparison to those who completed treatment between three months and one year ago?

3. What do patients perceive as the most helpful aspect of treatment? Is one type of relaxation perceived as more helpful than the other?
4. How does the relationship between improvement and the frequency of brief and extended relaxation compare to the relationship between improvement and other variables such as sex, age, pretreatment headache frequency, number of sessions, and years since completing treatment?

Method

Subjects

The subjects consisted of 102 fee-for-service patients with mixed migraine-muscle contraction headache who had just completed a comprehensive biofeedback and cognitive-behavior therapy program at a private multidisciplinary headache treatment center between 3 months and 4 years previously, and who responded to a mailed follow-up questionnaire. Diagnosis was determined by the referring neurologist. The mixed headache syndrome was defined as the presence of both migraine and muscle contraction headaches in the same patient (Saper, 1983).

Treatment Program

Treatment had consisted of individual sessions with one of the authors. The program incorporated both finger temperature feedback and EMG feedback from facial, neck, and shoulder regions. Subjects were provided with a set of six relaxation tapes including standard relaxation exercises (autogenic phrases, imagery, abdominal breathing, progressive relaxation) as well as explanations of the treatment rationale and instructions on using self-talk in managing stress and emotional reactions to pain. Subjects were instructed to practice relaxation with the tapes or on their own for 15 minutes twice a day. They were also instructed in the practice of frequent periods of brief relaxation and body awareness for between 10 seconds to a minute or so at a time. In addition, the program focused on other behavioral changes appropriate to the individual patient, such as slowing down, becoming more assertive, and the rehearsal of biofeedback skills in simulations of real life situations. Twenty-nine percent of the subjects completed 5 sessions or less, 43% completed 6-10 sessions, 17% completed 11-15 sessions, and 12% completed 16 or more sessions. (Note that the total adds up to more than 100% due to rounding up.)

Follow-up Questionnaire

On part of an eight-page, multiple choice follow-up survey, respondents were asked to rate "headache improvement since biofeedback training" on a 6-point scale (none, 1-24%, 25-49%, 50-74%, 75-99%, and 100% – no headaches). Since Cohen and McArthur (1981) had previously shown that patients experiencing both migraine and muscle contraction headaches consistently differentiate both types of pain, the questionnaire also asked each respondent to indicate the extent of his or her agreement with the statement "biofeedback skills helped me cope more effectively" for each type of headache on a 5-point scale, from "strongly agree" to "strongly disagree." A 3-point scale was provided ("most of the time, " some of the time," and "not at all") to indicate the extent to which biofeedback skills had helped with seven additional parameters for each type of headache: remaining calm during the headache, reducing intensity, reducing duration, aborting the headache, taking less medication, preventing headaches previously triggered by stress, and preventing headaches previously triggered by other factors.

In order to assess the use of brief relaxation, the questionnaire asked, "How frequently do you think about relaxation for *brief periods* of a few seconds up to several minutes at a time?" and offered 7 choices: "not at all," "less than once a week," "once or twice a week," "several times a week," "once or twice a day," "three to ten times a day," and "more than ten times a day." Use of extended relaxation was assessed by asking "How frequently do you practice biofeedback skills for *10 minutes or longer* at a time?" In this case, there was a 6-point scale, from "not at all" to "less than once a week," "once or twice a week," "several times a week," "once a day," and "twice a day."

Procedure

The survey was mailed to 310 individuals randomly selected from a total of 730 headache sufferers who had been referred for biofeedback at Michigan Headache and Neurological Institute, P.C. during the time of the study. Out of these, 193 questionnaires were returned for a response rate of 62%. Forty-two of the returned questionnaires (22%) were incomplete and not used in the final analysis, primarily because the person had not followed through on the referral or had discontinued treatment after the initial evaluation. This left a total of 154 usable questionnaires. Of these, the largest response was from the group of patients with mixed headache (66%), followed by those with diagnoses of migraine (25%), muscle contraction headache (5%), and other (4%). Only the mixed headache results are reported here.

Subject Characteristics

The sample was predominately female (83%), with a mean age of 33.5 years, a median of 33, and a range of 13 to 73. Prior to treatment, 33% had reported constant head pain and 34% reported pain that was daily but not constant, making a total of 67% with some type of daily pain. One fourth of the patients had been previously hospitalized on an inpatient headache unit. The subjects were distributed across three follow-up periods: (a) between 3 months and 1 year since the time of treatment (33%), (b) 1-2 years (39%), and (c) 2-4 years (28%).

Results

Type of Relaxation and Improvement

Overall improvement. The relationship between overall improvement and the frequency of both brief and extended relaxation is shown in Table 1.

Table 1
Percentage of Mixed Headache Patients Continuing to Practice Brief and Extended Relaxation: Relationship to Overall Improvement

Relaxation		Overall Improvement		
Type	Frequency	$\geq 50\%^a$	$< 50\%^b$	χ^2
Brief	Daily	69%	39%	8.64^{**}
Extended	Weekly	53%	32%	4.70^{*}

$^a n = 54$ $^b n = 44$
$^* p < .05$ $^{**} p < .005$

As illustrated, brief relaxation emerged as the more critical factor. Patients who continued the application of brief relaxation on a daily basis were much more likely to meet a criterion of at least 50% improvement than those who did not, with over two thirds of the clinically improved patients reporting continued conscious thoughts about relaxation on at least a daily basis. In contrast, despite strong encouragement to continue the regular practice of *extended* relaxation twice a day following the conclusion of treatment, only slightly more than half of these patients had continued to utilize at a frequency of once a week or more.

Type of headache control. Table 2 depicts the correlations, expressed as phi coefficients, between the frequency of each type of relaxation and specific categories of improvement or control over migraine and muscle contraction headache.

As shown, more frequent brief relaxation periods were significantly related to "coping more effectively" and "remaining calm" during both migraine and muscle contraction episodes. The frequency of brief relaxation was also significantly associated with the degree of muscle contraction headache control in the areas of reducing intensity, aborting headache, taking less pain medication, and preventing stress-related headaches, as well as preventing migraine headaches triggered by factors other than stress. In contrast, the frequency of extended relaxation was only related to "coping more effectively" with muscle contraction headache, and reducing the duration of migraine. The difference in the number of significant correlations with type of headache control for brief versus extended relaxation was statistically significant ($\chi^2(1) = 5.24, p < .025$).

Reductions in preventive medication. Eighty-four percent of the subjects had used preventive medications for headache at some point during their medical treatment. At the time of follow-up, 67% of these had reduced or eliminated their preventive medication. As shown in Table 3, there was a significant relationship between success in

Table 2

Correlations (Phi Coefficients) Between Type of Headache and Improvement in Mixed Headache Patients and Frequency of Brief and Extended Relaxation.

Type of Improvement	df	Type of Relaxation Brief	Extended
Cope more effectively	24		
Migraine[a]		.40****	.25
Muscle-contraction[b]		.37***	.32**
Remain calm	12		
Migraine[c]		.35*	.21
Muscle-contraction[b]		.43***	.31
Reduce intensity	12		
Migraine[c]		.22	.30
Muscle-contraction[d]		.34*	.18
Reduce duration	12		
Migraine[c]		.26	.34*
Muscle-contraction[b]		.28	.21
Abort headache	12		
Migraine[c]		.29	.29
Muscle-contraction[d]		.35*	.30
Take less pain medication	12		
Migraine[c]		.30	.27
Muscle-contraction[e]		.34*	.19
Prevent stress headache	18		
Migraine[a]		.28	.21
Muscle-contraction[b]		.34*	.22
Prevent other headache	18		
Migraine[a]		.27	.24
Muscle-contraction[d]		.28	.28

[a]$n = 96$ [b]$n = 92$ [c]$n = 97$ [d]$n = 91$ [e]$n = 90$

*$p < .05$ **$p < .01$ ***$p < .001$ ****$p < .0001$

Table 3

Percentage of Mixed Headache Patients Continuing to Practice Brief and Extended Relaxation: Relationship to Reductions in Preventive Medication.

Relaxation Type	Frequency	No Change[a]	Reduced[b]	Preventive Medication Eliminated[c]	χ^2
Brief	Daily	29%	62%	75%	10.28*
Extended	Weekly	25%	41%	45%	2.27

[a]$n = 24$ [b]$n = 29$ [c]$n = 20$

*$p < .01$

reducing preventive medication and daily use of brief relaxation, but no relationship with extended relaxation. There was no significant difference in the use of daily brief relaxation among those who eliminated versus those who only reduced their reliance on preventive pharmacotherapy (χ^2 (1, N = 49) = 0.89, n.s.).

Maintenance of Relaxation Over Time.

Most patients continued to practice brief relaxation frequently, regardless of how much time had passed since the conclusion of therapy, but there was a significant decline in the percentage continuing to practice extended relaxation one year or more after treatment, as illustrated in Table 4.

Table 4
Percentage of Mixed Headache Patients Continuing to Practice Brief and Extended Relaxation at Different Levels of Frequency: Relationship to Time of Follow-Up

	Time of Follow-up		
Relaxation	< One year[a]	≥ One year[b]	χ^2
Brief			
Several times/week	88%	79%	1.15
Daily	52%	55%	0.12
Extended			
Weekly	64%	35%	6.91*
Daily	55%	21%	11.51**

[a] n = 33 [b] n = 67
* $p < .01$ ** $p < .001$

Among those completing treatment over one year ago, four out of five continued to practice brief relaxation at least several times a week, and over half were continuing to practice it daily. In contrast, only about one-third were still practicing extended relaxation even once a week, and only one out of five used it on a daily basis.

Patient Perception Data

When asked to select which of five possible choices "was of most help to you in controlling headaches," patients were much more likely to identify "brief relaxation periods during the day" (25%) than "regular practice of relaxation for 10 minutes or more at a time" (8%), (χ^2 (1, N = 30) = 8.52, $p < .005$). Most respondents (43%) identified "awareness of thoughts and feelings related to headache" as of most help, with 68% selecting either "awareness" or brief relaxation. "Behavior changes" (slowing down, becoming more active, becoming more assertive) and "developing a more positive outlook on things in general" were each selected by 12% of the sample. Despite its central role in the treatment program, extended relaxation was actually the least popular choice.

There was no significant difference in the percentage of clinically improved versus less improved patients that identified brief relaxation (29% versus 21%), or extended relaxation (10% versus 5%), as the most helpful aspect of treatment. However, when the three behavioral categories of brief relaxation, extended relaxation, and "behavior changes" were grouped together, there emerged a significant difference in the distribution of choices between those who met the 50% improvement criterion and those who did not: 66% of the former group selected one of the three behavioral categories, in contrast to only 31% of the less improved (χ^2 (1, N = 91) = 5.62, $\rho < .025$). Although more patients selected "awareness" than any other individual choice, the percentage identifying awareness as the most helpful aspect of treatment did not differentiate the clinically improved and less improved groups (40% versus 44%).

Other Variables and Improvement

Sex. There were no sex differences in overall improvement, with 56% of both females and males each reporting at least 50% improvement.

Age. In order to determine whether there was any relationship between age and improvement, subjects were grouped into five age ranges: 13-20 (n = 13), 21-30 (n = 29), 31-40 (n = 32), 41-50 (n = 16) and 51 and older (n = 10). A chi-square analysis did not show any significant difference in the distribution of patients meeting the 50% improvement criterion among the different age brackets (χ^2 (2, N = 100) = 3.27, n.s.).

Pretreatment headache frequency. A chi-square analysis was performed on the distribution of patients meeting the 50% improvement criterion across the three different categories of pretreatment headache frequency (constant, daily but not constant, and intermittent pain). The results were non-significant (χ^2(2, N = 99) = 2.15, n.s.).

Number of treatment sessions. Subjects were grouped into four categories according to the number of treatment sessions completed: 1-5 (n = 29), 6-10 (n = 42), 11-15 (n = 17), and 16 or more (n = 11). Based on this grouping, there was no demonstrated relationship between the number of biofeedback sessions and the percentage of patients meeting the 50% criterion of overall improvement (χ^2 (3, N = 99) = 5.50, n.s.).

Years since completing treatment. For the sample as a whole, 56% of the subjects reported at least 50% overall headache improvement. The percentage of subjects meeting the 50% criterion of improvement did not differ significantly across the three time periods: 64% in the 3-month to 1-year group, 49% for the 1- to 2-year group, and 57% for the 2- to 4- year group (χ^2 (2, N = 100) = 1.72, n.s.).

Discussion

In summary, the analyses show a consistent and strong relationship between one aspect of behavior – the frequency of brief relaxation – and headache control for a group of medically referred mixed headache patients, most of whom had been suffering from chronic daily pain. The frequency of extended relaxation declined significantly over time, was less strongly related to outcome at follow-up, and was generally perceived as less helpful than other aspects of treatment. However, frequent periods of extended practice for 10-20 minutes may be important during the acquisition of relaxation and biofeedback skills, and may be related to the maintenance of improvement for some patients (cf. Silver et al., 1979). The results do provide empirical support for clinical emphasis on the use of brief relaxation in daily life.

As discussed in recent reviews of the headache and biofeedback literature by Chapman (1986) and Lake (1983), there is mixed evidence for a systematic relationship between changes in muscle tension or hand temperature during biofeedback and headache improvement. Is it possible that the frequency with which patients integrate biofeedback skills into their ongoing lives is of more significance than the degree of control achieved over muscle tension or hand temperature during training? This question deserves further research.

The maintenance of improvement over time was encouraging. At least one previous large-scale biofeedback follow-up study on patients treated at a headache center found a significant decrement in treatment outcome as a function of the time elapsed since training (Diamond et al., 1979). The failure to find a relationship between the number of sessions and improvement is consistent with Holroyd and Penzien (1986), but contrasts with results from some questionnaire studies (Diamond & Montrose, 1984; Hudzinski & Levenson, 1985).

The failure to find an association between age, sex, and treatment outcome is interesting. A recent meta-analytic review by Holroyd and Penzien (1986) of 37 prospective behavioral studies of tension headache that relied on daily headache records found mean client age to be the best predictor of improvement, accounting for 30% of the outcome variance. They also found a correlation between outcome and the percentage of females in the sample that approached significance ($\rho < .06$). In other words, younger female patient tended to get better results. Age and sex have also been shown to be important predictor variables in some large-scale retrospective follow-up studies of muscle contraction, migraine, and mixed headache patients who had been treated in medical settings (Diamond, Medina, Diamond-Falk, & De Veno, 1979; Diamond & Montrose, 1984; Hudzinski & Levenson, 1985).

The lack of an association between outcome and pretreatment headache frequency also stands in contrast to some previous findings. For example, one prospective study of cognitive behavioral therapy for chronic headache found that subjects who experienced continuous or near-continuous pain during their waking hours were not responsive to treatment (Bakal, Demjen, & Kaganov, 1981). This group comprised 33% of the sample in our other two groups with daily (but not constant) or intermittent pain. However, the subjects studied by Bakal and his colleagues were not using preventative medication, while as noted above many of our patients did use prophylactic drugs at some point during their treatment, which may help account for the reported improvement among those with continuous pain prior to therapy.

As noted above, most patients identified "awareness of thoughts and feelings related to headache" as the most helpful aspect of treatment. In a follow-up study of 79 participants in the Menninger Foundation's five-day biofeedback program, Sargent et al. (1980) found that "continuing to practice body awareness" was related to significant reductions in headache frequency, severity, and medication use, as well as ability to sustain improvement and overall change in headache condition. However, apparently only the continuation of practicing body awareness but not the frequency of such practice was assessed in the Menninger study. In our survey, patient emphasis on awareness was not related to improvement, with 40% of the clinically improved patients and 44% of those who failed to meet the 50% criterion of improvement identifying awareness as the specific aspect of treatment that was of most help in controlling their headaches.

It is important to note that the results reported here must be interpreted within the limits of a retrospective questionnaire study. Global estimates of improvement have been shown to be significantly correlated with improvement as measured by a comparison of follow-up and baseline daily headache records (Blanchard et al., 1985; Lake et al., 1979). Also, Andrasik and his coworkers found that global estimates of improvement using a visual analogue scale were not statistically different from improvement measured by daily report (Andrasik, Burke, Attanasio, & Rosenblum, 1985). However, the correlations between the frequency of relaxation and headache improvement may differ when improvement is measured by retrospective estimate versus daily headache record (cf. Lake et al., 1979).

Finally, although it is tempting to conclude that the frequency of brief relaxation is a causal factor in headache control, it is important to remember that correlational analyses cannot prove causality or the direction of effects. This study does provide empirical support for future research incorporating the systematic assessment of both the frequency of brief relaxation and headache activity with daily record-keeping, as well as the direct manipulation of brief relaxation frequency in controlled research designs.

ACKNOWLEDGEMENTS. We gratefully acknowledge Michigan Headache and Neurological Institute, P.C., for the funding of this study, and particularly thank the director, Joel R. Saper, for personal and professional support. Kenneth E. Guire of the Statistical Research Laboratory at The University of Michigan School of Public Health provided much appreciated computer analyses and statistical assistance.
Jeffrey D. Pingel is now associated with Ohio University.

References

ANDRASIK, F., Blanchard, E.B., Neff, D.F., & Rodichok, L.D. (1984). Biofeedback and relaxation training for chronic headache: A controlled comparison of booster treatments and regular contacts for long-term maintenance. *Journal of Consulting and Clinical Psychology, 52*, 609-615.

ANDRASIK, F., Burke, E.J., Attanasio, V., & Rosenblum, E.L. (1985). Child, parent, and physician reports of a child's headache pain: Relationships prior to and following treatment. *Headache, 25*, 421-425.

ATTANASIO, V., Andrasik. F., & Blanchard, E.B. (1987). Cognitive therapy and relaxation training in muscle contraction headache: Efficacy and cost-effectiveness. *Headache, 27*, 254-260.

BAKAL, D.A.. Demjen, S., & Kaganov, J.A. (1981). Cognitive behavioral treatment of chronic headache. *Headache, 21*, 81-86.

BLANCHARD, E.B. & Andrasik, F. (1985). *Management of chronic headaches: A psychological approach*. New York: Pergamon.

BLANCHARD, E.B., Andrasik, F., Evans, D.D., Neff, D.F., Appelbaum, K.A., & Rodichok, L.D. (1985). Behavioral treatment of 250 chronic headache patients: A clinical replication series. *Behavioral Therapy, 16*, 308-327.

BLANCHARD, E.B., Andrasik, F., Neff, D.F., Saunders, N.L., Arena, J.G., Pallmeyer, T.P., Teders, S.J., Jurish, S.E., & Rodichok, L.D. (1983). Four process studies in the behavioral treatment of chronic headache. *Behavioral and Research Therapy, 21*, 209-220.

BUDZYNSKI, T.H., Stoyva, J.M., Adler, C.S., & Mullaney, D.J. (1973). EMG biofeedback and tension headache: A controlled outcome study. *Psychosomatic Medicine, 6*, 509-514.

CHAPMAN, S.L. (1986). A review and clinical perspective on the use of EMG and thermal biofeedback for chronic headaches. *Pain, 27*, 1-43.

COHEN, M.J. & McArthur, D.L. (1981). Classification of migraine and tension headache from a survey of 10,000 headache diaries. *Headache, 21*, 25-29.

DIAMOND, S., Medina, J., Diamond-Falk, J., & DeVeno, T. (1979). The value of biofeedback in the treatment of chronic headache: A five-year retrospective study. *Headache, 19*, 90-96.

DIAMOND, S. & Montrose, D. (1984). The value of biofeedback in the treatment of chronic headache: A four-year retrospective study. *Headache, 24*, 5-18.

FORD, M.R., Stroebel, C.F., Strong, P., & Szarek, B.L. (1983). Quieting response training: Long-term evaluation of a clinical biofeedback practice. *Biofeedback and Self-Regulation, 8*, 265-278.

FULLER, G.D. (1977). *Biofeedback: Methods and Procedures in Clinical Practice*. San Francisco: Biofeedback Press.

HOLROYD, K.A. & Penzien, D.B. (1986). Client variables and the behavioral treatment of tension headache: A meta-analytic review. *Journal of Behavioral Medicine, 9*, 515-536.

HUDZINSKI, L.G. & Levenson, H. (1985). Biofeedback behavioral treatment of headache with locus of control pain analysis: A 20-month retrospective study. *Headache, 25*, 380-386.

LAKE, A.E. III (1983). Biofeedback and headache management. In J.R. Saper, *Headache disorders: Current concepts and treatment strategies* (pp. 191-231.) Boston: Wright-PSG.

LAKE, A., Rainey, J., & Papsdorf, J.D. (1979). Biofeedback and rational-emotive therapy in the management of migraine headache. *Journal of Applied Behavior Analysis, 12*, 127-140.

LIBO, L.M. & Arnold, G.E. (1983). Relaxation practice after biofeedback therapy: A long-term study of utilization and effectiveness. *Biofeedback and Self-Regulation, 8*, 217-227.

MARTIN, P.R. & Mathews, A.M. (1978). Tension headaches: Psychophysiological investigation and treatment. *Journal of Psychosomatic Research, 22*, 389-399.

REINKING, R.H. & Hutchings, D. (1981). Follow-up to: "Tension headaches: What form of therapy is most effective?" *Biofeedback and Self-Regulation, 6*, 57-62.

SAPER, J.R. (1983). *Headache disorders: Current concepts and treatment strategies*. Boston: Wright-PSG.

SARGENT, J.D., Solbach, P., & Coyne, L. (1980). Evaluation of a 5-day non-drug training program for headache at the Menninger Foundation. *Headache, 20*, 32-41.

SCHWARTZ, M.S. (1987). *Biofeedback: A practitioner's guide*. New York: Guilford.

SHELLENBERGER, R. & Green, J.A. (1986). *From the ghost in the box to successful biofeedback training*. Greeley: Health Psychology.

SILVER, B.V., Blanchard, E.B., Williamson, D.A., Theobald, D.E., & Brown, D.A. (1979). Temperature biofeedback and relaxation training in the treatment of migraine headache: One-year follow-up. *Biofeedback and Self-Regulation, 4*, 359-366.

STEGER, J.C. & Harper, R.G. (1980). Comprehensive biofeedback versus self-monitored relaxation in the treatment of tension headache. *Headache, 20*, 137-142.

Medical Psychotherapy
1988, Volume 1, pp. 131-141

© 1988 by
Hans Huber Publishers, Toronto

Group Assertion and Contingent Time-Out Procedures in the Control of Assaultive Behaviors in Schizophrenics[1]

EUGENE G. PENISTON
VA Medical Center
Fort Lyon, Colorado

PAUL J. KULKOSKY
University of Southern Colorado
Pueblo, Colorado

Chronic schizophrenic inpatients exhibiting a high frequency of assaultive behaviors were assigned either to a group that received group assertive training (GAT) combined with contingent time-out (TO) and positive verbal reinforcement procedures, or to a control group that received standard medical treatment. Total assaultive behaviors were significantly reduced in patients after nine months in the GAT program, but controls showed no significant changes in these behaviors. The results confirm the effectiveness of a combination of assertive training, contingent TO, and the positive reinforcement in the control of assaultive behaviors in chronic schizophrenic inpatients.

Introduction

A major problem associated with chronic schizophrenic inpatients on locked psychiatric units is assaultive behavior. Assaultive behavior varies from physical attacks, fighting, cruelty, and noncompliance, to successful suicide (American Psychiatric Association, 1980; Hewitt & Jenkins, 1946; Roback, Frayn, Gunby, &

Inquiries or reprint requests should be directed to Eugene Peniston, Clinical Psychologist, Psychology Service (116B), VA Medical Center, Fort Lyon, Colorado 81038.

1 Special thanks to Fort Lyon VA Medical Center for support of study and to Carol A. Hunter, M.D., Chief, Psychiatry Service (116A), for her assistance. Also, special thanks to Roberta Moritz, R.N., HSRO, Quality Assurance Coordinator for her assistance.

Tuters, 1972; Tate and Baroff, 1966). The legal risks associated with physical assault (DeLeon, 1961; Hagen, Mikolajczak, & Wright, 1972), and self-destructive behavior (Marten, Munoz, Gentry, & Robins, 1970; Russo, Carr, & Lovaas, 1980), have received much attention in the legal community (Applebaum, 1983; Davis v. Hubbard, 1980; Reid, Bollinger, & Edwards, 1985; Romeo v. Youngberg, 1982; Wyatt v. Stickney, 1972). Some studies, however, have addressed the elimination of assaultive behaviors (Bach-y-Rita, Lion, Climent, & Ervin, 1971; Blackburn, 1968; Burchard & Barrera, 1972; Depp, 1976; Ekblom, 1970; Favell, McGimsey, & Schell, 1982; Kalogerakis, 1971; Peniston, 1975; Toch, 1969; Wolfgang, 1966). Reduction of assaultive behaviors directed at self and others is critically important in the treatment of psychiatric inpatients (Depp, 1976; Lion & Reid, 1983; Menninger, 1963; Silver & Yudofsky, 1987; Tardiff, 1984; Tardiff & Sweillam, 1982). A literature survey reported by Marten et al. (1970) found a 74% incidence of belligerent thoughts and assaultive behavior in a medically indigent psychiatric population. They defined belligerence as "... positive responses to questions concerning thoughts, verbalizations, and acts involving the use of force directed towards others." Sixty-six percent acknowledged verbal fighting and 61.4% physical fighting in the last five years. Furthermore, 41% of these subjects were reported to be self-destructive, that is, they presented thoughts of harming themselves or had made actual suicide attempts. Supporting this contention are the surveys of Silver & Yudofsky (1987); Rossi et al. (1985); and McKinley et al. (1981) that patients admitted to acute psychiatric units were shown to have aggression and irritability not only by the course of their illness, but also by associated situational, characterologic, organic, or toxic conditions.

The psychiatric management of aggressive impulses has been seen by Menninger (1963) as a critical goal of mental health practice. Previously attempted treatment procedures have consisted of four-point restraints while in seclusion, antipsychotic medications, and other restrictive measures, all of which have not proven therapeutically effective in the reduction of assaultive behaviors (Adler, Kreeger, & Ziegler, 1983; Lion & Reid, 1983; Soloff, 1983). Although the conventional rationale for continued psychiatric hospitalization depends of the concept of "dangerousness," defined as violent behavior or overt threats to inflict injury on another person or self (Andrew, 1980; Depp, 1976; Shah, 1978), it is interesting that few systematic investigations of "dangerousness" have been conducted on patients' assaultive behaviors in psychiatric facilities (Madden, 1983; Nigrosh, 1983; Werner, Terrence, Yesavage, & Seeman, 1984). Nor has there been much thought about altering ways that will reduce "dangerousness" to others by changing the precipitating or predisposing social environment or relationships of psychiatric inpatients (Depp, 1976; Massachusetts Department of Mental Health, 1980).

There are various behavioral approaches used in modifying assaultive behavior, including Differential Reinforcement of Other behavior (DRO) and Differential Reinforcement of Incompatible behavior (DRI) (Barkley & Zupnick, 1976; Fleming & Nolley, 1981; Franzen & Lovell, 1987; Harvey, Karan, Bhargava, & Morehouse, 1978; Repp & Dietz, 1974; Schnieder, Ross, & Dubin, 1979). Perhaps among the most promising are those that utilize isolation ot time-out contingent on undesired behaviors, an omission training procedure that has been studied widely since Leitenberg's (1965) review of the field. In most studies, the subjects were placed in a secluded room on the assumption that some social stimuli are sustaining the assaultive behavior (Benjamin, Mazzarins, & Kupfersmid, 1983; Bostow & Bailey, 1969; Buchard & Barrera, 1972; Franzen & Lovell, 1987; Oldham, Russakoff, & Prusnofsky, 1983; Pendergrass,

1971; Ullman & Krasner, 1965; White, Nielsen, & Johnson, 1972). In the overwhelming majority of investigations, contingent time-out (TO) has effectively suppressed the subsequent incidence of physical assaultive behavior. Behavioral researchers have investigated a number of treatment strategies designed to eliminate self-injurious behavior. These have ranged from extinction (Myers, 1975), to contingent electric shock (Lovaas, Schaeffer, & Simmons, 1965; Romanczyk & Goren, 1975), often employed in a treatment package with other techniques (Baumeister & Rollings, 1976; Carr, 1977; Dorsey, Iwata, Reid, & Davis, 1982; Repp, Dietz, & Speir, 1974; Rincover & Devancy, 1982; Smoler, 1971). Alternative behavioral approaches, such as modeling, desensitization, and assertive training have also been shown to be effective in the management of self-defeating or injurious behaviors (Ferster, Nurnberg, & Levitt, 1962; Goldiamond, 1965; Homme, 1965; Lazarus, 1971; Lazarus & Serber, 1968; Marks, 1976; Peck, 1977; Thoreson & Mahoney, 1974; Watson & Tharp, 1972). Several investigations have indicated that assertive training involving rehearsal, feedback, modeling, and reinforcement, is an effective self-control procedure for problems marked by impulsive and self-defeating behaviors (Rimm & Masters, 1974; Rimm, Snyder, Depue, Haanstad, & Armstrong, 1976). Self-control can be thought of as a process by which individuals set up contingencies in their environment to change specific behaviors in themselves (Goldiamond, 1965; Skinner, 1953).

Developing a therapeutic method to control aggressive behaviors was the primary programming objective of this study. A group assertive training (GAT) program (Rimm et al., 1976; Sarason & Ganzer, 1973; Wolpe, 1958; Wolpe & Lazarus, 1966), and brief TO contingent on belligerent thoughts (Benjamin et al., 1983; Bostow & Bailey, 1969; Lamont, Gilner, Spector, & Skinner, 1969; Peniston, 1975), in conjunction with positive reinforcement (Repp & Dietz, 1974), for acceptable behavior, was employed for control of impulsive and self-defeating aggressive behaviors. Since each procedure has been shown to be effective in the treatment of assaultive behavior, the present study employed a clinical package combining all three in order to maximize treatment effectiveness.

Method

Population

The GAT program, consisting of assertive training procedures in conjunction with TO for assaultive behaviors and positive reinforcement for non-assaultive behavior, was conducted at the VA Medical Center, Fort Lyon, Colorado, a catchment area for the states of Wyoming, Utah, and Colorado. Patients admitted to the locked psychiatric wards share one basic characteristic – they are deemed to be at serious risk of physical harm to themselves or others, and have recorded repeated assaults, self-injury, serious property damage, or out-of-contact behavior.

The GAT program was initiated on a specially staffed locked psychiatric ward housing 30 male veterans. Participants (Ps) were 28 male inpatients, all less than 54 years old and diagnosed as chronic schizophrenics (American Psychiatric Association, 1980). The mean length of present hospitalization was 6.07 years. The Ps were all on anti-psychotic medications (i.e., phenothiazines), in most cases at a well stabilized maintenance dosage. Ps were recruited for treatment based on data obtained from staff documentation that indicated a high frequency of special incident reports of exhibited physical assaults on staff or other patients and/or self-injurious behavior during a 9-month duration.

The GAT group had a mean chronological age (CA) of 40.28 years with a standard error (SE) of 3.42. The Control (CON) group had a mean CA of 43.71 years with an SE of 3.87.

Procedure

Subsequent to the initiation of treatment, all 28 Ps were assessed for the number of physical assaults and self-injurious behaviors reported daily on the special incident forms, a required detailed VA Medical incident report form (VAF 10-2633) used for reporting assaultive behaviors occurring on open and locked wards. A specific individual (i.e., Head Nurse on the unit) was assigned the task of completing the form and submitting it to the VA Medical Center's Quality Assurance Coordinator no more than 24 hours after an incident had occurred. The report was detailed on not only the individuals involved, but also the exact physical means of assault and the extent and location of injury, if any.

The Ps were grouped into pairs matched as closely as possible for age and years of education. One person from each pair was randomly assigned to either the GAT ($n = 14$) or CON ($n = 14$) group.

The study consisted of a pre-assessment data collection period, 72 half-hour GAT sessions, and a post-assessment data collection period. During the pre-assessment period, the total number of Ps' assaultive behaviors (physical assaults and/or self-injuries) was calculated for each group (GAT and CON) across a 9-month interval from March 1, 1984 to December 1, 1984. During the post-assessment data collection period, their total assaultive behaviors were calculated following the last treatment session (a 9-month interval from February 1, 1985 to October 31, 1985), and at a 6-month follow-up phase (an interval from November 1, 1985 to April 1, 1986). The pre- and post-assessment data were collected and reviewed daily.

The VA Medical Center's Quality Assurance Coordinator (QAC) was responsible for collecting and analyzing the data. The QAC was not informed about assignment of Ps to treatment groups. A Research Assistant (clinical psychologist) also reviewed all Special Incident Reports of any assaultive behaviors towards other persons or of self-injury. The two observers (QAC and Research Assistant) collaborated on all Special Incident Reports and provided reliability data. The presence or absence of the specific target behaviors was determined by key phrases such as "hit," struck," and "assaulted" (cf. Silver & Yudofsky, 1987). Percent agreement was obtained by dividing weekly interval agreements between the observers by agreements plus disagreements and multiplying by 100. Inter-observer agreement ranged from 96% to 100% across all weekly intervals in which reliability was assessed.

Only the GAT Ps completed the 72 half-hour sessions after the pre-assessment data collection period, and were seen two times a week for nine months. The CON group was simply assessed and did not receive any specific behavioral treatment, but continued to receive medical treatment, i.e., prescription of anti-psychotic medications and application of involuntary restraint and seclusion.

Assertive Training

Following the pre-assessment data collection period, the Experimenter (E) and Co-therapist (CT) read to GAT Ps a graduated series of hierarchy constructions (situations) composed of actual threatening interpersonal events that had resulted in assaultive behavior toward self or others on the locked ward. The GAT Ps were asked to participate in therapy sessions involving a sequence of rehearsal, modeling, feedback, and reinforcement, with subsequent verbalization (as described by Rimm & Masters, 1974). The E and/or CT read three graduated threatening interpersonal events several times weekly during a therapy session, until each P's assertive response to the aversive event failed to elicit anxiety on four consecutive presentations. The E role-played the P's response; then the P responded; the E then provided reinforcement for positive aspects of the response and corrective feedback. Under conditions of role reversal, the E modeled an appropriately assertive response; then again role-played the threatening patient and again the P responded. This procedure was followed until both E and P judged that the latter was responding appropriately, and with a minimum of anger and anxiety. An appropriately assertive response was direct and straightforward but non-threatening, delivered in a self-assured manner. An illustration of a threatening interpersonal event read to the GAT group involved a patient's commanding voices (auditory hallucinations) telling him to hit or choke the person next to him, because he was intruding into his personal space. Assaultive behavior sometimes results from such intrusions (Newman & Pollack, 1973). An example of a good assertive response to this event might be as follows: "I will ignore the commanding voices," or "I will tell the Ward Nurse that I am about to lose control of myself; would you put me in the TO room until I have regained control of my behavior." Each of the targeted interpersonal events was dealt with in a similar fashion, emphasizing contingent TO by the P for "out-of-control" impulses. Each P in the group was given feedback in the form of positive verbal reinforcement and modeling of appropriate behavior by the E.

Contingent Time-Out Procedures

Group assertion training in conjunction with the TO procedure was used to control the P's aggressive thoughts of hitting others and/or harming self. These specific target behaviors were pre-selected, and were all of a highly disruptive or negative nature. The TO room (12 ft. by 8 ft.) was located near the dayroom on the ward away from the main activity area. Whenever the P demonstrated that he was about to lose control of his behavior (e.g., loud talking, pacing up and down the hallway, or cursing), his assertive response was to immediately request the Ward Nurse to place him into TO until he had regained control. At the P's request, he was immediately removed and placed in the TO room for 15 min, or until he was quiet or had demonstrated that he was in control of his behavior. Ps were only put in the TO room when they requested it. Also, as a safety precaution and to monitor the P's change in behavior, the Primary Therapist (PT) assigned to the P remained outside the TO room door, but remained quiet and out of sight at all times. The P was then returned to the dayroom accompanied by the PT and given some form of verbal reinforcement, such as "very good, you did not lose your temper," or "you were able to maintain control over your angry feelings," associated with a pat on the back. When the P demonstrated the appropriate behavior, that is, not becoming "out-of-control" in threatening interpersonal situations, the PT immediately (1-2 min) praised him, then presented a positive form of verbal reinforcement every hour.

Results

Data (Pre-/Post-assessment scores) were analyzed with split-plot analysis of variance followed by the Newman-Keuls procedure, with $p < 0.05$ as significant. Table 1 displays mean (± standard error) total number of physical assaults and self-injuries derived from VA records of special incidents for participants in experimental (GAT) and (CON) groups during the 9-month pre- and post-treatment assessment periods. A 2 (GAT x CON groups, between subjects) x 2 (physical x self assaults, within subjects) x 2 (pre- x post-assessment period, within subjects) split-plot analysis of variance revealed significant main effects of treatment group ($F(1, 26) = 7.17, \rho < .05$), type of assault ($F(1, 26) = 81.87, \rho < .05$), and assessment period ($F(1, 26) = 31.25, \rho < .05$). The statistical analysis further indicated significant interactions of treatment group and assessment period ($F(1, 26) = 27.22, \rho < .05$), type of assault and assessment period ($F(1, 26) = 32.39, \rho < .05$), and treatment group, type of assault, and assessment period ($F(1, 26) = 36.57, \rho < .05$). However, the interaction of treatment group and type of assault was not significant ($F(1, 26) = 3.80, \rho > .05$).

Comparisons of individual pairs of means with the Newman Keuls procedure revealed no significant difference in total assaultive behaviours between means of groups GAT and CON at the pre-assessment period ($\rho > .05$). However, Group GAT showed significantly fewer assaultive records in the post-assessment period compared to Group CON ($\rho < .05$). Further, Group GAT showed a significant decline in assaultive records in the post-assessment period compared to the pre-assessment period ($\rho < .05$). Group CON did not show a significant change in assaultive episode reports across the experiment ($\rho > .05$).

Table 1

Mean (+ standard error) physical assaults and self-injuries of subjects receiving group assertive training (GAT) or control (CON) treatments, in the pre-assessment and post-assessment testing periods.

	PRE-ASSESSMENT		POST-ASSESSMENT	
	PHYSICAL	SELF	PHYSICAL	SELF
GROUP GAT	6.64 + 0.9	0.85 + 0.42	1.00 + 0.31	0.28 + 0.22
GROUP CON	6.28 + 0.86	1.00 + 0.33	5.92 + 0.58	1.14 + 0.4

Breakdown of reports into categories of physical assaults and self-injuries indicated that physical assaults were much more frequent than self-injuries. Self-assaults were recorded at a low frequency throughout the experiment and did not differ significantly on any comparison between or within groups (ρ's $> .05$). Physical assaults showed significant declines in the GAT group on comparisons between and within groups (p's $< .05$).

Discussion

The data analyses of this experiment indicate that group assertion plus contingent time-out and positive verbal reinforcement significantly reduced total assaultive behavior (i.e., physical and self-assaults) in a group of schizophrenic patients on a locked psychiatric ward. In contrast, a control group that received only traditional medical treatment for assaultive behavior (i.e., restraints, involuntary seclusion, antipsychotic medications, and other restrictive measures), showed no significant changes. The significant result achieved by the combination of assertion and contingent TO procedures is a clear indication of its therapeutic effectiveness in treatment of violent schizophrenic inpatients. These results are compatible to those of Rimm et al. (1976), Goldiamond (1965), and Benjamin et al. (1983).

A continued six-month follow-up period yielded evidence of sustained benefit. Of the 14 inpatients who participated in the GAT treatment group, ten have been discharged into community-foster homes, three are on an open psychiatric ward awaiting placement outside the hospital, and another was transferred to a public medical hospital, while the control group inpatients showed no change in their status of either assaultive behavior or hospitalization.

This study attempted to show how the combination of the behavioral techniques of assertion, contingent time-out, and positive verbal reinforcement can significantly reduce assaultive behavior that had been previously treated by restraints, involuntary seclusion, antipsychotic medications, and other restrictive measures with no apparent therapeutic gains. Our findings clearly warrant additional studies involving greater numbers of subjects and longer term follow-ups, to evaluate the mechanism of the therapeutic effect (e.g., the contribution of placebo factor or the Hawthorne effect), and its long-term effectiveness.

Index Terms: group assertion, contingent time-out, assaultive behaviors, schizophrenia.

References

ADLER, W.N., Kreeger, C., & Ziegler, P. (1983). Patient violence in a private psychiatric hospital. In J.R. Lion & W.H. Reid (Eds.), *Assaults within Psychiatric Facilities*, (pp. 81-89). New York: Grune and Stratton.

APPELBAUM, P.S. (1983). Legal considerations in the prevention and treatment of assault. In J.R. Lion & W.H. Reid (Eds.), *Assaults within Psychiatric Facilities*, (pp. 173-190). New York: Grune and Stratton.

AMERICAN PSYCHIATRIC ASSOCIATION (1980). *Diagnostic and Statistical Manual of Mental Disorders* (3rd ed.). Washington, D.C.: American Psychiatric Association.

ANDREW, J.M. (1980). Are left-handers less violent? *Journal of Youth and Adolescents, 9*, 1-9.

BACH-Y-RITA, G., Lion, J.R., Climent, C.E., & Ervin, F.R. (1971). Episodic dyscontrol: A study of 130 violent patients. *American Journal of Psychiatry, 127*, 49-54.

BARKLEY, R.A., & Zupnick, S. (1976). Reduction of stereotypic body contortions using physical restraint and DRO. *Journal of Behavior Therapy and Experimental Psychiatry, 7*, 167-170.

BAUMEISTER, A.A., & Rollings, Q.P. (1976). Self-injurious behavior. *International Review of Research on Mental Retardation, 8*, 1-34.

BENJAMIN, R., Mazzarins, H., & Kupfersmid, J. (1983). The effect of time-out (TO) duration on assaultiveness in psychiatrically hospitalized children. *Aggressive Behavior, 9*, 21-27.

BLACKBURN, R. (1968). Emotionality, extraversion, and aggression of paranoid and nonparanoid schizophrenic offenders. *British Journal of Psychiatry, 115*, 1301-1302.

BOSTOW, D.E., & Bailey, J.B. (1969). Modification of severe disruptive and aggressive behavior using brief time-out and reinforcement procedures. *Journal of Applied Behavior Analysis, 2*, 31-37.

BURCHARD, J., & Barrera, F. (1972). An analysis of time-out and response cost in a programmed environment. *Journal of Applied Behavior Analysis, 5*, 271-282.

CARR, E.G. (1977). The motivation of self-injurious behavior: A review of some hypotheses. *Psychological Bulletin, 84*, 800-816.

DAVIS V. HUBBARD (1980). 506 F. Supp. 915 (W.O. Ohio).

DELEON, C.A. (1961). Threatened homicide: A medical emergency. *Journal of Medical Association, 53*, 467.

DEPP, F.C. (1976). Violent behavior patterns on psychiatric wards. *Aggressive Behavior, 2*, 295-306.

DORSEY, M.F., Iwata, B.A., Reid, D.H., & Davis, P.A. (1982). Protective equipment: Continuous and contingent application in the treatment of self-injuries behavior. *Journal of Applied Behavior Analysis, 15*, 217-230.

EKBLOM, B. (1970). *Acts of Violence by Patients in Mental Hospital*. Uppsala, Sweden: Scandinavian University Press.

FAVELL, J.D., McGimsey, J.F., & Schell, R.M. (1982). Treatment of self-injury by providing alternative sensory activities. *Analysis and Intervention on Developmental Disabilities, 2*, 83-104.

FERSTER, C.B., Nurnberg, J.I., & Levitt, E.B. (1962). The control of eating. *Journal of Mathematics, 1*, 87-109.

FLEMING, A., & Nolley, D. (1981). A comparison of techniques for the elimination of self-injurious behavior in a mildly retarded woman. *Journal of Behavior Therapy and Experimental Psychiatry, 12*, 81-85.

FRANZEN, M.D. & Lovell, M.R. (1987). Behavioral treatments of aggressive sequelae of brain injury. *Psychiatric Annals, 17:6*, 389-396.

GOLDIAMOND, I. (1965). Self-control procedures in personal behavior problems. *Psychological Reports, 17*, 851-868.

HAGEN, D.Q., Mikolajczak, J., & Wright, R. (1972). Aggression in psychiatric patients. *Comprehensive Psychiatry, 13*, 481-487.

HARVEY, J.R., Karan, O.C., Bhargava, D., & Morehouse, N. (1978). Relaxation training and cognitive behavioral procedures to reduce violent temper outbursts in moderately retarded women. *Journal of Behavior Therapy and Experimental Psychiatry, 9*, 347-357.

HEWITT, L., & Jenkins, R.L. (1946). *Fundamental Patterns of Maladjustment*. Springfield, Illinois: State of Illinois.

HOMME, L.E. (1965). Perspectives in psychology: XXIV. Control of coverants, the operants of the mind. *Psychological Record, 15*, 501-511.

KALOGERAKIS, M.G. (1971). The assaultive psychiatric patient. *Psychiatric Quarterly, 45*, 372-381.

LAMONT, J.E., Gilner, F.H., Spector, N.J., & Skinner, K.K. (1969). Group assertion training and group insight therapies. *Psychological Reports, 25*, 463-470.

LAZARUS, A.A. (1971). *Behavior Therapy and Beyond*. New York: McGraw-Hill.

LAZARUS, A.A., & Serber, M. (1968). Is systematic desensitization being misapplied? *Psychological Reports, 23*, 215-218.

LEITENBERG, H. (1965). Is time-out from positive reinforcement an aversive event? *Psychological Bulletin, 64*, 428-441.

LION, J.R. & Reid, W.H. (Eds.) (1983). *Assaults within Psychiatric Facilities*. New York: Grune and Stratton.

LOVAAS, O.I., Schaeffer, B., & Simmons J.Q. (1965). Building social behavior in autistic children by use of electric shock. *Journal of Experimental Research in Personality, 1*, 99-109.

MADDEN, D.J. (1983). Recognition and prevention of violence in psychiatric facilities. In J.R. Lion & W.H. Reid (Eds.), *Assaults within Psychiatric Facilities*, (pp. 213-223). New York: Grune and Stratton.

MARKS, I.M. (1976). The current status of behavioral psychotherapy: Theory and practice. *American Journal of Psychiatry, 133*, 253-261.

MARTEN, S., Munoz, R.A., Gentry, K.A., & Robins, E. (1970). Belligerence: Its frequency and correlates in a psychiatric emergency room population. Read at the 1970 meeting of the American Psychiatric Association. San Francisco, CA.

MASSACHUSETTS DEPARTMENT OF MENTAL HEALTH, OFFICE OF MANPOWER PLANNING AND DEVELOPMENT (1980). *Training in the Prevention and Management of Violence: A Survey of Massachusetts Programs*. Cambridge, MA: Human service Training and Development Consortium.

MCKINLAY, W.W., Brooks, D.N., Bond, M.R., Martinage, D.P., & Marshall, M.M. (1981). The short-term outcome of severe blunt head injury as reported by the relatives of the injured person. *Journal of Neurology, Neurosurgery, and Psychiatry, 44*, 527-533.

MENNINGER, K. (1963). *The Vital Balance*. New York: Viking Press.

MYERS, D.W. (1975). Extinction, DRO, and response cost procedures for eliminating self-injurious behavior: A case study. *Behav. Res. Ther., 13*, 189-191.

NEWMAN, R.C., & Pollack, D. (1973). Proxemics in deviant adolescents. *Journal of Consulting and Clinical Psychology, 40*, 6-8.

NIGROSH, B.J. (1983). Physical contact skills in specialized training for the prevention and management of violence. In J.R. Lion & W.H. Reid (Eds.), *Assaults within Psychiatric Facilities*, (pp. 265-285). New York: Grune and Stratton.

OLDHAM, J.M., Russakoff, L.M., & Prisnofsky, L. (1983). Seclusion: Patterns and milieu. *The Journal of Nervous and Mental Disease, 171*:11, 645-650.

PECK, C.L. (1977). Desensitization for the treatment of fear in the high level adult retardate. *Behavior and Research Therapy, 15*, 137-148.

PENDERGRASS, V. (1971). Effects of length of time-out from positive reinforcement and schedule application in suppression of aggressive behavior. *Psychological Record, 21*, 75-80.

PENISTON, E.G. (1975). Reducing problem behaviors in the severely and profoundly retarded. *Journal of Behavior Therapy and Experimental Psychiatry, 6*, 295-299.

REID, H.W., Bollinger, M.F., & Edwards, G. (1985). Assaults in hospitals. *Bull Am Acad Psychiatry Law, 13*, 1-4.

REPP, A. & Dietz, S. (1974). Reducing aggressive and self-injurious behavior of institutionalized retarded children through reinforcement of other behavior. *Journal of Applied Behavior Analysis, 7*, 313-325.

REPP, A., Dietz, S., & Speir, N. (1974). Reducing stereotypic responding of retarded persons by the differential reinforcement of other behavior. *American Journal of Mental Deficiency, 79*, 279-284.

RIMM, D.C. & Masters, J.C. (1974). *Behavior Therapy: Techniques and Empirical Findings*. New York: Academic Press.

RIMM, D.C., Snyder, J.J., Depue, R.A., Haanstad, A, & Armstrong, M.J. (1976). Assertive training versus rehearsal and the importance of making an assertive response. *Behavioral Research and Therapy, 14*, 315-321.

RINCOVER, A. & Devancy, J. (1982). The application of sensory extinction procedures to self-injury. *Analysis and Intervention in Developmental Disabilities, 2*, 67-81.

ROBACK, H., Frayn, D., Gunby, L., & Tuters, K. (1972). A multifactorial approach to the treatment and ward management of a self-mutilating patient. *Journal of Behavior Therapy and Experimental Psychiatry, 3*, 189-193.

ROMANCZYK, R.G., & Goren, E.R. (1975). Severe self-injurious behavior: The problem of clinical control. *Journal of Consulting and Clinical Psychology, 43*, 730-739.

ROMEO V. YOUNGBERG (1982). No. 76-3429 (E.D.Pa. 1978), 644F .2d 147 (3d Cir. 1980), vacated and remanded, 102 S. Ct. 2452.

ROSSI, A.M., Jacobs, M., Monteleone, M., Olsen, R., Surber, R.W., Winkler, E.L., & Wommack, A. (1985). Violent or fear-inducing behavior associated with hospital admission. *Hospital Community Psychiatry, 36*, 643-647.

RUSSO, D.C., Carr, E.G., & Lovaas, O.I. (1980). Self-injury in pediatric population. In J. Ferguson & C.B. Taylor (Eds.), *Comprehensive Handbook of Behavioral Medicine*. Holliswood, New York: Spectrum Publications.

SARASON, I.G. & Ganzer, V.J. (1973). Modeling and group discussion in the rehabilitation of juvenile delinquents. *Journal of Counseling Psychology, 20*, 442-449.

SCHNIEDER, H.C., Ross, J.S.G., & Dubin, W.J. (1979). A practical alternative for the treatment of tantrum and self-injurious behavior. *Journal of Behavior Therapy and Experimental Psychiatry, 10*, 73-76.

SHAH, S.A. (1978). Dangerousness: A paradigm for exploring some issues in law and psychology. *American Psychologist, 33*, 224-238.

SILVER, J.M. & Yudofsky, S.C. (1987). Documentation of aggression in the assessment of the violent patient. *Psychiatric Annals, 17*:6, 375-384.

SILVER, J.M. & Yudofsky, S.C. (1987). Aggressive behavior in patients with neuropsychiatric disorders. *Psychiatric Annals, 17*:6, 367-370.

SKINNER, B.F. (1953). *Science and Human Behavior*. New York: Macmillan.

SMOLER, S. (1971). Use of operant techniques for the modification of self-injurious behavior. *American Journal of Mental Deficiency, 76*, 295-305.

SOLOFF, P.H. (1983). Seclusion and restraint. In J.R. Lion & W.H. Reid (Eds.), *Assaults within Psychiatric Facilities*, (pp. 241-264). New York: Grune and Stratton.

TARDIFF, K. (1984). Characteristics of assaultive patients in private hospitals. *American Journal of Psychiatry, 141*:10, 1232-1235.

TARDIFF, K. & Sweillam, A. (1982). Assaultive behavior among chronic inpatients. *American Journal of Psychiatry, 139*:2, 212-215.

TATE, B.G. & Bardoff, G.S. (1966). Aversive control of self-injurious behavior in a psychotic boy. *Behavior Research and Therapy, 4*, 281-287.

THORESON, C.D. & Mahoney, M.J. (1974). *Behavior Self-Control*. New York: Holt.

TOCH, H (1969). *Violent Men: An Inquiry into the Psychology of Violence*. Chicago: Aldine.

ULLMANN, L.P. & Krasner, M.J. (1965). *Self-Directed Behavior: Self-Modification for Personal Adjustment*. Monterey, California: Brooks Cole.

WERNER, P.D., Terrence, L.R., Yesavage, J.A., & Seeman, K. (1984). Psychiatrists' judgments of dangerousness in patients on an acute care unit. *American Journal of Psychiatry, 141*:2, 263-266.

WHITE, G., Nielsen, G., & Johnson, M. (1972). Time-out duration and the suppression of deviant behavior in children. *Journal of Applied Behavior Analysis, 5*, 111-120.

WOLFGANG, M. (1966). *Patterns in Criminal Homicide*. New York: Wiley.

WOLPE, J. (1958). *Psychotherapy by Reciprocal Inhibition*. Stanford, CA: Stanford University Press.

WOLPE, J. & Lazarus, A.A. (1966). *Behavior Therapy Techniques: A Guide to the Treatment of Neuroses*. Oxford: Pergamon.

WYATT V. STICKNEY (1972). 325F. Supp. 781, 344F. Supp. 373 (M.D. Ala.).

Medical Psychotherapy
1988, Volume 1, pp. 143-149

© 1988 by
Hans Huber Publishers, Toronto

Crisis in Midlife Among Osteopathic Physicians

W. RANDALL RATLIFF, JAMES R. HALL, AND JERRY C. MCGILL
Texas College of Osteopathic Medicine

JOEL ALTER
Santa Rosa, CA

KATE WYATT
Fort Worth, TX

In a random sample of 139 male osteopathic physicians, five factors believed to be important in midlife transition were identified using an objective questionnaire, the W.A.R.M. Transition Inventory. These were: Job Involvement, Rootedness, Sense of Control, Romantic Satisfaction, and Sexuality and were identified using factor analysis with varimax rotation with final oblique rotation. When these five midlife factors were related to age, physical symptoms, and mental symptoms, results indicated that age was related moderately only to Rootedness and Job Involvement, mental symptoms were related to Sense of Control, and physical symptoms were unrelated to any of the factors. The low to moderate correlation of midlife factors with age calls into question the notion of a common, universal timetable for adult development. It appears that one cannot predict crisis in transition from age, as suggested by stage theory.

Introduction

The concept of a human life cycle with regular sequences or stages has been a subject of psychological thought since the time of Erik Erikson (1964) and Carl Jung

Inquiries or reprint requests should be directed to Dr. W. Randall Ratliff, Department of Psychiatry and Human Behavior, Texas College of Osteopathic Medicine, Camp Bowie at Montgomery, Fort Worth, TX 76107.

Dr. Joel Alter was formerly with the Department of Surgery at the Texas College of Osteopathic Medicine. He is now in private practice in Santa Rosa, CA.

(Campbell, 1971). The concept of the "male midlife crisis," a transitional period usually identified as occurring somewhere between the ages of 35 and 55, has been of particular interest during the last decade. The transition time is seen by most writers to be characterized by fluidity of biological, psychological, and sociological changes and to be experienced as distressing.

Levinson (1978), in studying men between the ages of 35 and 45, described a concept of life structure that evolves through a sequence of alternating periods of stable structure-building periods of six to eight years and of transitional structure-changing periods of four to five years. In the periods of transition, the past is reappraised either consciously or unconsciously, and the future is reconsidered in light of new possibilities or redirection. Vast upheaval and crisis-like distress may occur, resulting in some men making significant changes in lifestyle, interpersonal relationships, or occupation.

Another position is that of Vaillant and Milofsky (1980), who described men between the ages of 40 and 50 as leaving the compulsive, unreflective business of their occupational apprenticeships to return to a more turbulent search of the world within, similar to the effect of adolescence on the preadolescent period. Important to the position of Vaillant (1977) is the point that radical change does not occur often – crisis is an exception rather than the rule. Men in midlife are characterized by maturation and evolution of mature defenses. Most men make adaptive changes throughout the life cycle; the age at which a given stage is mastered varies enormously.

Even though there is a significant theoretical (Brim, 1976; Dubbert, 1979; Gould, 1978; Halberg, 1977; Levinson, 1978; McGill, 1982; Mayer, 1978; Sarason, 1977; Schlossberg, 1987; Sheehy, 1976; Vaillant, 1977) and clinical (Collin, 1979; Ciernia, 1985; Gutmann, 1976; Vaillant & Milofsky, 1980) literature on the midlife transition, there have been few attempts to objectify or quantify this process for empirical study. The present study investigated the nature of the midlife experience through the development of a measurement procedure that could be applied across populations. Male osteopathic physicians, whose earlier years were characterized by striving for high achievement and fulfillment of a dream, were targeted as a group of highly committed individuals whose midlife experience might be of particular interest in understanding the transitional phenomenon. Two previous studies (Pfeiffer, 1983; Medalie, 1984) have emphasized adult development of physicians, and another two of dentists (Born & Nelson, 1984; Hark, Waldman, Born, & Cytrynbaum, 1986), but few of these studies were empirical and objective regarding the measurement of transitional factors.

Method

Subjects were 139 male osteopathic physicians who returned completed questionnaires that had been sent to a random sample of 300 drawn from a listing of 1041 osteopathic physicians with addresses in the state of Texas. Questionnaires were returned anonymously; there was no place for name on the form and the cover letter directed the respondent *not* to put his name on the materials. The questionnaire consisted of three parts.

Part I dealt with demographic characteristics, including age, medical specialty, year of graduation, marital status, marital history, birth order, and age of children. Part II consisted of a 43-item Likert-like scale dealing with physical and mental symptoms commonly associated with stress and distress, such as tension headaches, overeating, low back pain, worrisome thoughts, etc. Respondents were asked to mark the frequency of such symptoms within the last 30 days, using a 4-point scale with anchors of *none, some, often*, and *always*. The W.A.R.M. Transition Inventory (Wyatt, Alter, Ratliff, & McGill, 1986), consisting of 73 items on midlife transition, made up Part III. Response categories for the transition inventory were *true, uncertain*, and *false*.

Results

The average age of subjects was 42 years, with a standard deviation of 10.4 and a range from 25 to 77.

Fifty-one percent of the subjects were first-borns, 27% were second; 13% third; 6% fourth; and 3% fifth or more. At the time of data collection 81% were married, 10% divorced, 1% separated, 1% cohabitating, and 7% never married. Thirty-one subjects failed to respond to the item on number of marriages; of those who did respond, 45% had been divorced at least once and 55% had never been divorced. Fifteen percent had been divorced two or more times. Twenty-five percent had children 5 years old or less; 37% had children 5 to 12 years old; and 37% had children 13 to 22 years old. Fifteen percent had grandchildren.

Table 1
Physical and Mental Symptoms of Physicians

Item Content	Percent Level One	Percent Level Two	Mean Severity	Rank
Worrisome thoughts	55	17	.75	1
Fatigue	53	18	.74	2
Overeating	50	15	.66	3
Alcohol consumption	50	12	.66	4
Angry feelings	53	11	.65	5
Aching neck/shoulder	45	14	.64	6
Nervousness	43	12	.57	7
Trouble falling asleep	42	13	.57	8
Low back pain	45	11	.56	9
Irritability with others	45	7	.53	10
Early morning awakening	32	9	.47	11
Feelings of depression	33	8	.45	13
Periods of depression	32	9	.45	13
Stomach indigestion	37	7	.45	13
Tension headaches	37	4	.42	15

The items of Part II, the symptom checklist, were subjected to a factor analysis with varimax rotation, with final oblique rotation to maximum simple structure using the ROTOPLOT procedure developed by Cattell (1978). Based on a scree test (Cattell, 1978) only two factors were identified. These two factors were called Physical Symptoms and Mental Symptoms.

Table 1 shows the fifteen most frequently endorsed items in the symptom checklist, at two levels of endorsement. The symptom items had four response categories – none, some, often, and always. Level one in Table 1 shows the percent of physicians who endorsed at the *some* level or beyond, while level two indicates the percent who endorsed at the *often* level or beyond. The Mean Severity score in Table 1 is the mean for each item when scores of 0, 1, 2, or 3 were assigned on the basis of a none, some, often, or always, respectively.

More than 50% of the physicians admitted having worrisome thoughts, fatigue, overeating, alcohol consumption, and angry feelings at least some of the time in the last 30 days. This percent dropped greatly at level two – (indicating often having the symptom), ranging from 18% to 11%. Other symptoms reported often in the last 30 days by more than 10% were aching neck and shoulders, nervousness, trouble falling asleep, and low back pain. Symptoms reported with frequent occurrence (more than 30% of subjects at level one) were irritability with others, early morning awakening, feelings of depression, periods of depression, stomach indigestion, and tension headaches.

The 73 items of the W.A.R.M. Transition Inventory were subjected to a factor analysis with varimax rotation, with final oblique rotation to maximum simple structure using the ROTOPLOT procedure developed by Cattell (1978). A scree test (Cattell, 1978) identified five factors. Although dealing with a relatively small number of subjects, factor analysis provided a set of categories for describing the data.

The first factor, labeled *Sense of Control*, contained twenty items and seemed to reflect the subject's sense of control and expectation in life and work. The highest weighted items included, "I feel too constrained by circumstances" (.79), "I feel uncertain about myself these days" (.73), and "I wish I had more choice about whether to work or stay at home" (.68).

The second factor, labeled *Romantic Satisfaction*, contained eleven items reflecting the subject's level of comfort with his primary love relationship. The three highest weighted items were "My home is more an economic arrangement than a loving family" (.77), "I am very happy with my primary love relationship" (–.77), and "I am very close to my spouse or lover" (–.74).

The third factor was labeled *Sexuality*, and it contained twelve items related to the subject's perception of his sexual function. The items included "I am as virile, sexy, and attractive as ever" (.65), "I'd enjoy sex more if I were more attractive" (–.65), and "My age and experience make me a better lover than I was" (.61).

The fourth factor was labeled *Job Involvement*. The six items that loaded most heavily on this factor involved the subject's level of investment in his work environment. The items related to this factor included, "I frequently work on evenings and weekends" (.60), "Succeeding at work is very important to me" (.56), and "I enjoy beating the competition" (.47).

The final factor was named *Rootedness*. The eight highest loadings included statements related to the subject's feeling of community, personal satisfaction, and sense of belonging. The three strongest loadings were, "I'm active in professional, civic, and social affairs" (.47), "I'd like to live in this location for the rest of my career" (.46), and "My partner and I please each other sexually as well as ever" (.45).

Nine variables including Year of Medical School Graduation, Age, the five midlife factors (Sense of Control, Romantic Satisfaction, Sexuality, Job Involvement, and Rootedness) and the two symptom checklist factors of Physical Symptoms and Mental Symptoms, were analyzed by correlational analysis. The pairwise matrix of midlife factors is shown in Table 2.

The strongest relationship of the matrix of Table 2 is between Year of Graduation and Age, with a correlational coefficient of –.94 indicating a high degree of relatedness between the two. While this is not an unexpected finding, examination of Table 2 reveals that it makes little difference which one of the two is used to examine the relationship with other factors. Since change over time is crucial to the concept of midlife transition, either of these two can be used as the index to validate the transitional process.

Table 2
Midlife Factors Among Physicians

Factors	Year	Age	SCon	Rom	Sexy	Job	Root	Phy
Year								
Age	–.94*							
Sense of Control	–.16	.18						
Romantic Satisfaction	–.06	.06	.36*					
Sexuality	–.18	.18	–.42*	–.08				
Job Involvement	–.43*	.42*	.07	.10	.32*			
Rootedness	.45*	–.46*	–.27*	–.10	.06	.07		
Physical Symptoms	.07	–.05	.01	–.11	.02	.04	.04	
Mental Symptoms	.06	.07	.51*	.28*	–.27*	–.01	–.05	–.57*

*$p < .01$

Age (as well as Year of Graduation) is significantly related to two of the five midlife factors: Rootedness showed the highest degree of relationship (–.45), and Job Involvement was moderately related (.42). Sense of Control (.18), Sexuality (.18), and Romantic Satisfaction (.06) were not significantly related to Age. Age was also unrelated to Physical Symptoms (–.05) and Mental Symptoms (.07).

The pattern of factor correlations among the five midlife factors is interesting. Sense of Control correlates with both Romantic Satisfaction (.36) and Sexuality (–.42), suggesting that subjects who felt a loss of control also were experiencing romantic dissatisfaction and reduced sexuality. There is little correlation between the two factors of Romantic Satisfaction and Sexuality (–.08). Sense of Control and Job Involvement (.07) did not correlate. There is a modest correlation between Sense of Control and Rootedness (–.27). Finally, a modest correlation occurs between Sexuality and Job Involvement (.32). These correlations seem consistent with the idea that personal relationships, particularly the primary love relationship, are central to the subjects' sense of control during midlife.

Interestingly, Physical Symptoms did not correlate significantly with any of the midlife factors. Mental Symptoms, however, correlated significantly with three of them, with a strong relationship with Sense of Control (.51), and more moderate ones with both Romantic Satisfaction (.28) and Sexuality (–.27). Mental symptoms did not relate to Job Involvement (–.01) or Rootedness (–.05). Despite the lack of a relatedness of midlife factors and Physical Symptoms, a strong negative relationship between Physical Symptoms and Mental Symptoms (–.57) was found.

Discussion

The data point to the existence of five factors among the items commonly reported in the midlife literature. These factors are related to job, feeling of rootedness, sense of control, romantic satisfaction, and sexuality. What is less clear is the extent to which these items clearly are age-related or merely indicative of general life adjustment regardless of age. At least two of the factors (Job Involvement and Rootedness) tend to vary with age.

Several alternative explanations are possible. First, this sample of physicians may represent a relatively homogeneous population, which reduced the variability regarding age. Second, it is possible that there is a great amount of individual variability regarding midlife adjustment. Rather than midlife crisis representing an event that occurs invariably within a certain age range (e.g., 35 to 45), the crisis may represent a developmental stage that occurs at highly variable ages, but with a uniform sequence. This would not have been apparent in a cross-sectional study such as this one. Further, the non-responding physicians may have been different from those who responded.

We are confident that the W.A.R.M. Transitional Inventory does sample a definable set of factors that can be used to study the so-called *midlife crisis* and transition. However, greater numbers of subjects are necessary to increase confidence in defining these factors. Moreover, in order to clarify the relationship to life change, and to further explore the relationship of these factors to the midlife crisis, additional data are needed including other population subgroups over a variety of age ranges. It is clear as well that longitudinal data are needed in order to follow the progression through the presumed developmental stages, to see if a consistent life change pattern exists in midlife.

References

BORN, D. O., & Nelson, B. J. (1984). Male dentists at midlife: An exploration of the one life/one career imperative. *International Journal of Aging and Human Development 18*, 219-235.

BRIM, O.G. (1976). Theories of the male mid-life crisis. *Counseling Psychologist, 6*, 2-9.

CAMPBELL, J. (Ed.). (1971). *The portable Jung*. New York: Viking.

CATTELL, R.B. (1978). *The scientific use of factor analysis in behavioral and life sciences*. New York: Plenum Press.

CIERNIA, J. R. (1985). Myths about male midlife crises. *Psychological Reports, 56*, 1003-1007.

COLLIN, A. (1979). Mid-life crisis and its implications in counselling. *British Journal of Guidance and Counselling, 7*, 144-151.

DUBBERT, J.L. (1979). *A man's place*. Englewood Cliffs, New Jersey: Prentice-Hall.

ERIKSON, E. (1964). *Insight and Responsibility*. New York: Norton.

GOULD, R.L. (1978). *Transformations*. New York: Simon and Schuster.

GUTMANN, D. (1976). Individual adaptation in the middle years: developmental issues in the masculine mid-life crisis. *Journal of Geriatric Psychiatry, 9*, 41-59.
HALBERG, E. (1977). *The Gray Itch*. New York: Omsbudsman.
HARK R.D., Waldman H.B., Born, D.O., & Cytrynbaum, S. (1986). Dentists at mid-life: Changing perceptions, new directions. *Journal of the American Dental Association, 113*, 19-27.
LEVINSON, D.J. (1978). *Seasons of a man's life*. New York: Knopf.
MAYER, N. (1978). *The male mid-life crisis*. Garden City, New York: Doubleday.
MCGILL, M. (1982). *Forty to sixty year old male: A guide for men and the women in their lives to see them through the crisis of male middle years*. New York: Simon & Schuster.
MEDALIE, J.H. (1984). Male midlife development. *Journal of Family Practice, 19*, 211-217.
PFEIFFER, R.J. (1983). Early-adult development in the medical student. *Mayo Clinical Proceedings, 58*, 127-134.
SARASON, S.B. (1977). *Work, aging and social change*. New York: The Free Press.
SCHLOSSBERG, N.K. (1987). Taking the mystery out of change. *Psychology Today, 20*, 74-75.
VAILLANT, G.E. (1977). *Adaptation to Life*. New York: Little, Brown.
VAILLANT, G.E., & Milofsky, E. (1980). Natural history of male psychological health: Empirical evidence of Erikson's model of the life cycle. *American Journal of Psychiatry, 137*, 1348.
WYATT, K., Alter, J., Ratliff, W.R., & McGill J.C. (October 1986). *Development of a measure of midlife change: The W.A.R.M. Transition Inventory*. Paper presented at meeting of the Texas Psychological Association, Dallas TX.

Medical Psychotherapy
1988, Volume 1, pp. 151-159

© 1988 by
Hans Huber Publishers, Toronto

Evoking Vocal Imitation in At-Risk Infants: An Experimental Analysis

LEILA REGINA DE PAULA NUNES, Ph.D.
Universidade Federal de São Carlos - Brazil

CLAIRE L. POULSON, Ph.D.
Queens College-City University of New York

The operant language-acquisition paradigm has been used to analyze some precursors of language development in the form of infant vocalizations. A substantial number of studies has shown the positive effects of social stimulation upon infant vocalizations, but functional analyses of infant vocal imitation have rarely been conducted. The present investigation was designed to identify the variables that should be manipulated to evoke vocal imitation in nonimitative infants who are at risk for developmental delay. Its purpose was to demonstrate the effects of some changes in the pattern of vocal mother-infant interaction on the frequency of matching infant vocal responses. One at-risk infant of 13 months of age and his low SES mother participated as subjects in a single-subject A-B design. Data on the parent's and the infant's responses, collected from videotaped sessions, showed that the introduction of treatment resulted in an increase in the percentage of both appropriate parent vocal modeling and matching infant responses.

Introduction

The operant language-acquisition paradigm has been successful in demonstrating how oral language can be taught to preschool children (Baer & Sherman, 1964), severely and profoundly retarded children and adolescents (Baer, Peterson, & Sherman, 1967), autistic individuals (Lovaas, 1977; Lovaas, Berberich, Perloff, & Schaeffer, 1966), and psychotic adults (Sherman, 1965). This paradigm has also been extended to analyze some precursors of language development in the form of infant vocalizations. In ef-

Inquiries or reprint requests should be directed to Leila de Paula Nunes, Universidade Federal de Sao Carlos, Rodovia Washington Luis Km. 235, Caixa Postal 676, 13560-Sao Carlos-Sao Paulo, Brazil.

fect, a substantial number of experimental studies has shown the positive effects of social stimulation upon infant vocalizations. Contingent adult vocalization, eye contact, and touching were successfully used as reinforcers to increase the frequency of normal and delayed infant vocal responding (Haughan & McIntire, 1972; Jones & Moss, 1972; Poulson, 1983, 1984, in press; Ramey & Ourth, 1971; Rheingold, Gerwirtz, & Ross, 1959; Sheppard, 1969; Todd, & Palmer, 1968; Wahler, 1969; Weisberg, 1963; Wiegerink, Harris, Simeonsson, & Pearson, 1974).

Nonetheless, deliberate treatment of infant vocal imitation – another important step in the operant training paradigm – has been experimentally investigated by only a few studies. Hursh and Sherman (1973), using 15- to 20-month-old normally developing infants, conducted a study in which the rate of a specific infant vocalization was brought under the discriminative control of an adult vocal model. Hursh and Sherman demonstrated that the combination of parents' modeling, praise, and repetition of infant-matched responses influences the rate of specific vocalizations already in the infant's repertoire.

Poulson, Nunes, Daurelle and Stiles (1966) replicated the Hursh and Sherman study using younger infants. The purpose of their study was to demonstrate that modeling vocal sounds, praising, playing with toys, and repeating the child's matched vocal responses can systematically increase the frequence of targeted vocal sounds of normally developing infants between 9 and 12 months of age. The data showed that massed presentation of modeling trials had very little effect on the emission of vocal matching behavior. Nonetheless, the modeling procedure did increase the frequency of both targeted and non-targeted vocalizations.

The studies reported so far have dealt only with middle-class normally developing infants. Considering that infants from economically disadvantaged families show a slower development in vocal imitation (Paraskevopoulos & Hunt, 1971; Wachs, Uzgiris, & Hunt, 1971), and that this seems to be associated with low frequencies of caretaker-infant vocal interactions (Tulkin & Kagan, 1972), research studies aimed at identifying the variables that make infants imitate their mothers' vocalizations should be conducted. The present investigation was designed to accomplish this objective. More specifically, our purpose was to demonstrate the effects of some changes in the pattern of vocal mother-infant interaction, on the frequency of matching vocal responses in an at-risk 13-month-old infant.

Method

Subjects

One low-income woman and her 13-month-old son participated as subjects. The mother, who had an older child considered to be language-delayed, was a recipient of public assistance and was under mental health care. The infant was 13 months old during his first session and 20 months old at the end of the study.

Setting and Apparatus

The study was conducted in the Infant Laboratory of the Kennedy Center at Peabody College of Vanderbilt University. The experimental room was a large room arranged like a living room with a couch, upholstered chairs, a coffee table, and an infant changing table equipped with supplies. An infant high chair was placed on the carpeted floor facing a folding chair that the parent used. A wooden table was placed between the parent and the child, and a set of easily manipulated toys and cups containing baby food were placed on plastic stools close to the parent. A VHS video system was set up in the room and operated by the experimenter.

Interobserver agreement

Data from the videotaped sessions were recorded on infant and parent responses by two independent observers, using an event-recording system. Interobserver agreement was analyzed on a point-by-point basis. The onset of entries made by the observers had to concur within 3 seconds to count as an agreement. Interobserver agreement data were calculated by dividing the number of agreements by the total number of observations, and multiplying by 100. Assessment of interobserver agreement occurred in at least 25% of sessions in each condition. The mean percentages of agreement on frequency of parent's models, model antecedents, model consequences, and infant responses were 81% (range: 65%-100%), 91% (range: 90%-95%), 79% (range: 58%-100%), and 85% (range: 75%-100%), respectively.

Procedure

Experimental Design

An A-B design was implemented with the mother-child dyad (Hersen & Barlow, 1977). Each condition, baseline, and treatment remained in effect until the graphed data showed a visually stable pattern (Baer, Wolf, & Risley, 1968). In spite of the weakness of the A-B design (it does not control for threats to internal validity such as maturation), it was used because this was an exploratory study in which the effectiveness of some instructional procedures used by the mother was under investigation.

Independent and Dependent Variables

The independent variables were the percentage per session of appropriate parent vocal models, the number per session of repetitions by the mother of infant vocalizations, and the number per session of parent vocal models paired with presentation of food or toy. An appropriate parent vocal model involved the following five dimensions: a modeling episode less than 6 seconds in duration, face contact between mother and infant, availability of time for the infant to respond, prompt or repetition of the model when the infant failed to match, and praise when the infant matched the model.

The dependent variable was the percentage per session of matching infant vocal responses to the mother's models.

Procedure

The mother-infant dyad experienced two phases: baseline and treatment. During the baseline the mother was asked to present the toys and talk to the baby as she normally would at home. Thirty-three sessions were conducted over a period of five months. During this period, the mother presented 19 different vocal sounds to be repeated by the infant (e.g. "hi," "dog," "huf-huf").

When treatment was introduced, two kinds of sessions were run each day – a training session and an experimental session. The training session was conducted first, with the purpose of increasing the frequency of infant vocalizations. Three procedures were used to accomplish this: a) repetition of infant spontaneous vocalizations by the mother, b) presentation of food or toy paired with a mother vocalization, and c) delivery of food or toy and repetition of infant vocalization following an infant vocal request. Fourteen sessions were conducted over a period of two months.

During experimental sessions the mother was instructed to present vocal models appropriately, i.e., according to the following five dimensions: short duration, face contact, time to respond, prompt, and praise. Sixteen sessions were conducted over two months, the same period as the training sessions. During these sessions, the mother presented 63 different vocal models. Twelve had already been presented during baseline, while 51 were now sounds.

Results

The absolute frequency of the mother's repetition of her infant's spontaneous vocalizations per session are presented in Figure 1.

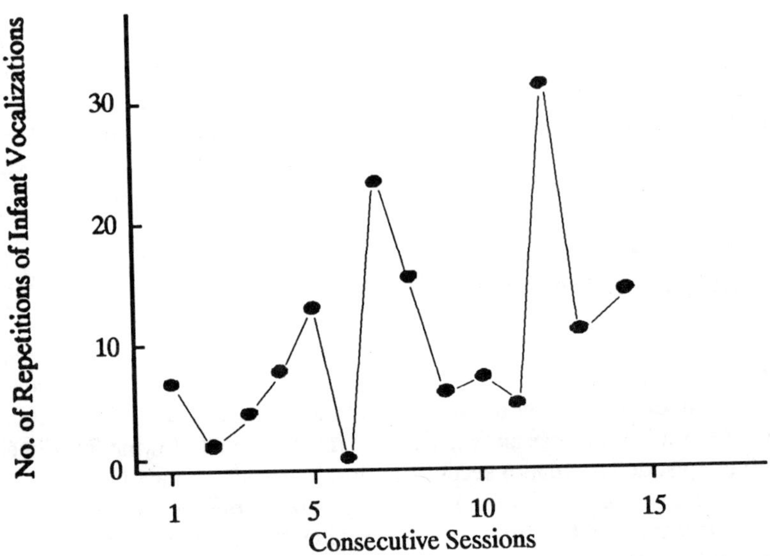

Figure 1
Number of repetitions of infant vocalizations by the mother during training sessions

The frequencies of repetitions increased consistently over the 14 training sessions. The absolute frequencies of both the mother's presentations of food or toys paired with a vocal model, and the infant's vocal requests per session, are shown in Figure 2.

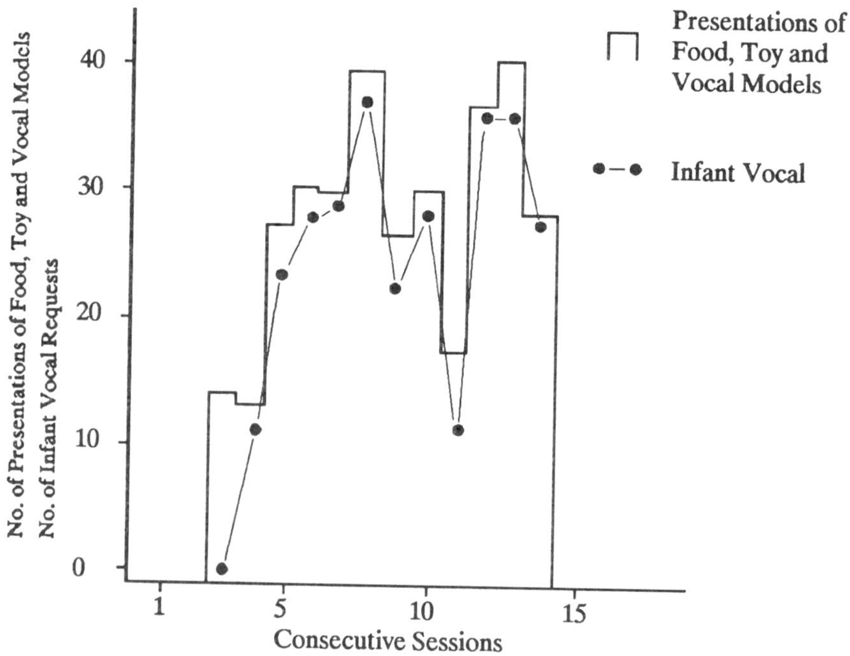

Figure 2
Number of presentations of food, toy and vocal models by mother and number of infant vocal requests during training sessions

Data showed that the mother maintained the presentations of food or toys paired with a vocal model on a regular basis. Infant vocal requests increased consistently over sessions.

The absolute frequencies of both infant vocal requests and the reinforcement provided by the mother to these requests per session are presented in Figure 3.

Data indicated that the infant kept requesting vocally either toys or food on a regular basis. Although the mother failed to provide these items upon request in some trials, overall she delivered reinforcement consistently over the sessions.

The percentages of appropriate vocal models displayed by the mother per session during each experimental condition are shown in Figure 4.

The percentage of appropriate vocal models remained at 0% during baseline condition. During treatment the percentage showed an increase to 64%, followed by a decrease to 25% and again an upward trend to 77%.

The percentages of matching infant vocal responses per session during each experimental condition are presented in Figure 5.

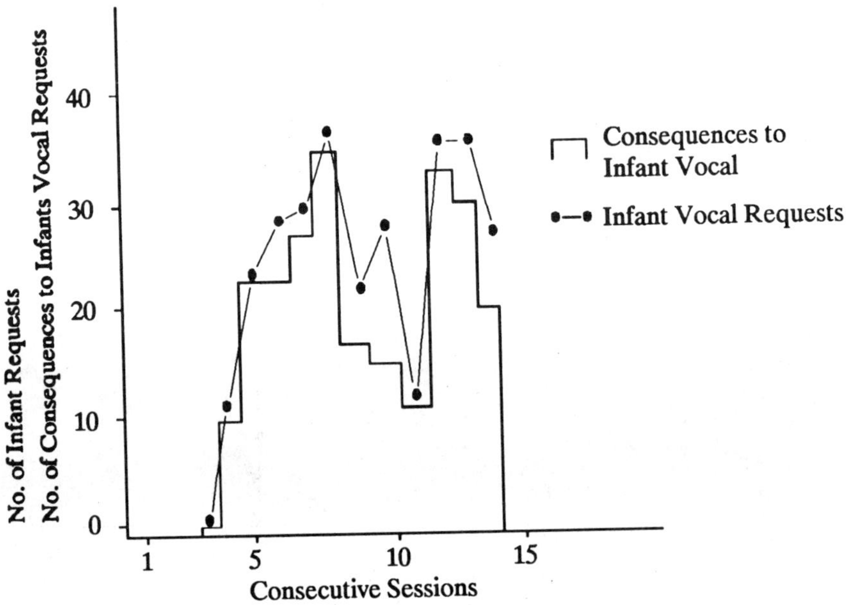

Figure 3
Number of infant vocal requests and number of consequences to vocal requests provided by the mother during training sessions

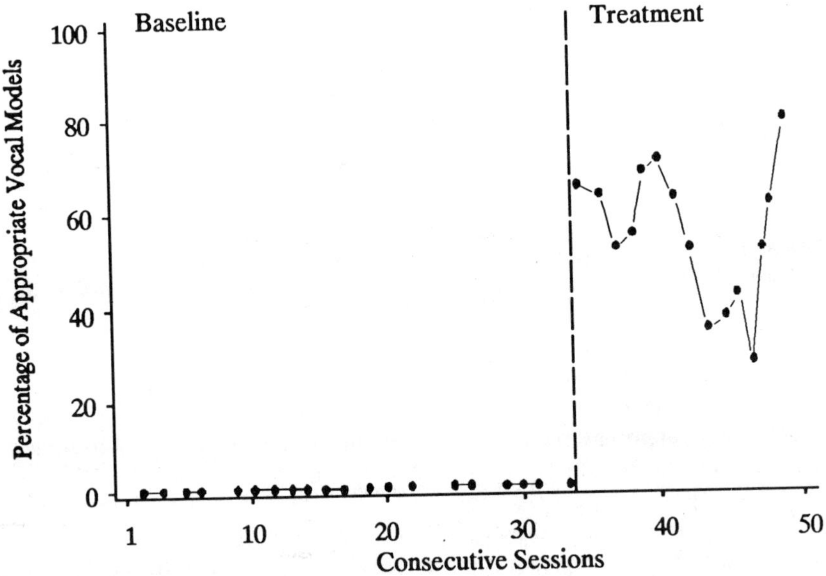

Figure 4
Percentage of appropriate vocal models delivered by the mother during baseline and treatment phases

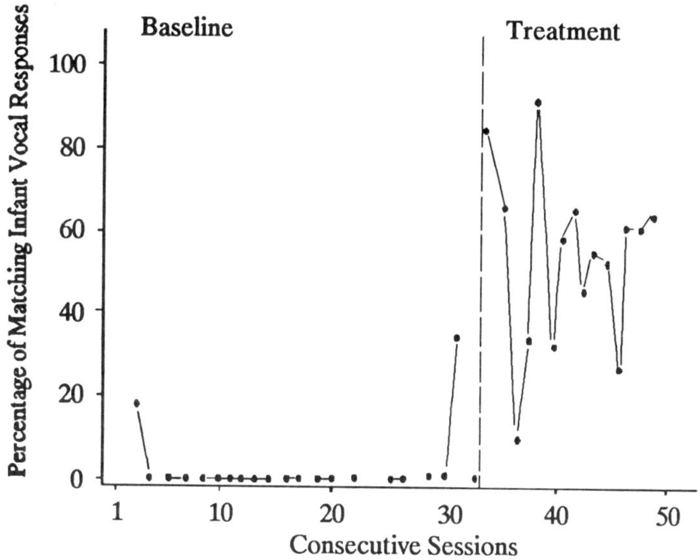

Figure 5
Percentage of matching infant vocal responses to vocal models presented by the mother during baseline and treatment phases

The matching infant responses remained at 0% in all baseline sessions but two. With the introduction of treatment, the percentage showed a clear upward trend.

In sum, during experimental sessions, the introduction of the treatment was associated with an increase in the percentage of both the mother's vocal models presented appropriately, and the infant's matching responses to these models.

Discussion

The purpose of this study was to examine the effects of a training package on matching infant responses to the vocal models presented by the mother. Data indicated that the treatment procedures were indeed implemented, and that an increase of vocal matching responses was associated with them.

Even though a component analysis would be necessary to indicate which specific procedure was accounting for the change in infant matching behavior, the effectiveness of the strategies used here has already been demonstrated in other investigations. The positive effects of the mother's repetition of her infant's vocalizations corroborate the results of a series of studies that have indicated that being imitated can greatly increase the probability of subsequent imitation by the child (Fouts, Waldner, & Watson, 1976; Hallahan, Kauffman, Kneedler, Snell, & Richards, 1977; Kauffman, Snell & Hallahan, 1976; Parton & Priefert, 1975).

The effectiveness of making access to food or toys contingent upon an infant vocal request in order to increase the frequency of such responses is consistent with the results of numerous investigations using incidental teaching procedures to teach functional language (Almeida, Nunes, Shores, & Warren, 1985; Warren & Kaiser, 1986; Warren & Rogers-Warren, 1985). The common element of studies on incidental teaching is that the children have to use language as a mediator to obtain something they want.

The effects of vocal modeling episodes presented according to the five dimensions described here (short duration, face contact, time for response, prompt, and praise) may have some support in a study conducted by Nunes (1985), in which the increase of motor models presented appropriately (i.e. according to these dimensions) was associated with an increase of infant matching responses.

In spite of the limitations of the research design used in the present study, the data suggest some strategies that parents could use to evoke vocal imitation in their infants. A replication of this study using a multiple baseline design across mother-infant dyads would provide more consistent data.

Considering that vocal imitation constitutes an important skill for language development (Bricker & Dennison, 1978), and that low SES infants who show a slower development of this skill may be at risk for language delay, the need for experimental, data-based studies to develop effective clinical infant interventions seems clear. It is hoped that the present investigation will aid in this.

References

ALMEIDA, M.A., Nunes, L.R., Shores, R., & Warren, S. (1985). *Adolescent tutors as language mediators for young language-delayed children*. Paper presented at the 11th Annual Convention of Association for Behavior Analysis. Columbus, Ohio.

BAER, D.M., Peterson, R.F., & Sherman, J.A. (1967). The development of imitation by reinforcing behavioral similarity to a model. *Journal of Experimental Analysis of Behavior, 10*, 405-416.

BAER, D.M., & Sherman, J.A. (1964). Reinforcement control of generalized imitation in young children. *Journal of Experimental Child Psychology, 1*, 37-49.

BAER, D.M., Wolf, M.M., & Risley, T.R. (1968). Some current dimensions of applied behavior analysis. *Journal of Applied Behavior Analysis, 1*, 91-97.

BRICKER, D. & Dennison, L. (1978). Training prerequisites to verbal behavior. In M.E. Snell (Ed.), *Systematic instruction of the moderately and severely handicapped children*. Baltimore: University Park Press.

FOUTS, G.T., Waldner, D.N., & Watson, M.W. (1976). Effects of being imitated and counterimitated on the behavior of preschool children. *Child Development, 47*, 172-177.

HALLAHAN, D.P., Kauffman, J.M., Kneedler, R.D., Snell, M.E., & Richards, H.C. (1977). Being imitated by an adult and the subsequent imitative behavior of retarded children. *American Journal of Mental Deficiency, 81*, 556-560.

HAUGHAN, G.M. & McIntire, R. (1972). Comparisons of vocal imitation, tactic stimulation, and food as reinforcers for infant vocalizations. *Developmental Psychology, 6*, 210-209.

HERSEN, M. & Barlow, D.H. (1977). *Single case experimental designs: Strategies for studying behavior changes*. New York: Pergamon.

HURSH, D.E. & Sherman, J.A. (1973). The effects of parent-presented models and praise on the vocal behavior of their children. *Journal of Experimental Child Psychology, 15*, 328-339.

JONES, S.J. & Moss, H.A. (1971). Age, state, and maternal behavior associated with infant vocalizations. *Child Development, 42,* 1039-1051.

KAUFFMAN, J.M., Snell, M.E., & Hallahan, D.P. (1976). Imitating children during imitation training: two experimental paradigms. *Education and Training of the Mentally Retarded, 11,* 324-332.

LOVAAS, O.I. (1977). *The autistic child: Language development through behavior modification.* New York: Irvington Publishers.

LOVAAS, O.I., Berberich, D.P., Perloff, B.F., & Schaeffer, B (1966). Acquisition of imitative speech by schizophrenic children. *Science, 151,* 705-707.

NUNES, L.R.P. (1985). Training teenage mothers to evoke imitation from their at-risk infants: an experimental analysis. Ph.D. Dissertation, Vanderbilt University, Nashville, TN.

PARASKEVOPOULOS, J. & Hunt, J. McV. (1971). Object construction and imitation under differing conditions of rearing. *Journal of Genetic Psychology, 119,* 301-321.

PARTON, D.A. & Priefert, M.J. (1975). The value of being imitated. *Journal of Experimental Child Psychology, 20,* 286-295.

POULSON, C.L. (1983). D.R.O. as a control procedure in the conditioning of infant vocalization rate. *Journal of Experimental Child Psychology, 36,* 471-489.

POULSON, C.L. (1984). Operant theory and methodology in infant vocal conditioning. *Journal of Experimental Child Psychology, 38,* 103-113.

POULSON, C.L. (in press). Operant conditioning of vocalization rate in Down's Syndrome. *American Journal of Mental Deficiency.*

POULSON, C.L., Nunes, L.R.P., Daurelle, L.A., & Stiles, R. (1986). *Experimental analysis of vocal imitation in normal infants.* Paper presented at the XVI Reunião Anual de Psicologia. Sociedade de Psicologia de Ribeirão Preto, São Paulo, Brazil.

RAMEY, C.T. & Ourth, L. (1971). Delayed reinforcement and vocalizations rates of infants. *Child Development, 42,* 291-297.

RHEINGOLD, H., Gewirtz, J.L., & Ross, H.W. (1959). Social conditioning of vocalizations in the infant. *Journal of Comparative & Physiological Psychology, 52,* 68-73.

SHEPPARD, W.C. (1969). Operant control of infant vocal and motor behavior. *Journal of Experimental Child Psychology, 7,* 36-51.

SHERMAN, J.A. (1965). Use of reinforcement and imitation to reinstate verbal behavior in mute psychotics. *Journal of Abnormal Psychology, 70,* 155-164.

TODD, G.A. & Palmer, B. (1968). Social reinforcement of infant babbling. *Child Development, 39,* 591-596.

TULKIN, S.R. & Kagan, J. (1972). Mother-child interaction in the first year of life. *Child Development, 43,* 31-41.

WACHS, T.D., Uzgiris, I.C., & Hunt, J. McV. (1971). Cognitive development in infants of different age levels and from different environmental backgrounds: An exploratory investigation. *Merrill-Palmer Quarterly, 17,* 283-317.

WAHLER, R.G. (1969). Infant social development: Some experimental analyses of an infant-mother interaction during the first year of life. *Journal of Experimental Child Psychology, 7,* 101-113.

WARREN, S.F. & Kaiser, A.P. (1986). Incidental language teaching: a critical review. *Journal of Speech and Hearing Disorders, 51,* 291-299.

WARREN, S.F. & Rogers-Warren, A.K. (Eds.) (1985). *Teaching functional language.* Austin, Texas: Pro-Ed.

WIEGERINK, R., Harris, C., Simeonsson, R., & Pearson, M. (1974). Social stimulation of vocalizations in delayed infants: Familiar and novel agent. *Child Development, 45,* 866-872.

WEISBERG, P. (1963). Social and nonsocial conditioning of infant vocalizations. *Child Development, 34,* 377-388.

Medical Psychotherapy
1988, Volume 1, pp. 161-172

© 1988 by
Hans Huber Publishers, Toronto

The Emotional Distress of the Artificial Insemination Patient

ALINE P. ZOLDBROD, Ph.D.
Private Practice

In approximately 40% of cases of couple infertility, the problems are due to the male partner. In such cases, couples may choose to try to achieve pregnancy by artificial insemination, either by husband (AIH) or by donor (AID). While much research exists on the psychology of infertility, little is written specifically about the experience of women who are inseminated, because of their concern with secrecy and confidentiality. This article describes the feelings of nine AI recipients. Although artificial insemination is a simple procedure technically, aspects of it are humiliating. In this study, it was found that in some cases, patients were not adequately prepared, and the mechanics of AI in a medical setting proved much more disturbing than they expected. The author's results agreed with those of prior investigators exploring the feelings of patients receiving other medical treatment for infertility: AI patients experienced a loss of libido, and felt a sense of loss of control over their lives and their bodies. In addition, new findings on the specific stresses of having artificial insemination emerged from this study: (1) patients felt shame at having medical personnel present at a "sex act"; (2) it was difficult to coordinate all the participants; (3) some patients experienced pain during insemination; and (4) feelings of stress and depression increased as the number of AI attempts increased. Implications of the findings for improvements in medical and psychological treatment of AI recipients are discussed.

Introduction

Despite the fact that every year thousands of couples choose to have a baby by artificial insemination, either by husband (AIH) or by donor (AID) (Curie-Cohen, Luttrell & Shapiro, 1978), there is no literature describing what the experience of insemination

Inquiries or reprint requests should be directed to Aline P. Zoldbrod, 293 Marrett Road, Lexington, MA 02173.

is like for the woman undergoing it, because of concerns about secrecy and confidentiality. For many women, however, the procedure causes emotional distress. While all illnesses and assaults upon one's body are experienced to one degree or another as narcissistic injuries, probably in no other condition is this experience more true than in infertility. Unfortunately, the mechanics of infertility treatment in a medical setting sometimes add insult to injury.

Subjects

This paper reports a case study of the emotional responses of nine women, aged 27 to 38, who underwent artificial insemination, two by their husbands and seven by donors – with mixed success. They vary from a 31-year-old woman who got pregnant after one insemination to a 36-year-old woman who has been trying AID for seven years! The couples' annual incomes ranged from $17,000 to $57,000. They came from settings both urban and rural, and they represented most regions in the United States.

These subjects are a sub-sample of all people responding to the researcher's "request for contact" in the national and local newsletters of RESOLVE,[1] the nation's largest support and advocacy self-help group for infertile people. The researcher asked RESOLVE members to write down "critical incidents" (positive and negative) they experienced in pursuing medical treatment for infertility. Because most people do not contact RESOLVE until they are already experiencing quite a bit of distress over their infertility, the research design probably makes for over-reporting of negative critical incidents. But given the paucity of information on patients' responses to AI, the data are worth reporting.

Review of the Literature

Much excellent research on the psychology of infertility in general can be found in the professional literature. But unlike some other medical or physical problems, infertility is a major life crisis. This is so because people who want to have children automatically assume that they are fertile. According to the Group for the Advancement of Psychiatry (1973, p. 83):

> A study has shown that children take it for granted that they will be fertile. So do most adults, until they find out differently. To change an image of oneself from a person who is fertile to that of one who is not is a painful process. Self-doubt has to be faced about the functioning of one's body...along with a feeling of shame and guilt. Such experiences tend to lower one's self-esteem, which is the biggest hazard of the ordeal.

---

1 The "request" appeared in the April, 1982, national RESOLVE Newsletter (Arlington, Massachusetts: RESOLVE, Incorporated). Subsequently, in early 1983, a longer version was published in many of the chapter newsletters. A "critical incident" was defined as "any interaction or treatment which stands out in your mind as especially helpful or hurtful to your mental or physical health, or, in your estimation, led to especially good or bad feelings about your overall treatment." People were invited to send in as many incidents as they wished.

Along with the assault to one's self-esteem, probably the single most important and common symptom of infertility is depression. Taymor and Bresnick (1979) report that this depression is frequently accompanied by feelings of anxiety, frustration, guilt, isolation, and obsession.

Feelings of anger are also common. Menning (1977) has written eloquently of the infertile couple's angry questioning of "why me?" and their subsequent attempt to figure out their "unknown sin" (was it someone's prior sexual indiscretions, fantasies, career ambitions, smoking or drugs?). Not surprisingly, many researchers have found that infertility impacts on marriage in a particularly negative way (Mazor, 1979; Menning, 1977; Walker, 1978). Even in situations where couples support and do not blame each other, the sexual act can become tinged with sadness because of the inability to procreate. During the infertility work-up, most people experience a temporary decrease in sexual desire or capacity, particularly when couples know that their "performance" will come under medical evaluation. (Menning, 1977, describes how infertile couples often fall into a pattern of fighting and sexual avoidance during the fertile period as long as their infertility persists.)

Several other negative concomitants of infertility have been documented in the literature. Mazor (1979) reports that couples lessen their involvement with their family networks because of intrusive questions as to when they will finally have a child, or because of the pain of repeatedly seeing siblings or cousins effortlessly give birth. Infertility also may have a bad effect on either or both of the partner's careers. The sheer energy needed to deal emotionally with an infertility crisis drains off the emotional investment necessary for career advancement. Major decisions as to whether to take promotions or transfers may be made on the basis of a reluctance by the couple to leave their infertility specialist or clinic. Because it is most often the woman who will be the caretaker when the baby does arrive, frequently it is her life that is put, seemingly forever, "on hold." Because she is hoping to become pregnant soon, she cannot in good faith start a new job, accept a promotion, or go back to school. One last important effect of infertility on the patient's life is the pervading sense of loss of control documented by Cooper (1979). She studied infertile women and found that her subjects perceived the locus of control over their lives as being external to a significantly greater extent than was the norm. Cooper also found that the longer a woman had been infertile, the less likely she was to feel in control of her life. These findings, in particular, have relevance for women undergoing artificial insemination.

The Literature on Artificial Insemination

While there is a lot written on the unresolved legal and ethical questions surrounding artificial insemination by donor (Simons, 1984), Barbara Menning, the founder of RESOLVE, is the rare professional who writes about the psychosocial issues of husband and donor insemination from the viewpoint of the couple and/or patient. Menning (1981) reports a number of problems experienced by AI patients: (1) she notes the fact that love-making during the time of seeking help can be sad, tentative, or loaded with feelings of doubt and guilt; (2) she describes the tremendous pain at the loss of continuity of the husband's genetic heritage; and (3) she describes how the couples using AID are very concerned about confidentiality. (The whole process of AID is especially secretive because most couples want the child's biological paternity to remain a secret. Keeping the secret, however, breeds even more emotional isolation than is usual in a couple coping with infertility.) We will find that several of Menning's findings are replicated in this study.

Artificial Insemination: Background Information

Artificial insemination by donor usually is chosen by couples because of total azoospermia, abnormal sperm, or because the husband has too low a sperm count. In some cases, it may be chosen because the husband's child would be at risk for a genetic disease such as hemophilia or Tay-Sachs. And it is sometimes used when the husband has previously had a vasectomy. Artificial insemination by husband is used for reasons such as an inability to deposit a normal semen specimen in the proper place, retrograde emission, or compromised motility.

The actual process of artificial insemination is very simple. However, since the patient is usually healthy, physicians and nurses often do not discuss the emotional strains of the procedure with her. In order to understand this emotional distress, one must remember that by the time women have begun artificial insemination, the majority of them are vulnerable and upset. They have just come through a long process of trying to become pregnant and the anxiety of wondering what is wrong. Although the husband's sperm count (a totally non-invasive procedure) should be obtained in the early stages of a medical work-up for infertility, at times this is not done. In addition, some of the women have fertility problems of their own,[2] so many of them have already been subjected to some painful, invasive medical tests. In summary, even before the inseminations had begun, the subjects of this report had the sense that their lives were out of control; they had, perhaps, experienced some painful medical interventions; and they were anxious and were probably depressed.

The Emotional Distress of Artificial Insemination Patients: Findings on Negative Incidents

Confidentiality

Patients were extremely distressed by breaches of confidentiality. At times, the medical personnel's insensitivity to their feelings was quite shocking to the researcher. One subject who had had AID reported that she was most chagrined when the urologist treating her husband came out to the waiting room and informed her, in front of the other patients, that her husband's sample showed no sperm and that he had to schedule a testicular biopsy. An AIH patient reported the following incident (of course, all names used here are fictitious):

---

2 For instance, here is what one respondent wrote as "type of infertility problem":
- diagnosis of sperm penetration problem by hamster test
- wife's chromosomal defect
- wife's luteal phase defect
- sperm antibodies in cervical mucus

> We were scheduled to come in to the clinic on a Monday and Wednesday. When we got to the reception desk on Monday, we were informed that Dr._____'s regular day off was now Monday, and that we couldn't possibly have an appointment. I explained that we were there for AIH and asked if the doctor had perhaps made other arrangements for another clinic doctor to take us that day. The receptionist proceeded to call out in a *loud* (her emphasis) voice to several other nurses standing around the clinic (and with many other patients in hearing distance), "Does anyone know anything about Dr.____'s artificial insemination patient, Janice White???" She called this out several times, always using my name and the terms "artificial insemination". We had several acquaintances going to the same clinic and the fact that we were trying AIH was something that was only known by a few close family members. We both wished we could sink through the floor and disappear. After calling our doctor's nurse the next day, she apologized and said the scheduling error had been made by her. The receptionist was reprimanded and our next appointment was given to us without cost. That was fine but did nothing to relieve the humiliation and pain we'd been through. . . .

Loss of Libido and Sexual Pleasure

As Menning previously reported, several subjects found their enjoyment of the sex act was severely inhibited. One Catholic respondent reported a loss of interest in sex because her knowledge that they weren't fertile made sex not permissible:

> Any interest or desire for sex which has been lost by us began well at the beginning of the infertility work-ups. This is due to the general feeling of "Why bother? It is not going to produce anything, anyway." I guess when you're a Roman Catholic, and so much about when sex is permissible and when it isn't is poured into you, it becomes difficult to tailor the "rules" to your own situation. You're rather reluctant to give yourself a break and make what you're doing OK in your own conscience.

Another AID patient told of an even more poignant example:

> . . . . Bill and I were on the beach, necking and petting. I got very turned on, so then we had to move to a place down the road, so we wouldn't be seen. By the time we actually made love a few minutes later, I wasn't turned on. My head was full of images of speculums and metal stirrups. . . . Sometimes I ask myself, is a kid worth this???

Loss of Control

All of the subjects reported feeling out of control of their lives in one way or another. Most of the time this problem was tied to reports of difficulties and errors in scheduling and to having to wait, wait, wait . . .

. . . . My doctor happened to be out of the office that day and he did arrange for another nurse to inseminate me. After my husband produced the semen, I waited for the nurse to come and do the insemination. After waiting half an hour, she finally arrived with an apology. She had forgotten that I was waiting. By the time that she did the insemination, the office was closing and there was no time for me to lie with my legs elevated for the required half hour. I went home feeling that the whole visit had been a waste.

Scheduling Difficulties

It seems that scheduling issues are extremely common during artificial insemination, since the whereabouts and activities of a number of independent human beings must be coordinated. An AIH patient relayed the following incident:

> Because of our jobs, my husband and I could not come in for the standard 9 A.M. appointments. Scheduling of medication and appointment times was a hassle right from the start. Although my doctor was part of a clinic, he wanted to have his staff do the insemination, and that meant working appointments around his day off and Sunday. As we needed to come in one day for the insemination, skip a day, and then come back the next for the second insemination, we had to be sure that the Clomid was started on the correct day. . . .

She went on to say:

> It's hard to describe how difficult the scheduling problems became. I was a school teacher at the time and my school was 35 miles from the doctor's office. Of course, I couldn't be gone mornings every month for 9 A.M. artificial insemination appointments. Also, my husband was working many miles from the office and never sure exactly what time he could get away. Both bosses had to be told a little of what was going on. . . . Neither of us enjoyed always asking permission to leave early. Fortunately, both bosses were very understanding of the situation.

Another AIH patient stated:

> Of course, time-wise, you are really inconvenienced. You have to juggle both your working hours around the doctor's schedule. You have to produce sperm without any feelings or sexual desire and pleasure. All this and the running around was exhausting and nerve-racking, not to mention unfulfilling.

One AID subject went to an excellent clinic in a large metropolitan area. The clinic used only fresh sperm. She always ovulated on weekends; however, her donor used to like to take weekends off and go out of town. Consequently, the insemination would often end up being done on Fridays or Mondays, not her most fertile time, since the first insemination was too early and the second too late. Of course, she always knew two weeks ahead of time when the insemination would need to be scheduled, given the timing of her last menstrual period. So for the second half of each month, she had to wait on tenterhooks to talk to the nurse, who would let her know "at the last minute" if she could be inseminated during her most fertile time (on the weekend), or whether her donor would be out of town!

Control Struggles and Scheduling

For women who liked to feel a sense of control over their bodies and over the process, the fact that the physician chose the insemination dates sometimes caused problems.[3] Methods of scheduling with physicians and clinics varied. In several cases, the women had to write to their physician, sending him or her their temperature charts from the preceding month. The physician would then write back, scheduling the appointments for the days he or she thought were correct and at the hours that were necessary according to the physician's schedule.

Some clinics did not offer service on weekends, which left some patients feeling that the inseminations were not happening on the right day. This pattern became more frustrating as the months went on without successful conception.

Scheduling difficulties also happened around holidays and doctors' days off. This led to obsessive concern with when one's next period might start. For instance, as one woman began to experience what she felt was pre-menstrual cramping, she began to look frantically in her calendar, hoping that her fertile days would not fall on a weekend or an upcoming holiday.

In one case, a professional woman who began insemination in her late 30s did not ovulate regularly. She was put on medication to make her more regular. In addition, she spent a lot of energy learning about the reproductive process and using imagery to try to regulate her ovulation. Her physician's policy was that she would send him her temperature charts, and then he would decide when to inseminate her. During one appointment, he looked at her mucus specimen and said that he did not feel that she was close to ovulation. She insisted that he inseminate her that day, for she felt that she was going to ovulate soon. Her physician, exasperated, said, "And what makes you think you're so damn fertile, anyway?"

Feelings of Shame and Humiliation During the Treatment

Several of the women felt ashamed and embarrassed by having to have strangers present at the "sex act." Here is what one patient had to say:

> The clinic where I am going for artificial insemination has a large nursing staff, who rotate their duties frequently, so that I have been inseminated, examined, injected, weighed, questioned, and poked at by at least a dozen different people besides my doctor. The nurse is often present when I am undressing or when the doctor is examining me. I feel that my privacy has been violated. There are just so many people involved

---

3 To make scheduling even more difficult, one study (Kohane, 1968) reported delayed ovulation in about 10-15% of donor-inseminated women, presumably due to the stress of the procedure.

> in my care. As our hopes dwindle, it is hard for me to maintain any equilibrium when I go to the doctor's office, and having to deal with a succession of strangers is difficult for me.

One patient said, much more descriptively, and angrily:

> I am just sick of spreading my legs. . . . When this process began, I just never dreamed I would have to spread my legs so many times for so many strangers.

Physical Pain During Insemination

Three women reported feeling pain during the insemination procedure. One AIH patient said:

> Artificial insemination not only takes all the emotional contact out of a couple and makes it very cold and regimental, but it is painful during the procedure and after.

Another woman said:

> The doctor did explain the physical procedure that would be performed, but did not mention that there would be cramping and other discomfort.

Another said:

> I guess I must have been really tight, because every time they put the speculum in, it hurt.

Increasing Stress with the Number of Inseminations

Cooper's (1979) findings on the relationship between the length of time a patient is infertile and the increasing sense of loss of control have particular relevance for artificial insemination patients. It seemed that the longer patients underwent the procedure with no resulting pregnancy, the more distressed they became. Most physicians tell women that they will become pregnant in from two to five menstrual cycles. This is apparently such common medical knowledge that these figures are even cited by Menning (1981) in her article on AID, where she states, "According to statistics, about 80% to 85% will achieve pregnancy, and it will take an average of five cycles for conception to occur."

Patients given this information expect pregnancy quickly. Three of the study participants mentioned getting pregnancy tests monthly after every insemination. Each sign and symptom was interpreted as a sign of pregnancy. Yet some women take much longer to get pregnant by insemination, and such patients would do better if they were told that not everyone conceives speedily. Here is what a patient said after many months of AID:

> I have had seven months with no pregnancy. I am going to adoption agencies now. I am not waiting. I went through all of this when we found out Sam's sperm count. I went through all of the sadness with him, and the waiting for him to be ready to have a kid. I thought it would happen right away. I thought I was pregnant and I had a test. Now it has been going on forever and ever, and I want to stop, and Sam wants to know, am I giving up already??

Another patient could barely stand the stress of four inseminations with her husband's sperm before she gave up:

> .... This critical incident occurred at our third insemination. It was a month after this incident that we decided to discontinue AIH. We actually went out to supper to celebrate the end of it. It seemed rather ironic to celebrate the ending of our last hope, but it had just been too trying emotionally....

Even the medical personnel seemed impatient. An AID patient in her thirties reported that after her fifth insemination was unsuccessful, the nurse commented to her, "I just can't *imagine* whatever is wrong with you!" This woman eventually became pregnant, but not until inseminations had gone on for over a year. She reported, "The nurse's lack of confidence that I would get pregnant made me feel defective, somehow. It disheartened me." It is probably no coincidence that the two artificial insemination patients who wrote in with mostly good things to say had gotten pregnant within the first two tries. In both cases, they wrote to submit positive critical incidents about physicians who went out of their way to time the inseminations to be done on the women's most fertile days. Nevertheless, as more women postpone getting pregnant, the population undergoing AI will grow older. Research shows that as women age, it takes them more menstrual cycles to conceive (Schwartz & Mayaux, 1982). Thus, one important finding of this study is to caution physicians not to encourage patients' expectations for a quick pregnancy. Some women may need to endure months and months of trying before they are rewarded with a pregnancy.[4]

Implications for Improved Medical and Psychological Treatment

Even though artificial insemination is technically a simple process, the women in this exploratory study reported quite a bit of emotional pain while undergoing it. While some of the stress appears to be inherent in the process of having infertility treated at all (e.g., general sense of loss of control, or loss of enjoyment in sex) the process of AI does seem to present its own special stresses. Some of these include special difficulties in coordinating all the participants; the experience of being humiliated by having so many strangers present during a "sex act;" control issues over timing the insemination; pain during the actual process; and increasing feelings of stress and depression as the number of cycles of inseminations increases.

---

4 With the possibility of contracting AIDS from artificial insemination, it becomes safer to use frozen sperm, which can be more thoroughly tested. There is some, albeit conflicting evidence that using frozen sperm may increase the number of cycles of insemination necessary to achieve pregnancy.

Patients who wrote in with either positive or negative critical incidents all had the same messages to give to the medical personnel with whom they were working. They desperately want their confidentiality to be respected. Although the process of AI is routine to the treatment team, it can be a terrible, humiliating ordeal to the patients. They want to be helped to feel respected and in control of their lives. As one positive respondent said:

> The doctor has shown respect for my need to have an intellectual grasp of the infertility problems which plague us. He has suggested books and resources and has spent time with diagrams to help us understand. Both of the doctors we have dealt with in . . . have treated us with respect.

Another patient wrote in happily reporting how her physician had let her choose the dates for insemination each month, rather than controlling the timing himself. Several of the subjects talked about wanting to "feel a part of the treatment team." Patients are eternally grateful to physicians who sensitively explain the emotional as well as the technical aspects of AI to them before proceeding. As one patient cited:

> The doctor was completely understanding and considerate when he first approached us with the whole thing, that we might have some religious or moral restriction to deal with (and we did) . . .

Another subject stated:

> Thankfully, our doctor warned us that it would be an emotionally trying experience, or the whole ordeal might have been even harder than it was.

Women should be told in a calm way that occasionally an artificial insemination may cause feelings of cramping; and patients need empathy when their hopes of pregnancy for the month are dashed. Then they need encouragement to go on, to be patient, if the physician still feels that there is a reasonable chance of conception. Older women, especially, need to be told to be patient. Finally, a large number of positive critical incidents cited had to do with physicians and nurses who went out of their way to schedule inseminations when the woman was most fertile, not just when it was the most convenient for themselves.

There are two important points to be made about psychological treatment. First of all, having a support group of other infertile people was cited as a major source of strength by several respondents. One woman suggested that physicians who deal with infertile couples immediately refer them to RESOLVE, not just after the patients are already angry or in crisis:

> I suspect that it often takes a blowup or tears before a doctor or nurse refers a patient to RESOLVE for support. Since it seems typical of infertiles to sit on such feelings for months or years, believing that "this month, we'll have a happy ending," I wish that RESOLVE were mentioned routinely on the first visit.

One patient used humor in talking about RESOLVE as an outlet:

> .... Several months after this interaction, we joined a RESOLVE support group, which restored my sense of proportion and humor.... I had years of pent-up bitterness and anger and self-pity to unload, as well as a shattered self-image to rebuild. The group served us well as a dumping ground and workshop. We learned to talk about our problems without tearful scenes – just as mildew was beginning to form on my husband's shoulders!

Mental health professionals should educate their colleagues that a self-help group for infertile patients exists.

Second, as more researchers study infertility, evidence mounts that the routine provision of psychological counseling along with medical treatment is extremely helpful, and that patients who participate in counseling are better able to persevere with infertility work-ups and treatment (Rosenfeld & Mitchell, 1979). The provision of individual psychotherapy may be especially important with artificial insemination patients, because of their concerns about confidentiality. (Even in RESOLVE chapters, groups of artificial insemination patients are relatively rare. Many artificial insemination patients prefer to get their support through totally confidential phone calls where the parties do not even know each other's last names.) To this end, professionals in the field of infertility should educate themselves to the special psychological risks to patients undergoing artificial insemination as treatment for infertility.

ACKNOWLEDGEMENTS. This paper was originally presented to the 1987 conference of the American Board of Medical Psychotherapy, Cancun, Mexico, May 8, 1987.
The author is grateful to the members of RESOLVE, Incorporated, who contributed their time and their experiences to this research.
The author is a psychologist in private practice and a member of the National Board of Directors, RESOLVE, Incorporated.

References

COOPER, S. (1979). *Female infertility: Its effect on self esteem, body image, locus of control, and behavior.* Boston: Boston University School of Education. Doctoral dissertation. Available through University Microfilms, order number 8005241.

CURIE-COHEN, M., Luttrell, L., & Shapiro, S. (1978). Current practice of artificial insemination by donor in the United States. *New England Journal of Medicine, 300*, 585-590.

GROUP FOR THE ADVANCEMENT OF PSYCHIATRY (1973). *The joys and sorrows of parenthood.* New York: Charles Scribner and Sons.

KOHANE, E. Therapeutic effects of emotionally caused delayed ovulation. Paper presented at the 6th World Congress on Fertility and Sterility, Tel Aviv, Israel, May 26-28, 1968.

MAZOR, M. (1979). Barren couples. *Psychology Today, 101*, 101-112.

MENNING, B. (1977). *Infertility: A guide for the childless couple.* New Jersey: Prentice-Hall.

MENNING, B. (1981). Donor insemination: the psychosocial issues. *Contemporary Obstetrics/Gynecology, 10*, 155-172.
ROSENFELD, D. & Mitchell, M. (1979). Treating the emotional aspects of infertility: counseling services in an infertility clinic. *American Journal of Obstetrics and Gynecology, 35*, 177-180.
SCHWARTZ, D. & Mayaux, M. (1982). Female fecundity as a function of age: results of artificial insemination in 2193 nulliparous women with azoospermic husbands. *New England Journal of Medicine, 306*, 404-406.
SIMONS, H. (1984). Infertility: Implications for policy formulation. In M. Mazor & H. Simons (Eds.), *Infertility: medical, emotional, and social considerations* (pp. 61-70). New York: Human Sciences Press.
TAYMOR, M. & Bresnick, E. (1979). Emotional stress and infertility. *Infertility, 2*, 39-47.
WALKER, H. (1978). Sexual problems and infertility. *Psychosomatics, 19*, 477-79 and 483-84.

Medical Psychotherapy
1988, Volume 1, pp. 173-180

© 1988 by
Hans Huber Publishers, Toronto

Professional Regulation in the U.S.: Task Force on Issues and Problems in Current Credentialing Practices

KENNETH N. ANCHOR
DEBORAH A. ABRAHAM
Vanderbilt University

Introduction

One of the major challenges facing mental health professionals in the 1980s and beyond is how to establish and maintain a meaningful system of credentialing. The current system for training practitioners, and licensing or certifying them to recognize competence and protect the public, is in a state of disarray. At present, professionals from such diverse educational and theoretical backgrounds as nursing, psychiatry, psychology, social work, and marital, family, and child counseling are all competing for independent recognition as providers of psychological services. Each discipline has its own system of credentialing, and few agree on the necessary requirements for demonstration of competency. Even within the various professions, credentialing requirements vary from state to state. This creates confusion in efforts to identify those who are, in fact, qualified to provide psychological services – a task that has become increasingly important due to recent concerns about the cost and quality of many health-related services.

Although the American Board of Medical Psychotherapy was established in 1982 to meet this need, much work remains to be done. Over the past few years, considerable concern has been expressed about professional regulation in general (Rose, 1983). Consumers and advocates are beginning to challenge the presumptive right of professions to decide alone the scope, manner, staffing, and site of service delivery. Evidence of the growing dissatisfaction with the cost and quality of many professional services can be found in the dramatic increase in the number of malpractice suits against physicians, psychiatrists, psychologists, and other professionals, and in new demands

Inquiries or reprint requests should be directed to Kenneth N. Anchor, Box 512 G.P.C., Vanderbilt University, Nashville, TN. 37203 for public participation in the activities of regulatory boards (Hogan, 1983). The charge is that professional regulation has been ineffective in assuring the public protection from the actions of incompetent, unethical, negligent, or dishonest practitioners. Rather, the critics argue that it has served to increase the cost of services, create shortages in the supply of these services, and discourage innovation in training and practice (Carroll & Gaston, 1983; Dorsey, 1983; Gross, 1978; Rayack, 1983; Trebilcock & Shaul, 1983).

As a result of the recent emphasis on professional accountability and quality assurance, practitioners can expect their services and credentials to be scrutinized by a number of parties, including the direct users of services, insurance carriers, peer review organizations, and government agencies. It is likely that where these services are found to be lacking in terms of serving the public interest or effective self-regulation, increased external control will be imposed.

Zemlick (1980) has pointed out that the best way to reduce the weight of review from those outside a profession is to increase credibility, visibility, and effectiveness of self-regulation within it. In pursuit of this goal, this article will explore some of the issues and problems in current credentialing practices, and recommend constructive remedies.

Current Credentialing Practices

Credentialing is a broad generic term that may be defined as the formal recognition of professional or technical competence. When applied to the mental health field, credentialing takes five basic forms: a) association membership, b) accreditation of educational/training programs, c) certification by a non-governmental agency or organization, d) licensure by an agency of government, and e) registration or listing on an official roster of credentialed personnel.

As these definitions attest, the five forms of credentials are intimately related. In many states and in many occupations, the award of a license is at least partially dependent on the individual having attended an accredited program of study. This is also true of certification and registration, the latter of which is based solely on evidence that other credentials (i.e., a certificate of license) have been attained. This interlocking system of control grew naturally from the philosophy that only members of a profession are competent to judge fellow members, and that only in this manner can the public be provided protection from harm. Whereas a *caveat emptor* attitude ("let the buyer beware") exists in most commercial enterprises, society expects more from members of a human service profession. Specifically, it expects members of such professions to be knowledgeable and trustworthy, to effectively regulate themselves, and to balance self-interests with the interests of the public at large.

Credentials accomplish the goal of protecting the public by providing the consumer with information as to the qualifications of service providers. That is, they are designed to assure the consumer that the practitioner has met certain entry level standards of competence as determined by his or her profession. Also, because credentialing involves the establishment of standards of practice and disciplinary procedures to make sure that practitioners abide by these standards, they provide a degree of quality assurance.

Although protection of the public is usually cited as the paramount rationale for credentialing, it does not account fully for the interest that so many professions have shown in developing a system of credentialing. (Wiens and Dorken, 1986, for example, estimate that more than 500 occupations are licensed at present and even more offer voluntary certification programs.) Rather, credentials are intrinsically linked to social and economic rewards in our society. Establishing a system of credentialing within a profession enhances the prestige of the field, increases an association's influence over its members and the public in general, and promotes the economic well-being of its members by limiting competition.

A number of problems in current credentialing practices can be identified that suggest that credentialing has not been as successful as intended in accomplishing its primary goal — that of public protection. These include problems in measuring competence, ensuring continued competence, and enforcing ethical practice. Each has important implications for the future of professional regulation and must be addressed.

Measuring Competence

As noted above, the main goal of professional regulation is to assure that those persons engaging in a given profession are, in fact, competent practitioners. In pursuit of this goal, boards require applicants to meet certain educational standards, to have a certain amount of experience, to complete written and/or oral examinations, and to fulfill various other requirements such as citizenship and residency. These requirements are based on the assumption that they are necessary for the competent practice of the profession. Unfortunately, there is little evidence to support this fundamental assumption (Danish & Smyer, 1981; Gross, 1978; Hogan, 1979; Koocher, 1979; Shimberg, 1981). In fact, the evidence that has been provided seems to suggest that advanced degrees, experience, and successful performance on exams make little difference in terms of clinical outcomes (Bernstein & Lecomte, 1981; Durlak, 1979; Hogan, 1983; Strupp & Hadley, 1979).

Although definitions of competence usually refer to some measure of knowledge, skill, and ability, its measurement has remained an elusive goal. Part of this problem is that so many different forms of psychotherapy exist, that defining the domain of practice in terms of essential skills or content areas is a formidable task. Corsini (1981), for example, has defined more than 250 discrete psychotherapeutic systems, each with differing aims, underlying assumptions, treatment foci, and methods for attaining and measuring desired outcomes. Thus, in the absence of more direct definitions of essential skills, boards have come to rely on an imperfect set of indices that are believed to have some relationship to (if not demonstrably predictive of) desired clinical outcomes. However, the validity of these indices as measures of competence is coming under increasing attack, and new, more reliable measures must be developed.

The validity of written examinations, for instance, has become the topic of frequent litigation. Disappointed applicants have challenged this requirement on several grounds, including: a) that exams are irrelevant to professional practice, b) that exams test only a very limited range of professional knowledge and skills, c) that the method of grading is subjective and arbitrary, and d) that cutoff scores bear no relationship to the minimal level of skill required for professional practice (Herbsleb, Sales, & Overcast, 1985). So far, applicants have not met with much success in overturning the decisions of boards on the basis of these arguments, but there is reason to suspect that this situation will change as increased emphasis is placed on quality assurance. Also, there is some evidence that a substantially higher percentage of blacks and older people fail written exams than do whites (in this case, the exam for psychology licensure) (Werner, 1980). Thus, there may be some basis for challenging written exams on the grounds that they discriminate on the basis of race and age, especially since there is no direct evidence that exams are positively correlated with competence.

Educational requirements have met with similar opposition. Bernstein and Lecomte (1981) argue that requirements for a doctorate or for graduation from an accredited program are indefensible in the absence of data showing that these requirements have any relationship to client outcome. Again, the courts have held that such requirements are constitutional, but only to the extent that they "bear a direct, substantial, and reasonable relationship" to professional practice (Oliver v. Commonwealth, 1979, p. 1387). As Herbsleb et al. (1985) have pointed out, the language used by the courts indicates that the issue has not been resolved with any degree of finality. To the extent that it can be shown that a substantial number of master's level service providers are as competent as doctoral level providers, the courts are likely to reconsider the rationality of this requirement.

The use of oral examinations as a measure of competency has received just as much criticism. Although they require applicants to apply the current body of knowledge and skills of a profession to hypothetical practice situations, and are, therefore, clearly related to practice, problems exist in the way these examinations are typically administered and graded. At the very minimum, a team of graders representing the field should independently evaluate the applicant on a set of predetermined objective criteria, and a written transcript of the questions and answers should be kept. (Recent court decisions have indicated that the fairness of oral exams can be challenged in cases where a single grader is allowed to determine whether a candidate passes or fails a given question, or where boards fail to provide applicants with an opportunity to show that grading is in error or that the exam is irrational – see Herbsleb et al., 1985.) The ideal situation would be to use a procedure in which graders reviewed anonymous transcripts of questions and answers to ensure that discriminatory biases were not operating in the evaluation of a candidate.

The problems associated with measuring competence should be of concern to all of us. Without evidence that requirements of credentials distinguish between qualified and unqualified and competent and incompetent practitioners, the credibility of a profession is damaged. It also becomes difficult to justify our services to consumers and insurance carriers. Moreover, it increases the probability that incompetent, unethical, or dishonest practitioners will be able to gain entrance into a profession, or that qualified ones will be excluded. Clearly, research is needed to identify the specific practitioner characteristics that successfully predict competent performance. It is likely that extending the scope of competency assessment to include "practical exams" (i.e., direct observation) over the range of activities associated with psychotherapy (such as diagnosing, developing treatment plans, testing, and so on) would be beneficial. Requirements for work samples for a credential are another step in this direction.

Continuing Competence

Even if current credentialing practice were effective in screening out unqualified practitioners, they provide no guarantee that a person who is licensed or certified at one point in time will remain a competent practitioner throughout his or her career. Dubin (1972), for example, has estimated that the half-life of a doctoral degree in psychology as a measure of competence is about 10 to 12 years. That is, using the analogy of radioactive decay, about 10 years after the receipt of a doctorate half of the knowledge that went into one's training is obsolete. In fields such as medicine and law the turnover is believed to be even more rapid, due to advances in medical technology and changing legal decisions (Jensen, 1979). Given the rapidity with which knowledge is outmoded and the growing demands for professional accountability, it is essential that boards develop and implement mechanisms to assure the continuing competence of those who hold credentials.

A number of strategies have been advanced to help assure that practitioners remain current. One of the more popular methods is participation in continuing education programs. Many boards presently require documentation of participation in seminars, workshops, or lectures as a condition of license or certification renewal. However, considering all the professions that exist, such provisions are more commonly the exception than the rule. Also, there is a growing recognition that the accumulation of a specified number of continuing education credits through attendance at lectures and seminars does not necessarily ensure that learning has occurred (Stigall, 1983). The 1977 Public Health Service Report on Credentialing acknowledged this problem, and recommended that "Instead of endorsing a single method such as continuing education, which itself is often unvalidated or of questionable relevance to continued competence, PHS urges that additional support be given to the development of more sophisticated approaches to continued competence which ultimately can be tied into a mandatory recertification or relicensure requirement. These approaches may include peer review through Professional Standards Review Organizations, reexamination, self-assessment techniques, and supervisory assessments, as well as continuing education" (U.S. Department of Health, Education, and Welfare, 1977, p. 17).

Efforts are currently underway to implement some of the newer methods in the mental health occupations. The American Psychological Association, for example, is in the process of developing a self-assessment program similar to that used by the American Board of Internal Medicine. As described in articles published in *The Medical Psychotherapist* (official newsletter of ABMP), self-assessment programs allow practitioners to identify knowledge and skill deficits through a series of tests covering various aspects of practice. Feedback is given as to any areas of weakness, and bibliographic references are provided to assist remediation. Although this kind of strategy has its advantages, its weakness lies in the fact that it is voluntary. Until boards require participation in such programs as a condition for relicensure or certificate renewal, it is likely that uneven interest and participation will predominate.

It can be predicted that consumers are eventually going to demand more assurance that practitioners have kept up with developments in their fields, than voluntary professional development procedures can provide. Thus, practitioners can expect to see more boards requiring periodic reassessment as a condition of continued licensure or certification. Medical boards have already begun implementing procedures to this effect, and other boards are likely to follow suit.

As efforts to improve and refine various systems of competency assurance continue, practitioners would be well advised to make a personal commitment to staying current. Professional standards and related legal codes are constantly changing, and awareness of these changes is essential for the competent practice of psychotherapy (and to reduce the risk of malpractice suits). Practitioners should also strive for an awareness of their own limitations in terms of areas of practice and special skills, and seek constructive remedies through both formal and informal means when skills are found lacking. Membership in professional organizations, participation in continuing education programs, reading relevant journals or textbooks in areas of interest, and attendance at scientific meetings are but a few of the means available to keep skills current.

Discipline and Enforcement

A third problem that threatens the future of professional regulation is the inconsistent enforcement of ethical codes and standards of practice by regulatory boards. Recently, a number of writers have severely criticized boards for their poor performance in this area (Hess, 1980; Hogan, 1983; Moore, 1978; Sinnett & Linford, 1982; Zemlick, 1980; Zitrin & Klein, 1976). Hogan (1979) for example, claims that discipline by psychology licensing boards has been "virtually non-existent." He reports that complaints to boards average only one a year for each year that a board has been in existence, and that up until 1972 only five licenses had been revoked. This is ironic, as competency assurance through self-regulation is the major justification for licensure.

Keith-Speigel and Koocher (1986) have summarized some of the specific criticisms leveled at the disciplinary functions of regulatory boards. These include: a) the assessment of "token penalties" that have no real impact, b) conflict of interest or bias among committee members, c) inadequate training and experience of most mental health professionals to function adequately in a quasi-judicial capacity, d) allegations of precedence of protective guild interests and due process rights of respondents over the welfare of complainants, e) extended time frame for adjudicating cases that may result in harm to the public in the interim, f) insufficient investigatory resources to do the job properly, g) timid procedures as a result of fears of lawsuits, and finally, h) reactive rather than proactive procedures.

Many of these criticisms are warranted and deserve immediate attention. Part of the problem is that boards are typically so overworked and underfunded that disciplinary enforcement is difficult except in the most flagrant cases of abuse or misconduct. These offenses, however, are usually already covered by general criminal or civil law. Thus, the disciplinary actions of boards tend to duplicate rather than supplement existing sources of control. Even though the process of investigating complaints, taking testimony, and conducting hearings is expensive and time-consuming, this important function must be performed with more vigor than it has in the past. The level of competency assurance that boards can provide to consumers is directly related to the speed and consistency of disciplinary actions.

Stigall (1983) suggests that efforts should be directed toward educating state legislatures and government officials to the need for providing sufficient resources to support the regulatory and disciplinary functions of boards (e.g., legal counsel and investigatory personnel). He argues that although boards are traditionally funded on the basis of fees paid by candidates and members, there may be justification for funding on the basis of general tax revenues since one of the main functions of boards is to protect the general welfare.

Another way that boards can increase their effectiveness in the area of discipline and enforcement is to define more precisely the boundaries of acceptable therapeutic practice. Ethical codes are often quite vague in terms of specifying what kinds of behaviors constitute incompetent, negligent, or unethical practice. Moreover, they often contain internal inconsistencies that lead to problems when attempts are made to apply them to specific problems. To expedite the enforcement of practice standards, an attempt should be made to develop rules of conduct that describe unacceptable behavior in less ambiguous terms than codes of ethics.

Clear disciplinary guidelines should also be established to ensure uniformity in handling cases. This would reduce the threat of malpractice suits against boards. The Virginia Board of Psychology has developed a set of guidelines along this line, and also distributes summaries of state statutes that relate to professional practice so that its members cannot claim ignorance of relevant laws (Wiens & Dorken, 1986).

Boards must also consider how to facilitate the receipt of consumer complaints. Clients often don't know that complaints can be filed or how to go about doing so. A solution to this problem can be found in recent suggestions that certification and licensure regulations should require "professional disclosure" (Simon, 1983). Professional disclosure requires practitioners to provide clients with a written statement summarizing relevant qualifications and experience, special interests and skills, fee schedules, and how a client can report possible complaints. Adoption of this kind of requirement would do much to reassure the public that psychotherapists are serious about maintaining high standards and are willing to submit themselves for review.

Finally, a mechanism for communication between boards needs to be developed so that incompetent, unethical, or dishonest practitioners can be quickly identified by all relevant credentialing bodies. There have been far too many cases of practitioners being disciplined or having a credential revoked for unacceptable behavior in one state or by one board, yet continuing to practice by simply moving to another state or operating under the auspices of another credential.

Summary and Conclusions

As this discussion has established, credentials do not guarantee adequate performance by every person credentialed. Rather, they reflect the general consensus of members of the profession that the credentialed practitioner has the basic qualifications necessary to deliver services with more consistency than the noncredentialed. Given the difficulty of defining and assessing the necessary requisites for the delivery of such an esoteric service as psychotherapy, credentialing cannot be expected to provide absolute protection to society. However, it has social utility because it increases the likelihood of the delivery of satisfactory services.

It is believed that both consumers and practitioners will ultimately benefit if careful attention is given to the problems described above. One thing is certain – if psychotherapists do not accept responsibility for their own regulation, outside systems of control will be imposed.

References

BERNSTEIN, B.L. & Lecomte, C. (1981). Licensure in psychology: Alternative directions. *Professional Psychology, 12*, 200-208.

CARROLL, S.L. & Gaston, R.J. (1983). Occupational licensing and the quality of service: An overview. *Law and Human Behavior, 7*, 139-146.

CORSINI, R.J. (Ed.) (1981). *Handbook of innovative psychotherapies*. New York: Wiley.

DANISH, S.J. & Smyer, M.A. (1981). Unintended consequences of requiring a license to help. *American Psychologist, 36*, 13-21.

DORSEY, S. (1983). Occupational licensure and minorities. *Law and Human Behavior*, 171-181.

DUBIN, S.S. (1972). Obsolescence or lifelong education: A choice for the professional. *American Psychologist, 27*, 486-496.

DURLAK, J.A. (1979). Comparative effectiveness of paraprofessional and professional helpers. *Psychological Bulletin, 86*, 80-92.

GROSS, S. (1978). The myth of professional licensing. *American Psychologist, 33*, 1009-1016.

HERBSLEB, J.D., Sales, B.D., & Overcast, T.D. (1985). Challenging licensure and certification. *American Psychologist, 40*, 11, 1165-1178.

HESS, H.F. (1980). Enforcement: Procedures, problems and prospects. *Professional Practice of Psychology, 1*, 1-10.

HOGAN, D.B. (1979). *The regulation of psychotherapists*. Cambridge, MA: Ballinger.

HOGAN, D.B. (1983). The effectiveness of licensing: History, evidence, and recommendations. *Law and Human Behavior, 7*, 117-138.

JENSEN, R.E. (1979). Competent professional service in psychology: The real issue behind continuing education. *Professional Psychology, 10*, 381-389.

KEITH-SPEIGEL, P. & Koocher, G.P. (1986). *Ethics in psychology: Professional standards and cases*. Hillsdale, New Jersey: Lawrence Erlbaum Associates.

KOOCHER, G.P. (1979). Credentialing in psychology: Close encounters with competence? *American Psychologist, 34*, 696-702.

MOORE, R.A. (1978). Ethics in the practice of psychiatry: Origins, functions, models, and enforcement. *American Journal of Psychiatry, 135*, 157-163.

OLIVER V. COMMONWEALTH, 404 A2d 1386 (Pa. 1979).

RAYACK, E. (1983). Medical licensure: Social costs and social benefits. *Law and Human Behavior, 7*, 147-156.

ROSE, J. (1983). Professional regulation: the current controversy. *Law and Human Behavior, 7*, 103-116.

SHIMBERG, B. (1981). Testing for certification and licensure. *American Psychologist, 10*, 1138-1146.

SINNETT, E.R. & Linford, O. (1982). Is there a crisis in professional self-regulation of the practice of psychology? *Professional Psychology, 13*, 332-333.

STIGALL, T.T. (1983). Licensing and certification. In B.D. Sales (Ed.), *The professional psychologist's handbook* (pp. 285-337). New York: Plenum Press.

STRUPP, H.H. & Hadley, S.W. (1979). Specific vs. non-specific effects in psychotherapy: A study of controlled outcome. *Archives of General Psychiatry, 36*, 1125-1136.

TREBILCOCK, M.J. & Shaul, J. (1983). Regulating the quality of psychotherapeutic services: A Canadian perspective. *Law and Human Behavior, 7*, 265-278.

U.S. DEPARTMENT OF HEALTH, EDUCATION, AND WELFARE (1977). *Credentialing health manpower*. (Publication no. 77-49). Washington, D.C.: U.S. Government Printing Office.

WIENS, A.N. & H. Dorken, (1986). Establishing and enforcing standards to assure professional competency. In H. Dorken (Ed.), *Professional psychology in transition*. San Francisco: Jossey-Bass Publishers.

WERNER, E. (1980). *A review of the examination for professional practice in psychology*. Sacramento, California: Central Testing Unit, California Department of Consumer Affairs.

ZEMLICK, M.J. (1980). Cosmetics for the face of the profession of psychology. *Psychotherapy, Theory, Research and Practice, 17*, 448-453.

ZITRIN, A. & Klein, H. (1976). Can psychiatry police itself effectively? The experience of one district branch. *American Journal of Psychiatry, 133*, 653-656.

Medical Psychotherapy
1988, Volume 1, pp. 181-182

© 1988 by
Hans Huber Publishers, Toronto

Counseling and Credentialing in the Field of Diabetes Mellitus

DIANA GUTHRIE
University of Kansas

Mental health therapists may work in various specialized fields, such as alcohol counseling, family counseling, and counseling related to specific chronic conditions. Each involves a potential for liability. In the field of diabetes, liability may result from inappropriate counseling or lack of counseling. An example of inappropriate counseling could be lack of communication with the client's physician when the client is on an insulin infusion pump and is either suicidal or incapable of handling such an instrument. Lack of counseling could be the exclusion of family members from the therapeutic process. If family members are not included, the adjustment of the diabetic client can easily be sabotaged by them.

The diabetes field is working increasingly with people involved in self-care. Many people who find self-administered urine tests distasteful have less of a problem with the more complex self-monitoring of blood glucose (Peterson et al., 1979), and now patients are sometimes asked to control the disease by matching insulin delivery to the biochemical requirements of their bodies. This puts them under a different type of pressure, and utilization of the services of a counselor is needed to assist not only in the adjustment to a chronic condition, but with the stress brought on by a more in-depth knowledge of the disease and its potential impact. Emotional upsets may interfere with the reading of meters or syringes; patients may choose to not take their medication or to take too much, or they may become confused and not follow directions correctly. Family members may offer inappropriate sweets or act in ways that make the person feel rejected.

The therapist may cause injury to a patient by providing improper supportive counseling. For example, a counseling approach may be inappropriate for improving a mental state that is due to abnormality of blood glucose levels. The therapist may give false hope during the counseling process, and lack of candor about emotional expectations could lead to accusations of negligence. Inavailability of the counselor might result in a crisis.

Many people give advice to the diabetes victim. Family members often become either too protective, or not supportive enough. Mental health professionals from

Inquiries or reprint requests should be directed to Diana Guthrie, University of Kansas, School of Medicine-Wichita, Dept. of Pediatrics, 1010 N. Kansas, Wichita, Kansas 67214-3199 counselor to psychiatrist should be involved throughout. As self-care aspects become more complex and society becomes more stressful, credible counseling will be increasingly needed. To become credible requires education, initial and ongoing. Most of all, it requires guidance and supervision. The health professional dealing with problems each day may get so immersed in the world of emotional adjustment that new approaches to guidance might be ignored or overlooked. These professionals, therefore, need continuing education not only related to their specialty field, but also in counseling skills.

This is especially true of the newer areas of diabetes management: behavior modification, biofeedback for stress management, and blood pressure control. There is increasing evidence of cognitive depression occurring at a greater rate in the diabetic population. However, this depression may actually deepen with the appropriate use of biofeedback (Fotopoulos, 1978), and behavior modification may result in an increase in compulsive behavior. In 1979, at a behavioral conference on people with diabetes mellitus concern was expressed about what needed to be studied. Problems with psychosocial adjustment and the need for more credible counselors were put near the top of the list (Hamburg, Lipsett, Inoff, & Drash, 1980).

Credibility requires education, policing, and feedback. Certification in some form thus becomes mandatory. The general public – and specifically the diabetic individual and his or her family – has no other way to determine the expected level of quality of the therapist without some accrediting process being involved. Ideally, this certification should be based on the assessment of actual practice. The sorrow is that the credentialing process does not include on-site assessment of therapists' skills. It is like the student who has straight A's in the classroom but is inept in the field.

There may be alternatives to on-site assessment, such as using videotapes. Along with this, individuals could be given the option of an oral or written examination, with a choice on the latter between essay or multiple choice answer format (some individuals overinterpret multiple choice questions). The inclusion of both an onsite or videotape evaluation and a paper-and-pencil test would assess not only actual practice, but the synthesis of knowledge into practice. To heighten professional accountability an added assurance would be the recommendation for including assessment of a knowledge base associated with each specialty field represented.

The process of credentialing is a challenge, and no single approach will meet all needs. Credentialing is expensive, but for all the negative arguments, the positive argument is it is needed. Quality care cannot be expected if it is not given by qualified people, and quality people cannot be scientifically identified except by an appropriate credentialing process.

References

FOTOPOULOS, S.S. & Sunderland, W.P. (1978). Biofeedback in the treatment of psychophysiologic disorders. *Biofeedback and Systematic Response, 3*(4), 331-360.

HANBURG, B.A., Lipsett, L.F., Inoff, G.E., & Drash, A.L. (1980). Behavioral and psychosocial issues in diabetes. U.S. Dept. of Health and Human Services, *NIH Publication*, 80-1993.

PETERSON, C.M., Jones, R.L., Dupuis, A., Levine, B.S., Berstein, R., & O'Shea, M. (1979). Feasibility of improved blood glucose control in patients with insulin dependent diabetes mellitus. *Diabetes Care*, 329.

Medical Psychotherapy
1988, Volume 1, pp. 183-185

© 1988 by
Hans Huber Publishers, Toronto

Professional Regulation: A Critique

LARRY E. BEUTLER, Ph.D.
University of Arizona

The American Board of Medical Psychotherapists task force has pointed to many of the problems of current credentialing procedures for mental health practitioners. They observe that there is a wide diversity of training programs, objectives, and standards existent in the field of psychotherapy, fostered by the varying motives of diverse professional associations. They also observe the low relationship between professional experience and training on the one hand, and treatment outcomes on the other, as an indication of the invalidity of credentials that are based solely upon professional degrees and experience. Finally, the authors question the validity of current written and oral examination procedures.

In the face of these critical observations, the board proposes the certification of *Medical Psychotherapy*, as a professional activity to be developed, based upon consensual ratings by a representative team of observers. Given the potential implication of these recommendations, I would like to provide a modest alternative viewpoint.

When the observed low relationship between a therapist's experience and treatment outcomes is used as a criticism of the procedure for credentialing members of a profession, at least two assumptions are invoked: (1) it assumes that treatment is the primary, only, or principal activity of the professional being credentialed; and (2) it assumes that the studies on which these conclusions are based adequately represent experience, training, and outcome.

Unfortunately, neither of the foregoing assumptions are justified. First, credentialing professionals, as opposed to activities, like psychotherapy, deigns to assess one's knowledge and diversity of skills, aside from treatment expertise. As applied to mental health disciplines, assessing familiarity with those dimensions that are relevant to personality assessment and diagnosis are also part of the process. To propose to certify or otherwise credential a single activity (e.g., medical psychotherapy) assumes that these other diagnostic and observational skills, as well as the knowledge behind them, are either irrelevant to or of lesser importance than the skill being credentialed. Even assuming that there is a low relationship between experience and psychotherapy outcome, there is still evidence to suggest that individuals seen by experienced and trained practitioners are less likely to be assigned to a treatment for which they are not appropriate than are those seen either by lay persons or by non-mental health practitioners (e.g., Andersen & Harthorn, 1987). To argue against credentialing on the

Inquiries or reprint requests should be directed to Larry E. Beutler, Dept. of Psychiatry, University of Arizona, Tucson, Arizona 85724.

basis of a low relationship between professional training and treatment outcome alone does a disservice to the breadth of any of the mental health disciplines.

The second assumption of the authors of the position paper is equally suspect. The studies underwriting the conclusions of low correspondence between experience and therapy outcomes have been criticized from a variety of perspectives (e.g., Kane, 1982; Phillips, 1982). One of the most telling and meaningful criticisms derives from the observation that all of these studies are based upon a single aspect of clinical functioning, that of psychotherapy, which is implemented only after a great many other treatment decisions already have been made. By the time patients are assigned to psychotherapy, a complex process of self-selection, diagnosis, and prognostication has been undertaken, which results in the treatment comparisons being made on very select groups of individuals who are predisposed to respond to a caring relationship. Without studying the process in its entirety, and by selecting only that slice of clinical activity that begins after a patient has been assigned to and accepted in a particular form of treatment, the relationship between experience and training on the one hand, and benefit on the other may well have been washed out by a truncated and homogenized sample.

This is not to say that there are no genuine problems with current credentialing practices or that the poor showing of experience is acceptable. The point is that criticizing credentialing simply misdirects the focus away from the more important issue of training for competence. The mental health disciplines have operated since their inception on what I term "the germ model" of education. That is, we assume that if we are exposed to an identified body of knowledge within a given time frame, we will catch it. Moreover, we assume that the more knowledge we're exposed to and the more unfocused practice we engage in, the more skill we will catch. This model of training simply doesn't help establish a consistent level of technical skill as applied to psychotherapy. On the other hand, there is ample evidence to support two related conclusions: (1) therapists who have consistently good outcomes and those who have consistently poor outcomes do differ in their perceptions of patients and in the interventions employed (Beutler, Crago, & Arizmendi, 1986; Orlinsky & Howard, 1986); and (2) treatment outcomes are consistently and quite highly related both to the therapist's expertness and to the degree to which he or she complies with the requirements of the treatment model being used (e.g., Luborsky, McLellan, Woody, & O'Brien, 1983; Luborsky et al., 1986; Beutler et al., 1986).

In the past decade, research has successfully operationalized psychotherapeutic treatments representing a wide variety of modalities and orientations. Treatment manuals exist for psychodynamic therapy (Luborsky, 1984; Strupp & Binder, 1984), Gestalt therapy (Daldrup, Beutler, Greenberg, & Engle, in press), interpersonal therapy (Klerman, Weissman, Rounsaville, & Chevron, 1984), cognitive therapy (Beck, Rush, Shaw, & Emery, 1979) and many others. At this point, it seems clear that by utilizing criteria-based training methods and highly specific manuals, therapists can be trained to achieve competency in these procedures and to improve their levels of effectiveness by doing so. Unfortunately, the position paper's authors' proposal that consensual evaluation be based upon ratings by a team of observers implies that raters trained in the "germ model" can agree upon those things that adequately represent good clinical practice. This proposal assumes both (a) a degree of consensus that does not appear to exist among clinicians, and (b) that clinicians can adequately observe the critical elements of treatment behavior. To the best of our knowledge based upon research to date, clinical raters can only accomplish the task of judging competence when they have been specifically trained to identify those elements that are critical to a specific treatment model that provides the basis for treatment.

These observations suggest some need to revamp our current training programs and to base them upon a competence educational methodology. If: (a) clinical activities can be manualized; (b) clinicians can be trained to comply with the structure of the manuals; and (c) doing so relates to more effective clinical outcomes than training acquired in the usual way, it would appear that more attention needs to be given to specific and criteria based training and credentialing. Rather than being certified or licensed solely in the generic way, as a profession or by a generic skill (e.g., psychotherapy), a more useful approach would be to identify specific areas of proficiency, including specific forms of psychotherapy and specific types of patient populations for which competence has been demonstrated. Instead of competence being assumed solely on the basis of generic training, it would have to be demonstrated within a given area. The burden may then come to rest, as it should, upon the clinician to demonstrate competence, rather than upon the public to disprove its presence.

References

ANDERSON, S.M. & Harthorn, B.H. (1987). *The Recognition, Diagnosis, and Treatment of Mental Illness by Primary Care Physicians*. Unpublished manuscript, University of California, Santa Barbara.

BECK, A.T., Rush, A.J., Shaw, B.F., & Emery, G. (1979). *Cognitive Therapy of Depression*. New York: Guilford Press.

BEUTLER, L.E., Crago, M., & Arizmendi, T.G. (1986). Therapist Variables in Psychotherapy Process and Outcome. In S.L. Garfield & A.E. Bergin (Eds.), *Handbook of Psychotherapy and Behavior Change* (pp. 257-310, 3rd ed.). New York: John Wiley and Sons.

DALDRUP, R.J., Beutler, L.E., Greenberg, L.S., & Engle, D. (in press). *Focused Expressive Psychotherapy: A Gestalt Therapy For Individuals With Constricted Affect*. New York: Guilford.

KANE, M.T. (1982). The Validity of Licensure Examinations. *American Psychologist, 8*, 911-918.

KLERMAN, G.L., Weissman, M.M., Rounsaville, B.J., & Chevron, E.S. (1984). *Interpersonal Psychotherapy of Depression*. New York: Basic Books, Inc.

LUBORSKY, L. (1984). *Principles of Psychoanalytic Psychotherapy: A Manual for Supportive-Expressive Treatment*. New York: Basic Books, Inc.

LUBORSKY, L., Crits-Christoph, P., McLellan, A.T., Woody, G., Piper, W., Liberman, B., Imber, S., & Pilkonis, P (1986). Do Therapists Vary Much in Their Success? Findings From Four Outcome Studies. *American Journal of Orthopsychiatry, 56*, 501-512.

LUBORSKY, L., McLellan, A.T., Woody, G.E., & O'Brien, C.P. (1983, July). *Therapists' Success Rates and Their Determinants*. Paper presented at the meeting of the Society for Psychotherapy Research, Sheffield, England.

ORLINSKY, D.E. & Howard, K.I. (1986). Process and Outcome in Psychotherapy. In S.L. Garfield & A.E. Bergin (Eds.), *Handbook of Psychotherapy and Behavior Change* (pp. 311-384, 3rd ed.). New York: John Wiley and Sons.

PHILLIPS, B.N. (1982). Regulation and Control in Psychology. *American Psychologist, 8*, 919-926.

STRUPP, H.H. & Binder, J.L. (1984). *Psychotherapy in a New Key*. New York: Basic Books, Inc.

[illegible]

References

[illegible]

Medical Psychotherapy
1988, Volume 1, pp. 187-189

© 1988 by
Hans Huber Publishers, Toronto

Comment on "Professional Regulation: Issues and Problems in Current Credentialing Practices"

ALAN H. ROBERTS, Ph.D.
Scripps Clinic and Research Foundation

The position paper of the Task Force on Professional Standards discusses a number of issues and problems in the credentialing of professionals. These are not of recent origin and have been with us since the establishment of even the earliest professions. Unfortunately, the difficulties are more easily stated than are the solutions. There are several reasons why these problems have become more obvious in recent years. One of these is surely economic. Psychology is, and always has been, the product of an affluent society. As our society becomes less affluent, more and more service professionals are scrambling for fewer and fewer available monetary resources.

A primary problem is that we cannot demonstrate convincingly that our unique education and training lead to substantially better service. There is little evidence, for example, that one kind of psychotherapy works better than another. There is even less evidence that one kind of training creates superior providers than another. It appears increasingly likely that the positive effects of psychotherapy depend more upon the persuasiveness, enthusiasm, and dedication of the therapist and the client than upon the more specific effects of a particular theory.

A more serious problem is that psychotherapists in general are not paying very much attention to the outcomes of their treatments or to the implications of research for what they do (Phillips, 1987; Roberts, 1985; Zilbergeld, 1986). None of the proposals in the position paper addresses this critical issue.

The position paper does propose some solutions, each of which is seriously flawed. It greatly oversimplifies matters to believe that our problems can be resolved by more credentialing, by rules requiring more continuing education, or by doing a better job of measuring competence.

It is naive to believe, for example, that proliferation of credentialing organizations will resolve the problems. Medicine has led the way in subspecialty credentialing, and

Inquiries or reprint requests should be directed to Alan H. Roberts, Scripps Clinic and Research Foundation, 10666 North Torrey Pines Road, La Jolla, California 92037.

physicians are still the largest group of professionals trying to cope with litigation. Requiring continuing education credits does little to assure enhancement of professional competence when too little attention has been paid to the quality of such education. Most people I know in psychology and medicine chose their courses in terms of cost, ease, and most often, where the meetings were held. There is no evidence that continuing education courses improve the quality of care: their requirement is more of a public relations gesture than an assurance that a professional is keeping abreast of current knowledge. Doing a better job of measuring competence also has great appeal, but unfortunately that can't be done until professional competence can be defined and measured.

Of the various proposals, the one recommending increased enforcement of ethical violations has the greatest chance of helping. The position paper points out several reasons why this enforcement has not been done: conflicts of interest, promotion of guild interests at the expense of social and client interests, lack of financial support for discipline, fears of litigation, etc. The reason it might help is that this action directly addresses the moral principles upon which ethical behavior depends.

Ethical codes are based generally upon three moral principles: beneficence, respect for autonomy, and justice (Faden & Beauchamp, 1986). The principle of beneficence basically requires that we promote good and prevent harm. The principle of respect for autonomy requires that we should respect the autonomous choices and actions of others. The principle of justice says that we should treat others in accordance with what is fair, due, or owed them.

Part of our problem is that we have relied too heavily upon beneficence in structuring our credentialing laws and ethical codes. These structures are based upon a view of our clients as troubled, sick, ignorant, vulnerable, and lacking the ability to judge the competence of professionals (cf. Roberts, 1965). This paternalistic emphasis has led to the development of rules and regulations to enforce the principle of beneficence to the relative neglect of the principles of autonomy and justice. Many of the problems addressed in the position paper become less salient if we place greater emphasis upon autonomy and justice. To do this, we need to provide mechanisms so that clients can exercise autonomous choices. We can require that clients be provided with enough information so that they can choose freely from among practitioners both within and outside a profession. This information should include the education and training of the practitioner, how he or she will function in the relationship, how long treatment will last, how treatment goals will be established, the responsibilities of both the client and the practitioner, risks and benefits of treatment, and the costs of service including overall costs, expected outcomes, and alternative available treatments. In short, the client should be provided with a contract in the form of an informed consent.

For this to be effective, clients must have access to justice. This means that they should be treated in accordance with what is fair and due, and have recourse if denied a good, service, or piece of information rightfully due. One of the major breakdowns in the current system of credentialing is that practitioners who treat their clients unjustly are not constrained or punished; the boards seem more concerned with protecting and shielding unjust practitioners in order to preserve the reputation of the profession, than they are in insuring justice for clients.

If clients are provided with sufficient basic information, they can make their own autonomous choices even if these choices are the "wrong" ones according to our views. It is more important to inform people than it is to protect them. Fully informed, they can generally take care of themselves.

Over 20 years ago, I published a paper on credentialing, ethics, and morality (Roberts, 1965). I still agree with about 85 percent of what I wrote then. The rest was off target and, because I overemphasized the beneficence principle, some of it is now downright embarrassing. The bottom line of that paper, however, still stands: you can't legislate morality.

The only effective ways to influence moral and ethical behaviors are through selection, teaching, and modeling. This means deliberate care in *selecting* students for these values, serving as appropriate *role models* for our students, and *teaching* moral and ethical values to them. In my opinion, little formal attention is paid to these in our graduate programs.

The problem is exacerbated by the proliferation of graduate programs that ignore balance in imparting the subject matter of psychology. We must therefore review and correct our teaching practices and content. If our students are going into practice without a healthy respect for science or an unwillingness or inability to apply emergent research to their practices, then we have failed them as teachers and models, we have failed our clients, we have abandoned our unique heritage, and we have lost our future.

References

FADEN, R.R. & Beauchamp, T.L. (1986). *A history and theory of informed consent.* New York: Oxford.

PHILLIPS, J.S. (1987). Science in the service of profession. *The Clinical Psychologist, 40,* 60-62.

ROBERTS, A.H. (1965). Professionalism, ethics and the social contract. *Rocky Mountain Psychologist, 1,* 11-14.

ROBERTS, A.H. (1985). Biofeedback: Research, training and clinical roles. *American Psychologist, 40,* 938-941.

ZILBERGELD, B. (1986). Psychabuse. *Science '86, 7* (June), 48-52.

Medical Psychotherapy
1988, Volume 1, pp. 191-202

© 1988 by
Hans Huber Publishers, Toronto

Credentialing Practices: Resistance to Innovation

RICHARD S. WEINER, Ph.D.
The Institute of Pain Management

Introduction

The typical health care delivery system in the United States, from the mid-nineteenth century to the early twentieth century, can be characterized as a period in which the allopathic treatment paradigm became paramount. Allopathic medicine embraces the rational, scientific, and mechanistic frame of reference. Such an epistomological orientation emphasizes reductionist techniques of analysis, action, and achievement. The underlying assumption is that through diagnosis (identifying a disease from its symptoms), pathology or disease entities can be discovered and then expiated. Researchers and clinicians have developed numerous narrow specialties for an ever-greater potential in discovering pathogens. Over time, this narrow perspective has resulted in very significant discoveries about human biology, sickness, and means of curing sickness. However, the same world view is myopic and renders unimportant many social, economic, and environmental factors that also influence health.

For example, the issue of chronic pain as a treatment problem has until recently been relegated to a "non-issue" status within the fragmented health care delivery system. It has not been clinically viewed as a separate and legitimate disorder; rather, it has received secondary consideration. The major emphasis has been upon the primary illness or accident, with the assumption that by treating that problem, the chronic pain problems would also be resolved. As a consequence of assigning chronic pain a non-issue status and developing a fragmented delivery care system, allopathic medicine has been unable to help many chronic pain sufferers.

This paper will examine potential formats for selecting and providing an alternative method of service delivery. In part, this will entail an attempt to compare and contrast the present state of the art with the possible benefits of alternative treatments, conceptually linked through a holistic frame of reference. In attempting this, there will be comments made regarding the resistance to change that credentialing entails.

Inquiries or reprint requests should be directed to Richard S. Weiner, The Institute of Pain Management, 1917 Memorial Drive, Suite A-2, Ceres, CA 95307.

Competing Paradigms

Health and efficient functioning are normal and natural conditions of the body. Homeostasis can be viewed as an internal state of equilibrium, whereby adjustments occur through a self-regulatory feedback method that is dependent upon sensory data derived from the body, mind, and spirit. For the typical chronic pain patient, homeostasis is distorted and adjustments are more difficult. The causes of such disharmony are many, but can be viewed as either self-initiated or externally initiated. An example of a self-initiated stressor may be playing tennis when one knows that one will "pay" for it later. An example of an externally initiated stressor may be barometric changes in the weather.

The present primacy of allopathic medicine is a result of policy decisions (or lack thereof), including allocation of resources. Such decisions, it can be argued, are the result of competing political, social, and economic influences. Within this milieu, scientific research or paradigmatic models also compete. Scientific paradigms, or in the present context medical models, offer solutions to problems viewed as legitimate by consensus. A model remains viable as long as no other competing explanation receives higher acceptance. Treatment paradigms are highly resistant to change: violations of expectation may be observed as anomalies, or may be forcefully consigned an explanation within existing models. Paradigms profoundly influence the perspective of practitioners: Kuhn (1970) describes a paradigm as a method of observing and ordering phenomena, and to this end, practitioners are educated (indoctrinated) to binding rules of standard practice. These rules define which problems are legitimate, and which forms of intervention-treatment are appropriate. Other problems are relegated to a nonscientific status or are considered anomalies.

This is how allopathic medicine has treated chronic pain. Chronic pain has not been viewed as a primary diagnostic category; rather, the allopathic medical model gives it non-independent status and frequently nonlegitimation. The paradigm views acute pain as legitimate, chronic pain as suspect. There has been no conceptual framework for recognizing the dimensions of chronic pain, and the instruments of the medical profession have reinforced its nonstatus role by not being able to diagnose it. In part, this has been a self-reinforcing or self-defeating process. The notions of the allopathic medical paradigm color the assumptions held by practitioners, and they in turn seek instruments, technology, and treatments that are consistent with the paradigm. Such technological determinism limits and directs explanations, treatments, definitions of observation, and future research.

As stated above, a paradigm remains primary so long as no competing paradigm is accepted as being better at explaining observable events. Reiser (1978) correctly points out that with each successive medical paradigm, old problems, techniques, and relationships are discarded. This may be an inevitable aspect of paradigm ascendancy, but it is unfortunate. The paradigm that frees the medical community of the arduous task of repeatedly "proving" basic tenets frequently devalues many tenable methods of previous discounted paradigms. The circumstances under which alternative methods of service delivery are embraced may, in fact, result in paradigm competition.

In the same light, a brief explanation will be offered suggesting that the lack of toleration inherent in the allopathic paradigm, as well as its primary powers of explanation, represent an extension of western imperialism and hegemony. Furthermore, the resistance to change that is characteristic of any paradigm is exaggerated in allopathy in a way that no prior paradigm has ever commanded. This is due to a pervasive technological determinism, which is rampant across all western disciplines to an extent never before achieved.

Evaluating a Paradigm – The Case of Chronic Pain as an Example

The goals of medical treatment are often difficult to agree upon. Throughout history, the procedures for goal fulfillment have consisted of accepted, legitimate methods and unaccepted, quasi-accepted methods. Methods that hold accepted status in a community share an underlying assumption that they are the proper and orthodox procedures. As such, they represent as aggregated dominant or cultural ideal. All other methods are typically viewed by the majority as inferior, unorthodox, and to be shunned. The cultural ideal represents the express wishes and desires of those actors involved.

However, some individuals have unequal influence on this decision-making. One criterion for reviewing and perhaps judging relative merit between treatment goals should be that of proximity to the treatment decision. One goal of giving order and purpose to one's environment is to reduce uncertainty, which historically has been viewed with much anxiety. In other words, through order the concept of a stable state can be conceived. Consequently, decision-makers have an interest in maintaining a stable state. This impacts how illness or health is defined and who may treat individuals considered sick.

This is true regardless of what paradigm is dominant at any given time. The manifestations of holding the status quo and evading change (anxiety) cut across all human activity. Activities that facilitate maintenance of the dominant or ideal are labeled good; activities that call assumptions into question are considered anomalies. There is a constant struggle between paradigms for dominance. At one level this may be viewed as power struggles between different sets of decision-makers, whose vested interests differ but may include political, economic, or resource allocation considerations. Depending upon the complexity of the culture, by which I mean the prevailing relationships and institutions, good and bad judgments give rise to prescriptions and proscriptions for behavior, and to sanctions for perceived violations. At any rate, these power struggles certainly represent competing views of the world and of order. Depending on the power of decision-makers and the instruments available for policy enforcement, views that are considered aberrations have historically been cast out. Methods to accomplish this have included excommunication; death to proponents; or exclusion from credentialing, accreditation, certification, licensure, and specialization. An example of the latter would be the conflict between the American Medical Association and the American Institute of Homeopathy. At the turn of the twentieth century, homeopathic medicine was challenging the allopathic position that treatment was dependent upon the discovery of a "single cause" of illness. For a number of years, physicians who practiced homeopathy could not be members of their local allopathic medical society, and in fact, the AMA forbade professional relationships between allopaths and homeopaths. Homeopaths were viewed as practicing nonscientific medicine.

Another criterion useful in reviewing and selecting[1] among alternative treatments would be the judgement as to which system provides a more stable state and reduces anxiety. It is for this reason that evaluation of perspective occurs. Therefore, the selection of a treatment methodology implies more than a simple choice of technique. A treatment modality is dependent upon assumptions of illness and causation, and fits within a particular world view. The choice of treatment reflects an understanding of illness that is supported by an agreement of the medical community.

Individuals differ in their perspective of how much anxiety is inherent in any situation. Furthermore, anxiety occurs at various levels of behavior. According to Maslow (1968) there is a hierarchy of basic human needs. These include: (a) bodily needs, (b) security protection, (c) interpersonal relations and belonging, (d) self-respect/self-esteem, and (e) self-actualization through developing talents and capacities. For most people, the focus of concern (anxiety) fluctuates in importance between these categories at any moment. However, chronic pain patients often become fixated at the lowest levels. Their most urgent concerns cause a focus upon bodily needs and security such as food, shelter, and paying bills. For some, interpersonal relations also take on excessive centrality. When this occurs, the self-regulating, self-pacing process of organismic growth is impeded. A comprehensive treatment plan must consider these needs and facilitate the removal of fixation in order for the individual to rekindle the growth process.

Consequently, it can be deduced that survival and the relative quality of survival produces groups with differing characteristics, needs, and world views. Much like the proverbial story of the blind men who touched different parts of an elephant and then reported different definitive truths, selection among alternative treatments highlights the relative importance and impermanence of medical paradigms. The explanatory power of a paradigm and its subsequent treatment modalities are intended to reduce anxiety.

Earlier in this paper, it was pointed out that the training of practitioners and technological determinism contribute to paradigm stability (resistance). Within a given medical paradigm, these factors feed on themselves and spawn institutions, interpersonal relations, clinical realities, modes of communication, and emphasis either upon treatment by an expert or upon self-cure. Thus, they also merit consideration as criteria for which selection of modalities appropriate to the treatment (of chronic pain) can be decided.

Historically, treatment paradigms have been influenced by unique social, political, and ecological factors. Different systems developed attributions intended to insulate members; however, insulation was always viewed as conditional and less than perfect. However, about six centuries ago the balance was fundamentally disturbed. This corresponds to the period following the European Renaissance. Beginning in 1415, European states began an assault upon the world, as seafarers began the search for gold and spices that led to increased imperialism. This military encroachment resulted in the dissemination of values and rules of order consistent with the industrial revolution. Never before had a single paradigm captured communities on a global scale. However, imperialism is not the present theme. I am concerned here with the reaction of the rest of the world to western influence and its consequences – the conse-

---

1 The choice of the term selection is rendered more meaningful when selection is observed as being a transient decision that obtains due to differently weighted impacting stimuli unique to the particular time and place in which the treatment is selected.

quences of co-optation and eventual termination of the various local schools of thought. With the introduction of western thought, indigenous ways of seeing the world and practicing mental health changed along with the social order (Chinweiza, 1975).

When Descartes conceptually separated the body, mind, and soul and described the functions of the body in mechanistic terms, the seeds of allopathic medicine were sown. Science became concerned with accurately reducing the body to its component parts. Disease could now be conceptually viewed in terms of bacteriological, biochemical, and pathophysiological problems. With the discovery of antitoxins and vaccines, it now became plausible to believe that science and research would cure any problems.

Eventually this revolutionary, optimistic, and omnipotent view would expend medicine's domain. Conceptually freed from the constraints of nature and religion, monopolistic rival professions were either absorbed or relegated to a fringe status. Judged as extramedical, such ancillary services were not tolerated; judged as quackery and guilty of violations of "science," certain practices were denied an opportunity to develop.

As the concept of human vulnerability changed, interpersonal and institutional changes accompanied the new image of clinical reality. Western medicine became bureaucratic, specialized, fragmented, and impersonal (Gordon, 1980). A professional cadre of health providers usurped the role of the family in the treatment of illness and pain. What formerly had been a participatory relationship between the sick person and the healer has evolved into a relationship whereby an "expert" does something to a "patient" who passively has the treatment done unto them. These were the new roles and relationships that would have a deleterious impact on the treatment of chronic pain. With the development of these roles began the "cosmic search" for the expert with the correct treatment. The assumptions and behavior inherent in these roles frequently encourage the chronic pain patient to assume and maintain a "sick" but nevertheless nonlegitimate role. When this behavior lingers beyond the period considered legitimate (acute), the patient runs the risk of being labeled a malingerer.

Healers who practiced their trade during eras when the paradigm allowed vulnerability did not have the burden of always being correct, for the final control was not typically seen as resting with performing scientific feats, but rather with a greater-than-human force. Nor did they have the arsenal of treatment available to today's physician. Consequently, early healers were viewed as catalysts – part of the whole. They had a revered status, but they had to maintain modesty. Present-day assumptions of eventual invulnerability through research redefine the role of healer as being closer to that of the ancient view of divinity. (Note: this perhaps fosters malpractice suits when there is the fall from the divine.)

Institutional changes occurred in response to the new emerging paradigm of single causation. Birth, death, and all medical treatments were shifted from the family home location and placed within the hospital setting, which has allowed further reductionist treatment. Technology and specialization could be concentrated for the ever-greater glory of final discovery.

In spite of the deep commitment of the western paradigm of health and to preferred types of treatment and instrumentation, a number of anomalies, discoveries, and crises are beginning to compete and form rival explanations. There is a need to put allopathic advances into an historical perspective. Cost/benefit and policy analysis can become part of such a revisionist historical inquiry.

Holistic Medicine

"...The holistic approach in medicine is a context and a set of principles to guide our attitudes toward health ..." (Hastings, Fadiman, & Gordon, 1980).

Presently, there exists no cogent holistic therapy regime. Holistic medicine refers to a loosely knit set of guiding assumptions or principles regarding health, therapy, body-mind relationships, social patterns, interpersonal dynamics, environmental analyses, and definitions of health. I believe that it would be safe to conclude that presently holistic medicine is in a pre-paradigm state. If holistic health emerges as a primary paradigm replacement, it will be because practitioners today will find holistic answers more helpful in reducing anxiety or unanswered questions. As previously pointed out, a change of paradigm implies the opening of new doors while possibly losing old truths forever. Such a shift will usher in different instruments, modes of diagnosis, and modalities of treatment.

While there exists no generic model for a holistic paradigm and no other strong paradigm competing with allopathic medicine, all of the facts and observations indicating anomalies in the treatment of chronic pain are equally plausible and, in fact, may never be understood. The allopathic paradigm with its reductionist base is unable to treat chronic pain as a problem, because the paradigm is a constraint that makes the problem unavailable for discovery across the multiple levels that require treatment. If my implementation of Kuhn's notion of the structure of scientific revolutions is correct, then I must conclude that chronic pain cannot be accommodated by the allopathic paradigm. Chronic pain is an unanswered "crisis"[2] confronting allopathy. Even if the allopathic medical paradigm "wished" to enlarge its scope to include chronic pain, it would be limited in its ability to do so. The reason for this is that it is part of a larger paradigm defining culture. It is part of a system.

Many of the problems faced by chronic pain patients require treatment that are structural and fundamental. Changes would be required in economic, political, and social areas. Thus, with the exception of incremental improvements in medical treatment, the condition will remain only partially treated. In all likelihood, this will be limited to refinements of technique intended for treating the "real" problem.

It is not my intent to malign allopathy, but rather to facilitate the discussion of credentialing using the example of chronic pain. Many of the achievements in medicine within the allopathic paradigm adequately serve a pluralistic mobile society such as ours, and positively serve the different interests, beliefs, and treatment needs in the populace. However, it still remains that until a treatment plan tailored to the individual (mindful of structural limitations) is implemented, no comprehensive treatment of chronic pain is likely.

Health Services

There are a host of health service providers serving the needs of chronic pain patients, including physicians (generalists and specialists), laboratory technicians, nurses, physi-

---

2 Kuhn uses the term here to describe events which, when combined, can trigger a crisis.

cal therapists, psychiatrists, psychologists, counselors, etc. However, services are fragmented and lack a cohesive case-management approach. Specialization of services for the chronic pain patient results in loss of unifying language, diminished interface among consultants, divergent assumptions of causality, and even different legal definitions as to what can or cannot be done. This has resulted in the establishment of an elite group (physicians) who are legally enfranchised to identify when a patient "legitimately" has pain, and when he or she is to be considered a malingerer. Specialization and diminished interface of perspectives also create a lack of opportunity for the infusion of new treatment ideas or theory development. As a result, chronic pain is rarely treated as a primary diagnostic concern, and many problems associated with it go unnoticed and untreated by medical practitioners.

Resistance to Innovation

As changes in diagnostic technology, service organization, specialization, and social relationships change in the treatment of illness (especially chronic pain) over the years, resistance has been encountered. Seventeenth century physicians made diagnoses and prescribed appropriate treatment on the basis of "subjective" evidence gathered primarily by listening to the patient's self-description of symptoms. Treatment would even be routinely prescribed through the mail on such a basis. Physicians rarely touched the patient, because this would have been considered a breach of the social rule of human dignity.

In the eighteenth century, physicians began to break down on these taboos and started to dissect dead bodies, looking for internal cause of pathology. Also, the development of percussion (listening to body sounds) was introduced. Often patients and older physicians argued against such techniques, and certain religious groups such as Orthodox Jews did not allow the practice of autopsy.

The nineteenth century saw the beginning of "objective" diagnostic technology, again with stiff resistance. In the twentieth century, the explosion of specialization and centralization of treatment around the hospital gave birth to new problems. In addition to creating new kind of pathology and developing different socially acceptable procedures, new stratifications in service delivery created problems that still remain unresolved. Frequently, specialists do not interface with each other, share no common language, hold widely differing theories of causation, and focus upon different findings with little or no systematic case management.

Research policies dominate the current medical model. Even the issue of what can be studied and by whom is beginning to be tightly controlled. Those making the case for placing such boundaries around patient care justify their position with the argument of insuring quality treatment. However, such restrictions serve as policy disincentive for the total treatment of the patient. Certainly a latent or hidden agenda behind licensure is sometimes vested interest in control of third party insurance payments, bringing insurance providers into the policy arena as a powerful interest.

The advent of specialization gave impetus to the articulation of professionalism. The rhetoric of upgrading standards has been used for the creation and maintenance of professional jargon within areas of specialization. In spite of the benefits that may derive from such a phenomenon, the process forces the loss of the human scale by creating an artificial mystification and unwarranted elevation of "scientific expectations."

Licensure requirements limit both the number and type of professionals allowed to practice. Frequently, licensure boards and even boards of insurance companies are controlled by medical specialists who exercise tight reins on certification. This has a limiting effect on research and treatment knowledge, inasmuch as only persons of similar minds are permitted to practice. Informal referral networks have exacerbated this problem. As credentialing is a major policy control strategy, it is worth examining further.

The unabridged edition of the Random House Dictionary defines a credential as "anything that provides a basis for confidence, belief, credit, etc." Thus, it would follow that a credential is not really a credential unless it leads to, or at least contributes to, a sense of confidence in a practitioner (Foster, 1977). It would be helpful to provide a brief definition of some of the accepted methods of credentialing.

Certification: This is a procedure for recognizing the ability of personnel in a profession by authorizing them to use a title adopted by the profession. Certification procedures usually rely upon a review of transcripts obtained from the completion of required courses.

Licensure: This method requires a governmental body such as a state legislature to regulate the practice and the title of the profession. Frequently, violators are met with legal sanctions. For this reason, most private practitioners prefer this means of limiting competition. Licensing boards often exercise quasi-legal power.

Accreditation: Another name for this procedure is "program approval." This occurs when an agency or association grants recognition of a school's program. Graduates are frequently listed in a registry.

The major issues surrounding licensure are described below, based upon the research of Carrol, Griggs, and Hallagan (1977) and broadened to include the licensure of any health professional. Does licensure result in the protection of the public from incompetent and unethical practitioners? Those in agreement with licensure feel that it assures minimum standards of education, training, internship, and experience. Without state licensure, there are no standards. Anyone may be called counselor, therapist, etc. Those in opposition claim that licensure sets minimum standards, but does not police their delivery. It is a one-shot deal that does not mandate continuing evaluation.

In addition to certification, licensure, and accreditation, one other means for insuring minimum competency exists that does not have stultifying effects on research and treatment. Stanley Gross (1977) has proposed "professional disclosure" as an alternative to these methods. Gross states that the assumption underlying licensure is that the public has to be "protected by" those who have specialist knowledge. The effort to insure quality of service raises three further questions: How does one differentiate the good from the bad practitioner? Where does one draw the line between the good and the bad? Who draws the line?

Shinberg, Esser, and Kruger (1972) trace the historical evolution of licensure to the efforts of nineteenth century medical practitioners to increase their status as well as their compensation. Prior to World War I, licensure procedures were institutionalized methods by which those who engaged in a practice controlled entry into the field (Selden, 1972). The public was led to believe that practitioners would disregard vested interests in order to regulate themselves in the interest of the public. Physicians were considered ethical, socially concerned, and learned individuals who could best develop objective and impartial broad national and social policy. Shinberg et al. concluded that, as a result, licensure today is considered a jealously regarded right that acts to maintain exclusive clubs and to support rigid bureaucracies. For instance, such policy has built-in headwinds for the development of comprehensive chronic pain treatments.

Not only does licensure not safeguard the public's interest, but its effects have frequently been felt as discrimination in the areas of age, sex, and race, by denying entry to certain groups into the profession. Furthermore, the public is harmed when unskilled practitioners become licensed, and when skilled but unlicensed individuals are denied access to practice. Roemer (1974) points out the policy implications of restricted access when, in spite of national shortages, there is an insufficiency of opportunity for members of minority groups, which thus also impacts service delivery to minority communities. The unnecessary length of training and the problems of mobility across state lines exacerbate this problem.

In arguing for professional disclosure as a policy alternative to licensure, Gross assumes that consumers can develop the capacity and responsibility to protect themselves. He believes that since the patient is best acquainted with his or her own problem, he or she is best able to evaluate competency. Consumer guide books can be plainly written with limited confusing jargon and made available for consumers so they can make comparisons. It is conceivable that one could argue that doing away with restrictive licensure laws would eliminate a market monopoly and make practitioners accountable to the community.

The method of professional disclosure that Gross supports includes the following steps: (1) disclosure should be made to prospective patients before any treatment for which a fee is charged, and it must be legible, on a printed form, and also posted conspicuously; (2) the fact that disclosure is required must be disclosed; (3) a notarized form should be filed with the Bureau of Business Licensure whenever a change is made and done yearly at a minimum; (4) disclosure should include education, school, time in practice, and areas of specialization.

Disclosure would not solve the problem of insuring quality service. However, neither have the accepted methods of certification, licensure, or accreditation. The advantage of disclosure is that innovative procedures and personnel are not stifled by the status quo rigidity of rules. Currently, in an area of concern such as chronic pain treatment, experimental methods with sufficient research evaluation must overcome not only limited knowledge, but resistance from vested interest groups.

From an economic standpoint, disclosure facilitates client choice within a relatively "free" market. All practitioners would be required to file the above-mentioned disclosure forms with the present Bureau of Licensure. The Bureau would be responsible for ascertaining the veracity of the information, thus insuring honest information dissemination.

Current Milieu

There has been a plethora of voices calling for increased professional accountability by establishing and maintaining additional credentialing requirements. Individuals trained in varying schools of thought have recently argued that through licensure and other credentialing means, they could "safeguard" the public, and have sought these means in order to restrain competition. There has been an increase in the argument recently that where there is licensure or means of credentialing that professional regulation has been ineffective in protecting the public. This has resulted in an increased call for professional accountability, quality assurance, oversight review organizations, and increased policing function by government agencies. To some extent there has also been a call for increasing the budget of the policing function for bureaucratic agencies.

The question must be asked, however: which public and which interest gets served in a political pluralistic society? It is easy to say that we all share the goal of defining good versus bad and weeding out the "bad" practitioner. However, as there are many types of problems and many individuals with different world views, it is frequently difficult to define what is good from what is bad. Furthermore, various social, cultural, and minority groups may find shamans, botanical doctors who practice with herbs, or religious explanations in keeping with their expectations for treatment. If there is a universally imposed requirement for "scientific treatment," such groups may be denied access to their historical treatments of choice.

In addition, historically public sector bureaucracies, when given increased budgets to expand staffing, have been quite successful in defining "the public's welfare" and thus enforcing new rules and regulations. Of course this results in a statistical increase in the police role of a bureaucratic agency. However, generally such bureaucracies are self-perpetuating and may not necessarily be "protecting the public" benignly.

The argument has been made that if mental health practitioners do not define and increase their own accountability, then "outside reviewers" will impose this upon them. On the surface, this is a neutral statement. It may not be bad to have consumers and impacted others exercise some ability for overview, if in fact such regulation must exist. It has also been argued that one role of credentialing boards should be to define more precisely boundaries of acceptable therapeutic practice. However, the problems inherent in such an assumption are many. The difficulty of defining what is competent from what is incompetent is but one. The ability to change and allow innovation is made more difficult if practitioners are constrained to certain boundaries and thus impose myopic world viewpoints. It is also erroneous to assume that such boards can "impartially and objectively" develop such regulations: in all likelihood, they would be based upon political power. Perhaps it would be better to allow the "free market" to allow consumers to have the freedom to choose (as described in Milton Friedman's book *Free to Choose*, 1979). In addition, we may be best guided by the words of Justice Louis Brandeis in Olmstead vs. United States, 277 U.S. 479 (1929) (in Friedman, 1979):

> Experience should teach us to be most on our guard to protect liberty when the government's purposes are beneficial. Men born to freedom are naturally alert to repel invasion of their liberty by evil-minded rulers. The greater dangers to liberty lurk in insidious encroachment by men of zeal, well-meaning but without understanding.

Conclusion

It may be that one of the reasons for the increased interest in accountability through licensure, accreditation, and credentialing is the belief that science in general and medical technology (including mental health) in particular is value-free. However, nothing can be further from the reality. Ivan Illich (1979) writes:

> Medicine is a moral enterprise and therefore inevitably gives content to good and evil. In every society, medicine, like law and religion, defines what is normal, proper, or desireable. Medicine has the authority to label one man's complaint as legitimate illness, to declare a second man sick though he himself does not complain, and to refuse a third recognition of his pain, his disability and even his death. It is medicine which stamps some pain as "merely objective," some impairment as malingering . . . morality is as implicit in sickness as it is in crime or sin.

Treatment decisions exist within a total context from which they are judged superior or inferior in power of explaining nature. A treatment provides for the means for achieving a stable state and the reduction of anxiety. In all likelihood, only when issues such as chronic pain are seen as "tautologies, statements of situations that could not conceivably have been otherwise" within a context, will such conditions no longer appear as spurious irritants and will ably serve as data for the negation of worn-out theories. If this condition obtains, practitioners will show an increased willingness to intervene with alternative methods of treatment. The proliferating version of treatment serves to loosen the foundations of allopathic treatment and may ultimately permit a new paradigm to emerge. The modes of paradigm solution will define the treatment enterprise. However, increased credentialing and increased practice restraint with the corollary of reducing which practitioner may legitimately see a client and treat that client will create resistance to improved comprehensive treatment.

Rather than arguing that improved credentials (a better mousetrap) is needed, what we may wish to argue is that a free market coupled with professional disclosure may serve to allow individuals to choose among various alternative methods of treatment while not unduly restraining the scientific (and other ways of knowing) the world.

There are costs – political, social, and economic – of any policy decision, whether for increased credentialing, or for allowance for alternative treatment delivery systems. As it appears that at present we are unable to have an absolute definition of good versus bad, merely holding a license that has demonstrated one's knowledge, skills, and ability, while not necessarily abetting moral turpitude or business greed, does not present an answer to the questions currently being raised. Thus, it may be better at this stage to allow the criterion of social utility to guide us towards a free market concept of service delivery. In the long run, this may be more effective, more economical, and more humane.

To respond to the current pressures to establish additional credentialing practices may be a reactive response rather than incorporating many of the ideas and experiences that we have learned to date. The challenge ahead is not to develop better methods of cost reduction, but to develop effective means of helping individuals, families, organizations, and communities adapt to an ever-changing and ever more stressful environment. We must help to educate policy decision-makers that the creation of turf and artificial limits on practice fail to account for the fact that no traditional discipline has organized its inquiry to encourage a comprehensive understanding for both individual and collective well-being.

Frequently it is only through an interdisciplinary and collaborative approach, which builds upon traditional school of thought but encourages creative and synergistic treatment, are we able to overcome the shortcomings inherent in any singular discipline. This applied orientation grows out of a belief that the dichotomies often posed between academics and practitioners, between the community of ideas and the community of experience, are false and dangerous. We should have learned by now that problems know no boundary, and efforts to restrict practice will only impede effective delivery of service. In facing the current challenge, we must seek to promote an open, experimental, and interdisciplinary approach to social learning – an approach that can synthesize ideas in new ways and expand the boundaries of established knowledge.

The search for usable knowledge provides no guarantees that individuals will act with the community's best interest at heart, but it does express a fundamental belief in the power of ideas to create new possibilities for a more human, compassionate, and responsive delivery system.

To respond to the current "crisis" facing mental health practitioners, developing additional credentialing practices is not the answer. Such action represents a continuing crisis of knowledge, values, and change. Only the unfettered free market can accommodate change and the explosion of knowledge inherent in our age of information without the constraints that licensure entails.

References

CARROL, M., Griggs, S., & Halligan, F. (1977). "The Licensure Issue: How Real Is It?" *American Personnel and Guidance Association Journal.*

CHINWEIZA, A. (1975). *The West and the Rest of Us.* New York: Vintage Books.

FRIEDMAN, M. & Friedman, R. (1979). *Free to Choose.* New York: Avon Publishers, New York, NY.

FOSTER, J. (1977). "What Shall We Do About Credentialing?" *American Personnel and Guidance Association Journal.*

GORDON, J. (1980). "The Paradigm of Holistic Medicine." In J. Fadiman & J. Gordon (Eds.), *Health for the Whole Person.* Boulder, Colorado: Westview Press.

GROSS, S. (1977). "Professional Disclosure: An Alternative to Licensure." *American Personnel and Guidance Association Journal.*

HASTINGS, A., Fadiman, J., & Gordon, J. (Eds.) (1980). *Health for the Whole Person.* Boulder, Colorado: Westview Press.

ILLICH, I. (1976). *Medical Nemesis.* New York: Bantam Books.

KUHN, T. (1970). *The Structure of Scientific Revolutions.* Chicago: University of Chicago Press.

MASLOW, A. (1968). *Tour of Psychology of Being.* New York: D. Van Nostrand Company.

REISER, S. (1978). *Medicine and the Reign of Technology.* Cambridge: Cambridge University Press.

ROEMER, R. (1974). "Trends and Licensure, Certification, and Accreditation." *Journal of Allied Health.*

SELDEN, W. (1972). "The Implication of the SASHEP for the Medical Profession." *American Journal of Medical Technology.*

SHINBERG, B., Esser, B., & Kruger, D. (1972). *Occupational Licensing and Public Policy.* New Jersey: Educational Testing Service.

Medical Psychotherapy
1988, Volume 1, pp. 203-205

© 1988 by
Hans Huber Publishers, Toronto

Response to ABMP Task Force Position Paper on "Professional Credentialing"

LOUIS A. PAGLIARO, M.S., Pharm.D., Ph.D., F.A.B.M.P.
Faculty of Pharmacy, University of Alberta

A valid system of professional credentialing, which correlates highly with the degree of professional competence that an individual practitioner possesses, is absolutely necessary to ensure optimal public health and safety. However, as self-evident as this statement should be, there are some who have questioned its practical application.

The arguments of Hogan (1983) and his proponents (e.g., Trebilcock & Shaul, 1983) of "laissez-faire" registration are extremely task-oriented and as such more applicable to the trades rather than to health care professions. For example, regardless of educational background, anyone who can pass all of the electrical code tests should probably[1] be licensed as an electrician. But *not* everyone who can pass a specific test should be licensed as a health care professional. There are many reasons for this sentiment. For one thing, tests for health care professionals *cannot* test every conceivable case that may be encountered in clinical practice.[2] Additionally, to function effectively as a health care professional one must *not* operate solely at the cognitive level of memory (e.g., What does code 14.3 say about this situation?), but must be able to operate at the cognitive levels of synthesis and integration (e.g., "Based on my clinical assessment and the patient's history, I would suggest the following . . ."). Tests of these types of cognitive operations are difficult to conduct and problematic to interpret. Thus, the registration of health care professionals needs more than a simple, singular licensing test in order to ensure competence and thus protect the public health and safety.

How then can one ensure competence with any degree of certainty? One may increase the certainty of a better correlation between some form of individual assess-

---

Inquiries or reprint requests should be directed to Louis Pagliaro, Faculty of Pharmacy, University of Alberta, 3118 Dentistry/Pharmacy Centre, Edmonton, Alberta, Canada T6G 2N8.

1 "Probably" is added here because I am not quite certain that someone diagnosed as a "pyromaniac" should be actively licensed as an electrician (at least I would not be comfortable if this individual were to wire my home)

2 Unlike tests for technicians, such as electricians, which can cover every code and hence every case that the electrician may encounter in future practice.

ment for registration as a health care professional and competence in the field of practice in much the same manner as increasing the multiple correlation statistic (i.e., by finding individual items that correlate positively and then using *several* of these items together). Thus, *in addition* to some form of testing[3] as a requirement for registration, one would *add* other items that correlate with professional competence. Most notable among these items would be, of course, educational preparation.[4] Other items (e.g., communication skills, empathy, specific personality traits), if demonstrated to correlate positively with professional competence, could be added to the equation (i.e., the list of predictive criteria) and thus increase the obtained correlation even further. Of course, no system will ever be perfect: statistically, there will always be Type I and Type II errors. However, by carefully choosing relevant criteria with which to evaluate health care professionals for registration and credentialing, one can ensure that the highest number of qualified practitioners are allowed to practice in the discipline and that the public's safety and health have been adequately protected.

Having arrived at this point, one realizes that it is not the end of the credentialing issue, but is actually a new beginning point. For once an individual health care provider is recognized as being competent in his or her chosen discipline and has obtained professional credentialing, the very next step is to ensure, within the limits of human potential and practicality, that as both the discipline and the individual change over time that he or she *remain* competent to practice (Dubin, 1972; Jensen, 1979).

Methods of maintaining and determining continuing competence must be carefully thought out, implemented, and periodically reviewed and revised in order to remain valid and reliable. At the onset, one might well include, perhaps as a starting minimum, required attendance and active participation in continuing education programs.[5] Other requirements might be deemed necessary in specific cases. For example, individual practitioners who remain professionally inactive for a period of twelve months or longer may be required to take a prescribed number of continuing education units or a prescribed refresher course, or even to be re-examined and re-pass the current credentialing examination before renewal of active licensure.

It would be naive to think that the implementation of the suggestions and recommendations outlined in this paper would provide a panacean solution to all of the issues and problems related to professional credentialing. However, it would be a good beginning.

---

3 Remember that testing need not be solely in written form. The best situation might well include both written and verbal tests of competence that measure problem solving skills in a case history type format.

4 Some, such as Berstein and Lecomte (1981) have pointed out examples of exceptional cases where individuals with less academic qualifications performed professionally equally or superior to those with higher academic credentials. However, one should note that these are exceptions to the rule. If this were not so, then there would be no need for an educational system and the granting of degrees would be a meaningless exercise. If anything, these exceptions point out not that one should devalue education, but rather that increased attention must be given to the application aspects of our current academic programs.

5 These continuing education programs could take a variety of forms such as seminars, professional conferences, university lectures, or self-study correspondence courses. A minimal annual number of units or contact hours, as determined by the profession, should probably be required.

References

DUBIN, S.S. (1972). Obsolescence or lifelong education: A choice for the professional. *American Psychologist, 27*(5), 486-498.

HOGAN, D.B. (1983). The effectiveness of licensing: History, evidence, and recommendations. *Law and Human Behavior, 7*(213), 117-138.

JENSEN, R.E. (1979). Competent professional service in psychology: The real issue behind continuing education. *Professional Psychology, 10*(3), 381-389.

TREBILCOCK, M.J. & Shaul, J. (1983). Regulating the quality of psychotherapeutic services: A Canadian perspective. *Law and Human Behavior, 7*(213), 265-278.

Medical Psychotherapy
1988, Volume 1, pp. 207-209

© 1988 by
Hans Huber Publishers, Toronto

Competency: Self-Imposed Professional Discipline

RAYMOND F. HANBURY, JR., Ph.D.
Mount Sinai Medical Center

As an involved member of the organization for medical psychotherapists, it is obvious to me that one of the concepts stressed is the interdisciplinary make-up of the professional group practicing psychotherapy. The points raised by Anchor and Abraham in their position paper, "Professional Regulation: Issues and Problems in Current Credentialing Practices", certainly do illustrate a particular dilemma both for professionals and for those who are consumers of our services. It would be difficult to disagree with the basic premises, concepts, and recommendations they put forth.

The present paper seeks to distinguish similarities and differences among various roles assumed by clinicians in fields such as psychology, psychiatry, and rehabilitation counseling. There is some overlap not only in the training but also in the actual tasks and responsibilities involved. Even with each discipline represented in the organization of medical psychotherapists, there are recognized subspecialties. For example, work in the addictive behaviors is a specialty that is receiving increasing recognition. It was not long ago that patients with this affliction, and often practitioners in the field as well, were looked upon as second-class citizens. That time is certainly past: addiction is no longer the problem of special groups, but is in the mainstream of society. A survey performed in order to assess what training in the field of alcoholism and substance abuse was offered by APA-approved clinical and counseling psychology programs (Selin & Svanum, 1981) indicated that students were receiving minimal training in the areas of addictions.

No one would refute that substance abuse, including alcoholism and all its related problems, poses a serious threat not only to the health of the individuals involved but also has serious ramifications to the family structure and society in general. This position is substantiated by such studies examining the total direct and indirect economic cost of alcoholism and substance abuse (Califano, 1979; Mayer, 1983); the overall loss in productivity (Quayle, 1983); and family destabilization and divorce rates among al-

---

Inquiries or reprint requests should be directed to Raymond F. Hanbury, Jr., Dept. of Psychiatry, Mount Sinai Medical Center, New York, NY 10029.

coholics (Matsunaga, 1983). Even with the apparent overt concern about public health and welfare manifested by both the general population and clinicians in various fields, during recent years the actual training and experience of practitioners to identify and treat individuals with such substance use disorders was found to remain minimal (Lubin, Brady, Woodward, & Thomas, 1986).

The reason for selecting this one particular disability is that it raises several issues that illustrate the need for members of various disciplines to assess and treat individuals from a biological-psychological-medical-sociological approach. Given the lack of training, exposure, and actual clinical experience with this population, the issue of determining competence to practice in some "specialty" in this field must be addressed. One method of assessing quality assurance is the peer review system. However, even the utilization of such experts depends on their personal commitment and ability to improve and increase skills in a field that is constantly updating its knowledge and findings.

Some areas of peer review systems for consideration are reliability, fairness, validity, and credibility (Sechrest, 1987). It is easy to understand the fact that reviewers may disagree with services and the treatment strategies simply based on their various theoretical orientations (Cohen & Oyster-Nelson, 1981). This mechanism of peer review goes past explicit criteria, and eventually goes to the point of using clinical judgement on certain issues, such as whether to continue therapy with an individual (Sechrest, 1987). Obviously there is a need for some type of nonbiased system in this area to assess services, but more intensive and extensive research is needed.

As was mentioned earlier, there are specialty areas within various disciplines. In the area of rehabilitation in particular, there has been a distinction made between multidisciplinary and interdisciplinary processes (Fordyce, 1981; Melvin, 1980). Fordyce summarized this in the following manner:

> . . . Both involve efforts by people from several disciplines; and both require that the people involved have at least passing familiarity with the knowledge and methods of the other disciplines. But interdisciplinary differs from multidisciplinary in that the end product of the effort – the outcome – can only be accomplished by a truly interactive effort and contributions from the disciplines involved. In a multidisciplinary exercise, two or more professions may make their respective contributions, but each contribution stands on its own feet and could emerge without the input of another.

The reason for making this point is that if people with disabilities are to be served by qualified and competent clinicians, it is essential to identify the training necessary for practice and be able to assess the performance and functioning of these individuals. Among the essential elements of an occupation that has acquired professional status is identification of a unique body of knowledge (Brubaker, 1977). However, as Hawley and Capshaw (1981) have observed, "deprofessionalization appears to be gaining momentum throughout the world of work; particularly in the human services." Only we can take the initiative and enhance the sense of professionalism among the various practitioners in the field of mental health. This must be accomplished without fragmentation or fission. When we consider the areas we have moved into, such as head trauma rehabilitation, work with AIDS patients, chronic mental illness, geriatrics, and addictive behaviours, it is of paramount importance to provide the essential training for students to not only acquire basic knowledge, but also to look at their own attitudes and value systems regarding working with people with any of these disabilities.

Once trained, it does become incumbent on individuals to establish a system to continue their education. Credentialing and licensure are obvious ways to insure that at least the minimum is being done. As Dr. Anchor has aptly pointed out, there are no guarantees as to the level of competence, but having a monitoring system is at least helpful so that consumers – and the field – have some protection.

References

BRUBAKER, D. (1977). Professionalization and rehabilitation counseling. *Journal of Applied Rehabilitation Counseling, 8*, 208-217.

CALIFANO, J. (1979). Presentation by Joseph A. Califano before the National Council on Alcoholism. *Alcoholism: Clinical and Experimental Research, 3*, 368-373.

COHEN, L. & Oyster-Nelson, C. (1981). Clinicians' evaluation of psychodynamic psychotherapy: Experimental data on psychological peer review. *Journal of Consulting and Clinical Psychology, 49*, 583-589.

FORDYCE, W. (1981). On interdisciplinary peers. *Archives of Physical Medicine, 62*, 51-53.

HAWLEY, I. & Capshaw, T. (1981). In Emener, W., Luck, R., & Smits, S. (Eds.), *Rehabilitation administration and supervision*, (pp. 281-303). Baltimore: University Park Press.

LUBIN, B., Brady, K., Woodward, L., & Thomas, E. (1986). Graduate professional psychology training in alcoholism and substance abuse. *Professional Psychology: Research and Practice, 38*, 151-154.

MATSUNAGA, S. (1983). The federal role in research, treatment, and prevention of alcoholism. *American Psychologist, 38*, 1112-1115.

MAYER, W. (1983). Alcohol abuse and alcoholism: The psychologists' role in prevention, research, and treatment. *American Psychologist, 38*, 1116-1121.

MELVIN, J. (1980). Interdisciplinary and multidisciplinary activities and ACRM. *Archives of Physical Medicine, 61*, 379-380.

QUAYLE, D. (1983). American productivity: The devastating effect of alcoholism and drug abuse. *American Psychologist, 38*, 454-458.

SECHREST, L. (1982). Research on quality assurance. *Professional Psychology: Research and Practice, 18*, 113-116.

SELIN, J. & Svanum, S. (1981). Alcoholism and substance abuse training: A survey of graduate programs in clinical psychology. *Professional Psychology, 12*, 717-721.

Information for Contributors

The journal gives preference to articles that report empirical or conceptual work in which behavioral or psychological methods of treatment are related to areas that are "medical" in the broad sense. However, articles will also be accepted that deal with the wider areas of disease prevention, health, and wellness, insofar as they relate to psychology and psychotherapy. The journal's purpose is to provide a forum for dissemination of scientific findings as well as practical information and conceptual integration of existing knowledge in the broad areas of overlap between health and disease on the one hand and psychology and the psychotherapies on the other. Selected book reviews in this area will also be considered.

MANUSCRIPTS should be six to thirty pages long. They must be double-spaced on one side of the page, and submitted in triplicate (one original and two photocopies) to Charles L. Sheridan, Ph.D., Co-Editor, *Medical Psychotherapy*, Department of Psychology, University of Missouri-K.C., 5100 Rockhill Rd., Kansas City, Missouri 64110. An abstract from 100 to 300 words should accompany the manuscript, and all the figures and artwork must be camera-ready. Manuscripts should be written in accordance with the current edition of the style manual of the American Psychological Association. The editorial review process ordinarily takes about three months. Further information about the submission of manuscripts can be obtained from either of the Editors. Inquiries to Dr. Sargent may be addressed to him at Box 829, The Menninger Foundation, Topeka, Kansas 66601. Authors of accepted manuscripts will be asked to submit, if possible, a copy of their article on diskette (further information will be provided at the appropriate time).

From C. J. Hogrefe Publishers

Crisis

International Journal of Suicide and Crisis Studies
Published under the auspices of the
International Association for Suicide Prevention (IASP)

Volume 9 No. 1 1988

Editor
Raymond Battegay

Assistant Editors
R. F. W. Diekstra, Thomas Haenel
Gernot Sonneck

Consulting Editor
Erwin Ringel

C. J. Hogrefe, Inc., Toronto/Canada

Crisis, founded at the 10th International Congress for Suicide Prevention and Crisis Intervention in Ottawa, Canada, is the first international journal in the field of suicide prevention and crisis counseling. For nine consecutive years *Crisis* has been serving as a comprehensive international forum for the exchange and discussion of information, investigations, and results of suicide research and studies from around the world.

The integrity of the contributions is guaranteed by the renowned international experts of the editorial board. The new expanded format includes developments in research, practical approaches to crisis intervention, the newsletter of the International Association for Suicide Prevention, updates on other organizations, book reviews, and news and announcements of interest to readers in suicide studies.

Appears in two issues per annual volume.

Suicide is often interpreted as the final and tragic consequence of a mental illness. However, it also has roots in such social factors as unemployment, migration, alcohol and drug abuse, loneliness in old age, and others. As the incidence of suicides continues to increase in our societies, worldwide research into the causes and prevention of suicidal behavior has become both more important to the professional and lay communities, and more extensive internationally. Consequently, the need exists to coordinate and disseminate the vital information generated by the activities of the diverse institutes and clinics concerned with this field.

For subscriptions, contact

HOGREFE INTERNATIONAL, INC.
Periodicals Manager

14 Bruce Park Ave.
Toronto, Ontario
CANADA, M4P 2S3
(416) 482-6339

P. O. Box 51
Lewiston, New York
USA 14092
(716) 282-1610

Subscription Rates:
Individuals: US $22.00/CAN $29.80
Institutions: US $30.00/CAN $40.00

Sample and back issues available

From Hans Huber Publishers

This interdisciplinary journal publishes articles dealing with the practice, research and theory of behavioral medicine and health enhancement. Contributions are published concerning applications of biofeedback training procedures and instruction as well as related methods in hospitals, mental health centers, schools, rehabilitation facilities, private practice, business, and industry. *Clinical Biofeedback & Health* seeks to foster insight into the adaptive and dysfunctional responses to living and working environments. Techniques for treating individuals and groups previously believed beyond professional assistance are also provided.

Following, are examples of contributions that have appeared in past issues:

- Current Issues in the Use of Biofeedback Treatment with Psychiatric Inpatients: A Review (Vol. 10, No. 1, 1987)
- Current Status of the ß-Endorphin and Self Regulation: Health Enhancement Through Applied Neurosciences (Vol. 10, No. 1, 1987)
- Stress Management and Biofeedback (Vol. 9, No. 2, 1987)
- Patterns of Neuromuscular Activity in Pain and Nonpain Patients (Vol. 9, No. 2, 1986)
- Health Changes in a Biofeedback and Stress Management Program (Vol 9, No. 1, 1986)

- Appears in two issues annually

For subscriptions, contact

Hogrefe International, Inc.
Periodicals Manager

14 Bruce Park Ave.
Toronto, Ontario
CANADA, M4P 2S3
(416) 482-6339

P. O. Box 51
Lewiston, New York
USA 14092
(716) 282-1610

Subscription rates:
Individuals: US $18.00/CAN $24.80
Institutions: US $36.00/CAN $49.00

Sample and back issues available

HOGREFE HUBER

Holroyd, K. A.; Athens, Ohio, USA
B. Schlote; Ulm, West Germany
H. Zenz; Ulm, West Germany
(Editors)

Perspectives in Research on Headache

1983, 248 pp., hardcover
ISBN 0-88937-006-0
US $32.00/CAN $43.50

This book is addressed to professionals working with people who suffer from pain, particularly headache. Authors from the United States, Canada, Germany, and Australia present current research in headache and delineate future directions in pain research.

Contents:

I: **Basic Research on Headache and Pain:** Neuroleptides and Pain/ Experimental Headache Syndromes/ Issues and Problems in Measuring Experimental and Clinical Pain

II: **Classification and Diagnosis of Headache:** Headache Assessment from a Severity Perspective/ The Empirical Validity of Clinical Headache/ Myogenic Headache/ Diagnostic Procedures for the Diagnosis of Myogenic Headache

III: **Medical Treatments of Headache:** Social Aspects of the Management of Headache Patients/ Drug Therapy of Chronic Headache/ Alternative Treatments in Chronic Headache/ Analgesic Withdrawl in Pain Therapy

IV: **Psychological Treatments of Headache:** EMG Biofeedback with Tension Headache: Therapeutic Mechanisms/ Cephalic Vasomotor Feedback Therapy: A Controlled Study of Migraneurs and Normals/ Biofeedback versus Cognitive Stress-Coping Therapy in Migraine Headache Patients/ A Behavioral Treatment Program (SEP) for Chronic Migraine Headache Patients/ Indications for Client-Centered Psychotherapy with Headache Patients/Behavioral Research on Headaches: Current Status and Future Directions

• "The book is valuable for two reasons: (1) it gives English-speaking readers access to unfamiliar research and might encourage further exchanges with European colleagues, (2) there are some good, concise review papers which would make excellent introductory reading. Of particular note are chapters by Bakal and Holroyd on their models of headache and the process of effective treatment respectively. There is also a good brief review by Wolfgang Kesser on the measurement of pain. Perhaps the most stimulating chapter is a fine conceptual analysis of 'myogenic headache' (tension or muscle contraction headache) by Claus Bischoff and Harald Traue. All in all I was pleasantly surprised by this book. It is well presented with excellent translations into English."

Reviewed by Stephen Morley in *The British Journal of Clinical Psychology* Vol. 23, Part 4, 1984.

Please send your order to:

HOGREFE INTERNATIONAL, INC.

12–14 Bruce Park Avenue
Toronto, Ontario M4P 2S3
Canada (416) 482-6339

Hans Huber Publishers

C. J. Hogrefe Publishers

P.O. Box 51
Lewiston, New York 14092
USA (716) 282-1610

New Publications from

MULTILINGUAL MATTERS LTD.
Bank House, 8a Hill Rd, Clevedon,
Avon, England, BS21 7HH.
☎ 0272 876519

NEUROTIC AND PSYCHOTIC LANGUAGE BEHAVIOUR

NEW BOOK

Edited by Ruth WODAK and Pete VAN DE CRAEN

"In what way can the study of (deviant) language behaviour contribute to a better understanding of both deviant and normal behaviour?", is one of the numerous questions treated in this collection of essays studying neurotic and schizophrenic language behaviour. The approach adopted here is interdisciplinary in the true sense: socio- and psycho-linguists, (social) psychologists, sociologists and psychiatrists have not only joined forces but have studied at least more than one discipline. As a result new approaches for the study of deviant language behaviour are offered. Although most contributors favour the view that human development is to a great extent influenced by communicative experience physiological aspects are not neglected either. The combination of interdisciplinary methodologies and a number of open approaches towards both the neurotic and schizophrenic syndromes provide new insights into the origins and therapies of certain form of deviant language behaviour.

Contents:

Introduction: Highways and Byways *by Pete Van de Craen.*

Part I Neurotic Language Behaviour

1. At last I know......: Sociolinguistic and Psycholinguistic aspects of the Therapeutic Process and its Effect *by Ruth Wodak*
2. Intervention in Psychotherapy: A Qualitative Analysis of Persuasive Theory *by Peter Nowak*
3. Confrontation in Psychotherapy: A Conversational Analysis *by Susanne Bleiberg Seperson*
4. A Study of the Verbal Interaction in the Initial Phase of Therapeutic Discourse *by Agnes Speck and Sabine Stitz*
5. Therapy Talk: 'start', beginning' and 'outset' *by Karin Kichler and Johanna Lalouschek*
6. 'When I was still very small, life was much easier': The Manifestation of Neurotic Disorders in a Projective Sentence *by Helmut Gruber*

Part II Schizophrenic Language Behaviour

7. "Grammar' and 'Language-game' as Concepts for the Analysis of Schizophrenic Communication *by Hans Rudi Fischer*
8. Paradoxical Injunctions in Everyday Language and in the Language of Science *by Stephan von Block*
9. Jargonaphasia and Schizophasia: An Essay in Contrastive Patholinguistics *by Günter Peuser*
10. Towards an Interpersonal Theory of Schizophrenia *by Brigitte De Decker and Pete Van de Craen*
11. Some Effects of Supportive Psychotherapy on Texts Written by Schizophrenics *by Klaus Schonauer and Gerd Buchkremer*
12. The Analysis of Dialogues with a Schizophrenic Patient *by Marie-Louise Kaesermann*
13. On the Problem of Accessibility in Conversations with Schizophrenic People *by Diek Van Bijsterveld*
14. Assertive Speech Acts in Psychotic Discourse *by William Van Belle*
15. The Language of Schizophrenics as a Reflection of Meanings Concealed by Culture and the Individual *by Janusz Wròbel*
16. Over-inclusion and Cognitive Disturbances in Schizophrenic Communication: An Empirical Study *by Karl-Ernst Bühler and Hildegard Vogt*

Notes on Contributors

Chapter Abstracts

Index

Approximately 416 pages; Publication early 1987

Hardback ISBN 0-905028-77-5 c. £39.00 US$69.00

Paperback ISBN 0-905028-76-7 c. £15.90 US$29.00

HOGREFE HUBER

Thornton, J.F.; Toronto, Canada
M.V. Seeman; Toronto, Canada
(Editors)

34

Schizophrenia: Understanding the Management
A Guide to the Medical, Legal and Social Complexities

1988, 200 pp., hardcover
ISBN 0-920887-17-1

in preparation

This volume provides concise and clear outlines for steps that can minimize the devastating effects of schizophrenia, and points out the pitfalls that patients and their caregivers can encounter. It is designed to help caregivers determine the stage at which their schizophrenic patient is operating, and makes suggestions for treatments. Decision trees and flow charts help the reader grasp the primary options available. This book will be valuable for all practitioners involved with schizophrenia. *Contents:* What is Schizophrenia? / Role of Family – burdens posed by illness and burdens posed by refusal to accept illness and need for treatment / Symptoms Accepted – Assessment, Diagnosis, Treatment, Medication, Symptom Resolution. Medical follow-up and associated long-term problems. Continuing care and Rehabilitation follow-up. What kinds of programs and follow-up offered / Symptoms not Accepted – Functioning level and behavior. Legal steps – Criminal Code, Mental Health Act, Civil Action, Guardianship.

Strauss, J.S.; New Haven, CT, USA
W. Boeker; Bern, Switzerland
H.-D. Brenner; Bern, Switzerland
(Editors)

Psychosocial Treatment of Schizophrenia
Multidimensional Concepts, Psychological, Family, and Self-Help Perspectives

1986, 320 pp., hardcover
ISBN 0-920887-10-4

US $39.00/CAN $49.00

This volume stems from the international symposium on the Psychosocial Management of Schizophrenia, held at the Psychiatric University Clinic in Bern, Switzerland, in 1985. The contributions by well-known North American and European scientists in the field reflect many new directions in understanding psychological and social aspects of schizophrenia, which are the basis for developing improved treatment:
Psychosocial factors affecting the long-term course of schizophrenia / Possible implications of the vulnerability hypothesis for the psychosocial management of schizophrenia / Basic disorders: Instability of cerebral functions / Toward a coherent multidimensional understanding and therapy of schizophrenia: Converging new concepts / Early intervention medication as an alternative to continuous depot treatment in schizophrenia / A controlled study of family therapy, social skills training and maintenance chemotherapy in the aftercare treatment of schizophrenic patients / Changing the family environment of schizophrenic patients / Skills training for the community adaptation of schizophrenics / Social skills training for the treatment of chronic schizophrenics / Basic symptoms and coping behavior in schizophrenia / The significance of basic disorders for treatment and rehabilitation / Assessing the impact of psychosocial treatments for schizophrenic patients: Reliability, validity, responsibility / The philosophy and practice of self-help for relatives of schizophrenic patients / Cognitive and behavioral interventions in the self control of schizophrenia / On self-help phenomena among schizophrenics / The role of patients in recovery of psychosis / Prospective possible developments in research and practice.

Please send your order to:

HOGREFE INTERNATIONAL, INC.

12-14 Bruce Park Avenue
Toronto, Ontario M4P 2S3
Canada (416) 482-6339

Hans Huber Publishers

C.J. Hogrefe Publishers

P.O. Box 51
Lewiston, New York 14092
USA (716) 282-1610

HOGREFE HUBER

Norman S. Endler; York University, Toronto, Canada
Emmanuel Persad; Clarke Institute of Psychiatry, Toronto, Canada

Electroconvulsive Therapy
The Myths and the Realities

1988, 160 pp, hardcover
ISBN 0-920887-20-1
US $27.00/CAN $36.00

1988 marks the fiftieth anniversary of the first electroconvulsive therapy treatment. A half-century later, ECT remains highly controversial as a therapeutic approach: while it is highly efficacious for treating some forms of mental illness, there is widespread concern and confusion regarding its immediate and long-term side effects.

This volume traces the development of ECT from its first application through to modern times, and explores the issues surrounding it from a number of different perspectives. Its major aim is to separate the myths from the realities: what ECT can actually do for those suffering from depression and other disturbances, and which dangers are perceived as opposed to real. It is aimed at mental health professionals, researchers, patients and their families, and the public.

Chapters include:
- History of ECT
- Indications for the use of ECT
- ECT versus other treatment modalities for depression
- Side effects and complications of ECT
- ECT and the brain
- Social and political issues affecting mental illness
- Legal and ethical issues
- Myths and realities
- The stigma of mental illness and ECT

The book finishes with a summary chapter and an extended bibliography that directs the interested reader to many sources beyond those cited in the text.

Please send your order to:
HOGREFE INTERNATIONAL, INC.
12-14 Bruce Park Avenue
Toronto, Ontario M4P 2S3
Canada (416) 482-6339

Hans Huber Publishers
C.J. Hogrefe Publishers

P.O. Box 51
Lewiston, New York 14092
USA (716) 282-1610

HOGREFE HUBER

Fiedler, K.; Giessen, West Germany
J. Forgas; New South Wales, Australia
(Editors)

27

Affect, Cognition & Social Behavior:
New Evidence and Integrative Attempts

1988, 350 pp., hardcover
ISBN 0-88937-016-8
US $ 59.00 / CAN $ 76.00

Understanding the relationships between feeling states, cognitive processes, and behavioral consequences has become a prominent theme for psychologists working in such diverse areas as memory, learning, motivation, emotion, social psychology, clinical psychology, and psychophysiology. Numerous journal articles and book chapters dealing with the influence of feeling on thinking, and vice versa, have been published and constitute one of the most popular research endeavors in recent years. However, the mood-and-cognition phenomena reported up to now, and the theoretical accounts proposed to explain these phenomena, still represent an incomplete picture of the richness of this intriguing issue. There is still much to be shown and much to be explained. The purpose of this book is twofold: first, to critically review the available evidence from different theoretical perspectives and, second, to present new ideas and original research that link the mood-and-cognition approach to person perception, social behavior, depressive illness, psychophysiology, and behavioral adaptation. The volume addresses scientists as well as students and practitioners in psychology, and should also be of interest to readers working in the fields of education, behavioral medicine, and artificial intelligence.

Frey, S.; Duisburg, Germany

Analyzing Patterns of Behavior in Dyadic Interaction

1988, 250 pp., hardcover
ISBN 0-920887-08-2
in preparation

There is no area of human behavior that has been subjected to more speculation, and at the same time has remained so difficult to investigate empirically, than the nonverbal component of the communication process. This text traces the controversial history of nonverbal research as it developed from the early personality-oriented "physiognomic" phase through the emotion-centered period of "expression-studies", to the modern communicational views. It offers a new understanding of nonverbal behavior as an "effector variable" in communication and provides the methodological means for its study. For the first time the full details on the "Bernese System", a highly efficient tool designed to permit a comprehensive study of the nonverbal and verbal processes operating in human interaction, are systematically explained.

Please send your order to:

HOGREFE INTERNATIONAL, INC.

12-14 Bruce Park Avenue
Toronto, Ontario M4P 2S3
Canada (416) 482-6339

Hans Huber Publishers

C. J. Hogrefe Publishers

P.O. Box 51
Lewiston, New York 14092
USA (716) 282-1610

SPECIAL ISSUE: THE JOURNAL OF MIND AND BEHAVIOR

The Sexual Body: An Interdisciplinary Perspective

by Arthur Efron, SUNY at Buffalo

The Sexual Body: An Interdisciplinary Perspective proposes an inherent bodily dimension to the concept of sexuality, and studies this within a wide variety of disciplines including psychology, psychoanalysis and its history, anthropology, biology, issues concerning the neonate and child sexual abuse. The discussion falls within the framework of Dewey's definition of inquiry as the creation of objects of knowledge rather than uncovering antecedent realities. Thus, multi-disciplinary insights into sexuality create new problems for inquiry, and these are pronouncedly relevant in the later stages of the sexual revolution, which this study maintains, is still in progress in most parts of the world.

CONTENTS

1. Introduction: The perspective of the sexual body.
2. Psychoanalysis as the key discipline.
3. Analogues of original sin: Postulate of innate destructive aggression.
4. Reichian tradition: A view of the sexual body.
5. Challenges to psychoanalytic theory: Recent developments.
6. Reinventing the asexual infant: On the recent "explosion" in infant research.
7. The adult sexual body: A missing theory.
8. The sexual body, psychoanalysis and science: Bowlby, Peterfreund and Kohut.
9. Lichtenstein, Holland and Lacan: Ambivalence toward the sexual body, cooptation and defiance.
10. World hypotheses and interdisciplinary sciences in intimate relation.

The Journal of Mind and Behavior, Volume 6, Numbers 1 and 2. $15.00, approximately 300 pages. This double issue may also be ordered as part of JMB Volume 6 at the regular yearly subscription rate. Discount available for orders of more than ten copies.

Yearly subscription rates: $45.00 for institutions, $25.00 for individuals. JMB appears quarterly.

ISSN 0271-0137 ISBN 0-930195-01-9

Circulation Department
THE JOURNAL OF MIND AND BEHAVIOR
P.O. Box 522, Village Station
New York City, N.Y. 10014

☐ Special Issue only.

☐ ____ copies of Special Issue at discount rate.

☐ Please enter my subscription to JMB starting with the current volume.

Name ____________________

Street ____________________

City and State ____________________

Please enclose purchase order or prepayment in US-Dollars. Checks must be drawn on American banks!

HOGREFE HUBER

39

Sethi, A. S.; Ottawa, Ontario, Canada
D. Caro; Ottawa, Ontario, Canada
R. S. Schuller; New York, New York, USA
(Editors)

Strategic Management of Technostress in an Information Society

1986, 425 pp., hardcover
ISBN 0-88937-012-5 US $36.00/CAN $44.00

This book collects the views of several outstanding scholars on the critical subject of coping with technostress in organizations. It reflects a deepening concern among researchers and organizational managers that the cumulative effects of information technology change in the workplace exact unacceptable levels of psychological, physical, and economic stress. The fundamental premise is that management has a positive responsibility to introduce information technology in a work environment in ways that will foster effective organizations and improve the quality of working life. With the advent of fifth-generation technologies into the work environment, a proactive and strategic management approach for the effective manager will become even more critical. Techniques for reducing and managing technostress include individual, organizational and societal strategies. This volume is an instrumental reference work for managers in both private and public sectors, health practitioners, counselors, human resource specialists, company doctors, and researchers.

Contents:
1. Introduction
2. A Strategic Choice Model of Technostress Management

PART I: Strategic Organizational Choices for Managing Technostress
3. Technology Strategy: The Role of Strategic Planning and Monitoring Systems
4. Integrating Technology Strategy with Corporate Strategy
5. Human Resource Strategies for Technostress Management
6. Social Support Strategies for Technostress Management
7. Social Change Strategies in Managing Technostress
8. Time Planning and Communication Behavior Strategies
9. Organizational Culture in Technostress Management
10. Integrated Information Systems: Work Design and Ergonomic Strategies

PART II: Strategic Individual Choices for Managing Technostress
11. Nutritional Strategies for Technostress Management
12. Fitness Strategies
13. Yoga for Technostress Management
14. Contempletative Strategies for Technostress Management
15. Biofeedback: A Therapeutic Perspective
16. Sleep and Dreams in Technostress Management

PART III: Strategic Societal Choices for Technostress Management
17. Strategic Societal Choices for Technostress Management
18. Conclusion: Toward Technological Renaisance

Please send your order to:

HOGREFE INTERNATIONAL, INC.

12-14 Bruce Park Avenue
Toronto, Ontario M4P 2S3
Canada (416) 482-6339

Hans Huber Publishers

C. J. Hogrefe Publishers

P.O. Box 51
Lewiston, New York 14092
USA (716) 282-1610

Order the authentic Rorschach Plates directly from the publisher.

Hermann Rorschach

Psychodiagnostik Psychodiagnostics

Tafeln - Plates

Medizinischer Verlag

Hans Huber, Bern

Medical Publisher

Distributed by

Hans Huber Publishers, Inc.
14 Bruce Park Avenue
Toronto, Ontario M4P 2S3

Order directly from our nearest office.
No shipping charges with prepaid orders: **US $65.00/ CAN $85.00**

Also available

Recording Blanks (100 sheets per pad) US $17.00/ CAN $23.00
Rorschach Location Charts (1 set of 5 charts): US $8.90/ CAN $12.00
Psychodiagnostics (9th ed.), by H. Rorschach: US $29.00/ CAN $39.00

CANADA
Hogrefe International
12-14 BrucePark Ave
Toronto, Ontario M4P 2S3
(416) 482-6339

USA
Hogrefe International
P. O. Box 51
Lewiston, NY 14092
(716) 282-1610

SWITZERLAND
Verlag Hans Huber
Länggass-Strasse 76
CH-3000 Bern 9
031-242533

GERMANY
Verlag Dr. C. J. Hogrefe
Rohnsweg 25
D-3400 Göttingen
0551-54045